CRITIQUE OF FANTASY, VOL. I

Before you start to read this book, take this moment to think about making a donation to punctum books, an independent non-profit press,

@ https://punctumbooks.com/support/

If you're reading the e-book, you can click on the image below to go directly to our donations site. Any amount, no matter the size, is appreciated and will help us to keep our ship of fools afloat. Contributions from dedicated readers will also help us to keep our commons open and to cultivate new work that can't find a welcoming port elsewhere. Our adventure is not possible without your support.
Vive la open access.

Fig. 1. Hieronymus Bosch, Ship of Fools (1490–1500)

Laurence A. Rickels

CRITIQUE OF FANTASY

VOLUME 1

Between a Crypt
and a Datemark

Brainstorm Books
Santa Barbara, California

CRITIQUE OF FANTASY, VOL. 1: BETWEEN A CRYPT AND A DATEMARK. Copyright © 2020 Laurence A. Rickels. This work carries a Creative Commons BY-NC-SA 4.0 International license, which means that you are free to copy and redistribute the material in any medium or format, and you may also remix, transform, and build upon the material, as long as you clearly attribute the work to the authors and editors (but not in a way that suggests the authors or punctum books endorses you and your work), you do not use this work for commercial gain in any form whatsoever, and that for any remixing and transformation, you distribute your rebuild under the same license. http://creativecommons.org/licenses/by-nc-sa/4.0/

First published in 2020 by Brainstorm Books
An imprint of punctum books, Earth, Milky Way
https://www.punctumbooks.com

ISBN-13: 978-1-950192-92-2 (print)
ISBN-13: 978-1-950192-93-9 (ePDF)

DOI: 10.21983/P3.0277.1.00

LCCN: 2020939532
Library of Congress Cataloging Data is available from the Library of Congress

Book design: Vincent W.J. van Gerven Oei
Cover image: "Palm Springs, CA," July 8, 2016. Photograph by moominsean.
Frontispiece: "Star Wars X: Boomer Remover," 2020. Photograph by Nancy Barton.

Contents

Introduction;
or, How *Star Wars* Became Our Oldest Cultural Memory   19

(The rundown of a Star Wars Effect recycling through the
aftermath of World War Two propaganda: *Independence
Day, Moonraker, Reign of Fire,* SPECTRE, *Jurassic
World,* and *Star Wars: The Force Awakens. Critique
of Fantasy* sets out to explore the borderlands of the
fantasy and science fiction genres, which the success of
Lucas's film first illuminated. The digital relation takes
over where Christianity left off grounding the fantasy
genre. Digital fantasy in the SF movies *The Martian* and
Gravity.)

Chapter 1
The Ethics, Poetics, and Practical Metaphysics of Waking
Dreaming   35

Be Careful What You Wish For   35
(Hebel's "Three Wishes" and fantasying's pedagogical
supplement. Tolkien tries to separate his fantasy genre
from the moral upbringing of children. He also tries to
overtake science fiction. But he ends up at two borders.)

No Strings Attached   41
(The match between Aquinas and Pinocchio schools the
will. Visiting the Aldiss, Barrie, and Collodi crypts. Kant
and the categorical imperative of mourning in *Groundhog
Day.*)

The Fantasies We All Know So Well   49
(Tolkien's "On Fairy-Stories" and Freud's "The Poet and Daydreaming." The notion of the datemark, the present moment that triggers the jump-cut to fantastic wish fulfilment, is the indelible stamp awaiting historicization, the half-life of fantasying and fantasy. The loser and winner of the contest take on new roles. Science fiction rereads in the ruins of its failed forecasts the deregulated ranging of fantasy, animated by the only fantasy that is true, the digital relation.)

The Mechanical Brain   58
(Introducing Gotthard Günther, who examines in Jack Williamson's 1946 novel *The Humanoids* the sci-fi prospect of a perfectibility of rational thought that would override willing and wishing. In the 1980 sequel *The Humanoid Touch,* however, fantasy is in the ascendant.)

The More the Merrier   68
(The Prime Directive of the humanoids leaves them where they lie. Bentham/Mill and *The Truman Show.* The showdown with utilitarianism motivates the American superhero in the ongoing struggle against the American psycho.)

Ghost-seeing and Clairvoyance   74
(Schopenhauer places the paranormal evidence of Mesmerism's impact on a sliding scale ranging from the night dream to paranormal states of waking dreaming. The question of the ghost, its impossible possibility, draws Schopenhauer's articulation of fantasy states onward.)

Chapter 2
Making a Wish   83

> *Calibrations of Beauty*   *83*
> (Hanns Sachs relates the postponement of the machine
> age in classical antiquity and its uncanny sequelae to the
> administration of doses of primary beauty within the arts
> of wishing in techno-culture. Sachs recognizes in typical
> psychotic delusions of techno-surveillance the emergency
> arrival of the machine of secondary narcissism. In the
> machine of Disney animation, however, there are new
> pitfalls of prettiness ensuing from the rotoscoping of live
> actors. The curbed sex appeal of cuteness in *Snow White
> and the Seven Dwarfs* sets the standard for subsequent
> films, including *A Scanner Darkly*.)
>
> *Mutual Daydreaming*   *92*
> (Sachs discovers in daydreams of collaboration and self-
> pity missing links in the evolution of art. Schnitzler and
> Kubrick explore daydreaming in common.)
>
> *Gender Fantasying*   *103*
> (Winnicott's crypt study of a male girl carrier and its
> illumination of Hamlet.)
>
> *The Secret in Mutual Daydreaming*   *110*
> (A secret is always kept in mutual daydreaming until
> its bearer lies on the couch. Sometimes the secret in the
> daydream held in common is a crypt. The example of
> Lord Henry and Dorian Gray.)
>
> *Flight to Reality*   *114*
> (Winnicott on fantasy's manic defense against the
> depressive position. Fantasy takes flight to reality, really
> an omnipotent fantasy about reality, from inner reality,
> the dread deadness inside. The depressive position of
> photography in *Blow-up*.)

Fantasying Fantasy   124
(Winnicott is led by his patient to find in the potentiation of daydreaming a way around the protest against waking living. Dissociated fantasying opens up through a fantasying of fantasy.)

Auguste Müller of Karlsruhe   135
(Schopenhauer refers repeatedly to the case of Auguste Müller, whose magnetic treatment brought to the fore her own clairvoyance. She becomes a therapist for the community and adjusts the vertical controls of her newfound stability through her dead mother's support and counsel. In the two adaptations of Jackson's *The Haunting of Hill House* the impasse of a daughter is circumvented, now through cinematic fantasying of fantasy in the secular setting of waking dream states, now through the special-effects-adorned Christian-digital ascendancy of fantasy heroism.)

Fantasy Island   142
(A precognitive relay of traumatic world histories transmits within a network of encrypted losses that counts *The Tempest* as entry and exit.)

Chapter 3
New Vampire Lectures   149

Zombie Wars   149
(The hypothetical reality of ghostly communication goes on and on: Dick's half-life, W. James's norm of falsification of evidence, and Ehrenwald's telepathic scatter. Between contact and attack, the psychic reality of vampirism goes into literature. American science fiction turns undeath into living death. Gertrude Stein wages zombie wars against centuries that are already at rest.)

The Psychopathy Test   157
(P.K. Dick's afterword to Jeter's *Dr Adder* takes swipes
at the Tolkien influence on science fiction via *Star
Wars*. Like Adder's novel, however, Dick's *The Zap
Gun* pursues fantasy heroism, which Dick sets on a
psychopathy test preliminary to successful mourning and
the innovations of substitution.)

All You Vampires   163
(Heinlein's "All You Zombies…" replaces the conceit of
mutation in Matheson's *I Am Legend* with time travel
and breaches the impasse between vampiric sole survival
and the zombie apocalypse.)

Countdown   171
(Heinlein's "By His Bootstraps" introduces a *Ding an
Sicht* into time travel's affinity with cinema. The mere
suffering of waiting around for the delivery of transport
into outer space must be transcended into something
other. The zombie, linked by Günther to the mechanical
brain, is the poster monster of the American way of
death, the countdown to second death. Variations on this
finite afterlife of a secular cosmos in *Dracula, Hamlet, I
Am Legend,* and *Interstellar*.)

Chapter 4
Where the Dead Are   183

Fantasia   183
(In early fragments on the coloration of fantasy Benjamin
anticipates his avowals of Scheerbart and Disney. The
verging of fantasy on science fiction in Scheerbart's
Lesabéndio draws inspiration from Fechner's animist
psychology. Scheerbart's cyborgs on Pallas and the
Hobbits of the Shire roll back the stone and stoners of
nihilism.)

Wish upon the Stars 195
(Kant's stargazing reflects a German Enlightenment understanding of the afterlife on the outer planets. The transport of the *Phantasiermaschine* through *Arrival* transmutes this understanding for science fiction. It's not the mathematical sublime but the horror of successful mourning that is in the ascendant in *Signs*.)

Fantasying and Haunting 206
(Kant tests his hypothesis that the main source of fantasying is the ghostly netherworld. Swedenborg is at once the greatest ghostseer and the greatest fantast.)

Arrival Time 211
(In Chiang's "Story of Your Life" the aliens recognize in Fermat's performative non-causal principle an overlap with their appreciation of goals that are already given. From page to screen – *Arrival* – the protagonist's memory of the unstoppable future now is complete, breaking only on the inability of her others to affirm a life of foregone conclusions.)

The Specific Emotional Situation 215
(The white lie in Rousseau's *Reveries of the Solitary Walker* is the byproduct of the run of time in language, of being out of time. Sachs elucidates fantasying and fiction as the ongoing retrieval of specific situations in which affect wasn't expressed. Lost and found affect in daydreaming undermines the success rate of mourning's work.)

Afterword
Go to China   223

> (The datemark of this study is shared with the centrality
> of China in movies from *Looper* to *Arrival*. It marks a
> period of transition and preparation, making the world
> good again, so the communist redemption of the third
> world can enter and realize the new worlds of science
> fiction. *The Great Wall, The Three-Body Problem,* and
> *The Wandering Earth*.)

Bibliography   235

Index   243

Acknowledgments

I must thank the editors I contacted at the university presses of California, Columbia, Fordham, MIT, and Northwestern for the rude awakening. After over a year of pitching my work as required like a beginner in a time-killing process of application, I recalled that recently two good friends in the Humanities, who have followed my work forever but, coasts apart in their CVs and current affiliations, do not know one another, recommended punctum books as the best address for my work. Thank you, Richard Burt and Daniel Tiffany.

One day I noticed that one of the punctum books editors had settled in Santa Barbara working closely with two of my close friends and former colleagues. Looking it up again online I saw that I knew a second editor from my stints at the European Graduate School. It is with the relief that comes from the lifting of repression and the prospect of a more integrated departure from my academic life that I thank Julie Carlson, Aranye Fradenburg Joy, Eileen A. Fradenburg Joy, and Vincent W.J. van Gerven Oei for making the happy end happen.

Critique of Fantasy visits endopsychic genealogy and endopsychic allegory on a few of the title's likely suspects but in large part on unsuspected trajectories. Two works by Ian McEwan offer bookends for framing the endopsychic claims I am staking. When Jonathan Lethem was at the American Academy in Berlin we began a series of exchanges accompanying his composition of *A Gambler's Anatomy,* which came to an end when he crossed the finish line. At the same time, I was concluding my study of slasher and splatter movies, *The Psycho Records,* and introduced some of its themes into our final exchange. Among the "psycho" influences that allowed him to get inside his protagonist's "anatomy," Lethem referred to McEwan's *The Innocent* (1990). The nightmare topos of the difficulties attending disposal of the murder victim is what the protagonist must work through in his amateur hours of dissecting the corpse. Four years later McEwan published a novel for or, rather, about children, *The Daydreamer*. From age ten to twelve we follow Peter Fortune's development through the developmental staging of his wish fantasies. He periodically enters daydream fantasy and departs from reality for a spell on the cusp of hallucination and delusion. In other words, his daydreams partake of night-dream reality. Although he ends up allegedly reconciled with growing up, his episodes were psycho. The protagonist of *The Innocent* is the fantast and his ultimate fantasy is that by making the body of his murder victim disappear his courtship of the dead man's wife can continue uninterrupted unto the happy end. But the fantasy isn't fulfilled, and the woman for whom he did it all can't have anything further to do with him. Whereas the 1994 novel *The Daydreamer* exemplifies the pitfalls of the obvious when it comes to fantasy, *The Innocent,* by allegorizing the wish for reunification within the deep cuts of making the past disappear, is a more nuanced sorting through of near-misses, which I am convinced both fantasy and critique demand.

When it was my turn in the exchange with Lethem, I proceeded in record time. This meant that other readings I was engaged in at that moment, and which were earmarked for the present study, crept into my sallies. Otherwise, however, I left the bulk of the booklet, in particular my swift readings of Lethem's oeuvre between science fiction and fantasy, out of this study, also because they depended on the context I shared with his authorship. *The Blot: A Supplement* (Anti-Oedipus Press, 2016) contains in nuce many of the theoretical conclusions I reach at greater length in the present study. I recommend it as souvenir of the journey going into *Critique of Fantasy*. I thank Jonathan Lethem for the season of brainstorming. My study is its byproduct.

Introduction; or, How *Star Wars* Became Our Oldest Cultural Memory

I have touched down in the *Star Wars* franchise on several occasions to illustrate a historical paradox I once dared name "Nazi Psychoanalysis."[1] Let me say right off that this study will not look more closely at the *Star Wars* movies.[2] Instead, it will explore a terrain between the science fiction and fantasy genres that the success of George Lucas's 1977 film illuminated and which remains to this day the cradle of blockbuster culture.

Orbiting around the B-line I will continue to make in this introduction, examples abound of what might be termed the "*Star Wars* Effect." Roland Emmerich, who was originally enrolled in film school in Germany to become a producer, switched his career goal to directing when he saw *Star Wars*. Did it take a German to recognize Lucas's refurbishing of Allied propaganda films? The Death Star, the unbeatable foe, is brought down by a makeshift alliance of unlikely victors, who win as losers, not as winners. That's Lucas's remix of the formula: to win as winner would be tantamount to filling the position the

1   See Laurence A. Rickels, *Nazi Psychoanalysis,* 3 vols. (Minneapolis: University of Minnesota Press, 2002).
2   My most sustained attempt to interpret the six *Star Wars* films can be found in *I Think I Am: Philip K. Dick* (Minneapolis: University of Minnesota Press, 2010), 71–74.

Nazis forever occupy in the global culture industry. If losers continue to prevail against empires of evil as the good and the brave, then the Nazis keep on winning as unrepentant winners. The 2020 pandemic incited US news anchors to cite from the famous broadcasts Churchill delivered during the Battle of Britain and encourage a population endangered by and as losers to rally around the prospect that they were now living *Star Wars*. *Star Wars* turned propaganda hype into archetype. Emmerich's blockbuster *Independence Day* (1996) testified to the instruction he took down from *Star Wars*.

The success of Lucas's movie encouraged the Bond franchise to hitch to its star the one Ian Fleming fiction that was exceptionally and untenably close to World War Two: *Moonraker* (1955). At the end of the movie *The Spy Who Loved Me* (1977), the next Bond film to be coming soon was already announced to be *For Your Eyes Only* (1981), the first film to turn to the short stories for material and title. But *Star Wars* placed *Moonraker* back on the books-to-film shelf. The producers recognized a way around the novel's direct hit of Nazi vengeance. In the 1979 movie, Sir Hugo Drax operates out of California from within a network of facilities for research and construction of space shuttle-like transportation next door to the French chateau he transferred to the American West stone by stone, like London Bridge.

In the novel, Sir Hugo Drax is a celebrity in the UK by dint of great wealth and incredible generosity. Drax has donated to his adopted home the ultimate defense rocket, "the Moonraker," which will restore British sovereignty in the Cold War context. That Drax all along planned to blast London with the lifetime-long held-back miracle weapon is a reprisal made all the more blatant by the blind spot it occupies. For, Drax's rocket scheme is such a foreign body – both as event in the book and, apparently, as book – that no one in Britain can recognize a Nazi victory rocket when only ten years after the war they see a big one being built atop the cliffs of Dover.

In the movie, the Nazi/"not see" Death-Star element is the eugenics prejudice guiding the selection of sole survivors to be transported in the flotilla of space shuttles to the restart position, the pure future of the species. But even the best laid plan is undone by Bond's Allied propaganda pitch to Drax's henchman, the giant named Jaws, who, suited up with his midget partner, thought he was going to get away with the purity brigade. The freakish victim takes his stand with Bond's triumph against all odds.

Does Lucas's admission or recollection of the influence of Joseph Campbell's *The Hero with a Thousand Faces* contradict the setting of the *Star Wars* success story in these historical prop departments? No. Although Campbell first published the book in 1949, it was upon its revised reissue in 1968 that he, like his model Carl Jung, found a larger following in the United States. Campbell benefited, therefore, from the era of change tied to the antiwar movement in the States. After the spirit of rebellion had gone into decline, Lucas brought it back, albeit reshuffled along the inner/outer fronts of World War Two propaganda. The stampede of family approval followed. Shortly after the appearance of Lucas's movie, new editions of Campbell's book displayed Luke Skywalker (Mark Hammill) on the cover.

The Hero with a Thousand Faces had already served as the main bookend propping up the media's mythologizing of President Kennedy's term in office as "Camelot." The former First Lady, in the meantime Jacqueline Onassis and Doubleday editor, arranged for the 1988 publication of *The Power of Myth*. The sequel to and summary of *The Hero with a Thousand Faces* was based on a transcript of Bill Moyers's long conversation with Campbell, which was filmed for TV on Lucas's Skywalker Ranch. Looking back upon this delegation (Campbell died shortly before the show aired), we could be inside a science fiction by Philip K. Dick, in particular *The Simulacra* (1964), which anticipated mass psychologization of primal scenes of a ruling middlebrowbeat and the consequent marketing of the reduction of myth and religion to the stages of grief – or, rather, of the hero's progress.

Another upgrading backstory you will hear from *Star Wars* idolators – adepts of the history of their own making in the digital archive – concerns Lucas's contact with Japanese art cinema. Since he had been unable to obtain the adaptation rights for the *Flash Gordon* franchise, in 1973 Lucas came up with a synopsis for a heroic space movie of his own, which reads like the plot line of Akira Kurosawa's *The Hidden Fortress* (1958). However, whatever all-nighter pressure he was under to slap together that summary, it didn't feature the franchise's distinctive traits, such as "the force," which only appeared in the final version. What remains from the cribbed synopsis are the two robots, who held the place of the bickering peasants. Too much information is the milieu of online outlines of interpretation. I found an afterimage of this unlikely lineage of influence in an interview with Andrei Tarkovsky's son. When he was a kid, he wasn't able to see *Star Wars* in the Soviet Union, so parental guidance told him the story and enacted it so he could watch it in his imagination. The next day his father showed him the movie that was available for screening: *The Hidden Fortress*.[3] What I take from this anecdote is that censorship, which gets passed along, promotes half-knowledge.

Star Wars introduces itself both in the timeless past of the fairy tale ("A long time ago") and in the future of outer space ("in a galaxy far, far away"). This conflation of defining traits of the genres is a compromise formation in light of the hostile takeover bid informing J.R.R. Tolkien's manifesto-essay "On Fairy-Stories." The breakthrough success of *Star Wars* collected its momentum in the contest between the new or renewed genre of fantasy, which Tolkien began championing in the 1930s, and the other genre component of Lucas's film, science fiction. The historical onset of the rivalry between fantasy and science fiction is crowded with literary examples. But as B-genres science fiction and fantasy were contemporaries of early cinema emerging out of the scientific and experimental study and recording of motion made visible. In an early work such as *The Time Machine* by H.G. Wells, the transport through time – the ununderstood crux of this literary experiment – was rendered through description of "special effects," the cinematic-fantastic component in the narrative, which reflected new developments and forecast the movies to come. *Critique of Fantasy* follows the rebound of wish fantasy between literary description of the ununderstood and its cinematic counterpart (for example, visual and special effects).

3   Marina Galperina, "Andrey Tarkovsky Loved *Star Wars* So Much," *Animal,* October 31, 2013, http://animalnewyork.com/2013/andrey-tarkovsky-loved-star-wars-so-much/.

Tolkien introduced his new view of a genre (as old as human consciousness, he upholds, but in the meantime confined to childhood) with a view to addressing a more adult readership. Works of fantasy tended to be reserved for children: that's how Tolkien's *The Hobbit* (1937) first circulated. Tolkien concluded "On Fairy-Stories" while composing *Lord of the Rings* (1954–55), which he hoped to pitch to a more mature audience. The new young-adult genre Tolkien launched did not begin to make it outside its own subcultural niche market and become a full-grown rival of science fiction on the adjacent shelves in the bookstore until the hypnotizing success of *Star Wars*. That it is hard to tag the genre content of Lucas's franchise fits the contest to which it owes its projection. In *Reign of Fire* (2002), fire-breathing dragons beset London in a future that sure looks like we're back in the Battle of Britain. In the bunker's scare – I mean, care – center, the kids are diverted by the puppet-play version of the *Star Wars* saga. The Darth Vader puppet pronounces: "I am your father," while all around the transfixed children gawk and gasp. In this future world, the story counts as mythic fairy tale.

We could observe the *Star Wars* Effect skewering together the 2015 return of three major franchises. SPECTRE is punctuated throughout by encrypted souvenirs of the films comprising the franchise chapter that opened in 2006 styling with a return to the 1960s. The integration of Germany at the front of the line of the ghost history of World War Two (even as the world turned the denial) packed the surprise appeal of the first season of Bond movies. In 2015, the first SPECTRE agent to report at the meeting – which is a remake of a scene in *Thunderball* (1965) that reintroduces Blofeld – speaks German and business as usual. Instead of the residual charging of the traumatic history of World War Two, however, a fantasy tale is introduced along the lines of Otto Rank's transfer of the import of the Freudian poetics of daydreaming to his own account of the myth of the birth of the hero. Young Bond, the adoptive brother, came to monopolize the father's love like the cuckoo deposited in the nest. Blofeld remains the crazed son crying out "cuckoo, cuckoo" whenever Bond is near. His criminality, which commences with the murder of the father, expresses one sibling's envy of the orphan brother, the true heir and hero.

We touch here on the family romance which, quickly put, is a fantasy Freud identified during his season of theorizing wish fulfillment. In *SPECTRE,* the authenticity of inheritance is asserted outside bloodlines, preserving the romance through its spiritual reversal: the adopted heir is the hero. The family romance is the fantasy of the child currently being raised by nice but modest foster parents (including uncles and aunts). The eventual ascendancy to hero status will disclose and reclaim the child's more elevated inheritance.[4]

By keeping it all in the family romance, the other films flashing in the back of the minds of the viewer–experts watching *SPECTRE* rebound within the compact underworld of the last three films, to which the return of Blofeld from the first season of the franchise subjects Bond, the bond with the viewer. That the viewer-expert knows the franchise and brings to the new

---

4 Rank made the family romance the rule of the heroic saga in *Der Mythos von der Geburt des Helden* (*The Myth of the Birth of the Hero,* 1914). It is by this introject in its makeup that Campbell's book seems to spring eternal following the splash made by Luke Skywalker. "Typically," Campbell says to Moyers in the TV special while flashing on images from *Star Wars,* "the hero is the orphaned son of royalty. Unaware of his true identity, he is consigned to a life of drudgery and exile." Or again: "the child of destiny has to face a long period of obscurity." These quotes did not make it into the book *The Power of Myth,* the selective transcript of the TV special. When Campbell goes on, still on TV, to identify this situation of the hero's childhood with Rank's Freudian thesis of the family romance and the myth of the hero's birth, he draws instead on the post-Freudian work Rank pursued focused on an origin of the hero in the womb, which becomes the foster placement he must jettison: "everyone is a hero in his birth. He has undergone a tremendous transformation from a little, you might say, water creature, living in a realm of amniotic fluid and so forth, then coming out, becoming an air-breathing mammal that ultimately will be self-standing and so forth, is an enormous transformation and it is a heroic act […]. It's the primary hero, hero form, you might say." The scenario skips the relational origin of life between mother and child. See "Ep. 1: Joseph Campbell and the Power of Myth – 'The Hero's Adventure'" (June 21, 1988), *Moyers Archive,* https://billmoyers.com/content/ep-1-joseph-campbell-and-the-power-of-myth-the-hero's-adventure-audio/.

screening all the information fitting a smaller screen, the portal to the digital archive, inflects each 2015 sequel with the return to an encrypted origin.

In *Jurassic World,* the child protagonists fall into a crypt storing all that remains of the visitor center from the first film, (1993). Out of the debris they assemble a rescue vehicle. The past belongs to the history of the films, while the present allows the story's "mythic" personalization by the viewers. Two brothers from competing eras of fantasy (the elder is a teen) shake their foster care and form an alliance to withstand on their own the derailment of the world (the separation of their true parents). The reproductive romance of the fantasy is split off into the DNA remixed in the labs to engineer the faux prehistoric animals. The secret raptor provenance is the hot spot of betrayal and allegiance in the heroic saga waged among the creatures.[5]

At the close of *Star Wars: The Force Awakens,* the young heroine, who doesn't yet know her true parents, embarks on a journey that crosses generations to draw benefit from the first film. The dark-side double and rival is the peer of the new viewer also in terms of his expertise and fandom, which he renews in secret recess with the skull and mask of Darth Vader, the grand or great father the family romance won for him. While the inter-references in the other two sequels are each a spolia more by metonymy, the haunted helmet–skull is in fact a leftover of the original masked heavy-breathing psycho-POV retrofitted in 2015 above the entry to the super-franchise, which imparts the family romance of heroism to all franchises that carry with them the digital know-how of their viewer fans.

---

5 While the specific *Jurassic Park* franchise is less vintage than the other two that came back for more in 2015, the adaptation and book reach back through the history of the fantasy and science fiction genres to earlier novels and their subsequent adaptations, which is not lost on the fans hunting for the "Easter eggs" of cross-reference in the digital archive. The title of Michael Crichton's sequel novel cited one of the precursors: Arthur Conan Doyle's *The Lost World* (1912). Jules Verne's *Journey to the Center of the Earth* (1864) and Edgar Rice Burroughs's *The Land that Time Forgot* (1916) are the bookends of Crichton's posthumously published prequel, set in the late-nineteenth-century United States, *Dragon's Teeth* (2017).

After Ridley Scott saw *Star Wars* he immediately shelved what he was planning, an adaptation of the medieval legend of "Tristan and Iseult," and accepted instead the offer to direct *Alien* (1979). What wowed him in Lucas's film was the new vista of special effects that the magic wand of fantasy was waving through, ultimately toward the anticipated innovations of digitization. His next film was *Blade Runner* (1982), the adaptation of P.K. Dick's *Do Androids Dream of Electric Sheep?* (1968), a movie that counts in its own right as history changing.[6] The two films follow separate trajectories that Scott later combined in his *Alien* prequels, *Prometheus* (2012) and *Alien: Covenant* (2017), which frame his eclectic career with the mix of science fiction and fantasy, the main "effect" that *Star Wars* taught him.

Science fiction failed to predict the future, and yet fantasy did not so much succeed as draw the benefit from the resemblance of basic fantasying to the new digital relation. If the fantasy that is true is no longer the Gospel (which was Tolkien's definition) but instead all that digitization holds in store, then fantasy becomes a genre without borders, the subsuming genre of "fiction."

The 1977 anticipation of the digital relation went into the continuation of the original *Star Wars* trilogy like a wish into its fulfillment. Lucas was intent on imparting digital perfectibility to his earlier special effects. But embellishing the same old films was not enough: their projection into the digital era required a greater frame of heroic saga or franchise, which he accomplished by a reversal that placed the beginning in the middle. Those first *Star Wars* films were revealed to be descendants of a heroic franchise in which the fantasy of the digital relation was a wrap with the surprise of true origins.

In addition to the topics foregrounded in psy-fi, notably, psychosis and mourning (or unmourning), adolescence is pivotal throughout my archaeology of the recent past. In *Critique of Fantasy,* it's clear right from the start that the work cut out for a poetics of daydreaming is the rescue of teen innovation from

---

6   In *Germany: A Science Fiction* (Fort Wayne: Anti-Oedipus Press, 2014), I assigned *Blade Runner* to the avant-garde of the return of German science fiction after decades of repression with(in) the recent past of the Cold War.

the turbulence of its throwaway prematurity. Freud drew the distinction between child's play, which can be out in the open since the underlying fantasy – the wish to be big or grownup – doesn't merit censure, and its substitute, the fantasying that takes over in adolescence and withdraws omnipotence into a stronghold that keeps private the wishes that are embarrassingly narcissistic, inartistic, and even antisocial.

The mix of B-genres to which the present study attends in tracking the ascendancy of fantasy is as nebulous as the triumphant genre's meaning or medium, which *is* fantasying. That our second nature as daydreamers is so slippery does not contradict that it is, according to Freud and Tolkien, the reason for art's existence. I have specialized before in engaging the outer limits of understanding. Psychopathy? Nobody knows. Asking people what they think daydreaming is might be a party game. Our second nature is either disowned or not known. And yet, out of the interior cacophony of "like, like" and "unfriend, unfriend," the reflux reflex of omnipotence, I am trying to discern, as did the psychoanalysts and philosophers before me, the evolution of the social relation that is art.

You can think anything, but once you enter upon the genre of thought that is wish-fantasy, the emerging daydream scenario is at once singular (in context) and apparently limited to a finite list of variations and types. While it seems that by now anything goes in A- and B-culture and the old precept that the solo wish fantasy is inadmissible no longer applies, the ways in which primary narcissism keeps on being altered and restaged for the social relation have become "diacritical," reliant on the biggest show in town: the public narcissism of small differences.

Freud upended the innocent/guilty impasse between fantasy altered by the stick and carrot of unattainable beauty and untenable, unsavory private daydreaming through a line of contrast that unfolds in time. In his poetics of the daydream, Freud supplied the notion of a datemark that belongs to the moment in the present that triggered the fantasying and indelibly stamped it. The constitutive arc in every daydream, which takes off from an idealized past and jump-cuts to the future of wish fulfillment so as to elide the present, is a bridge that will fall down. Fantasy is historicization waiting to happen, the mortal recoil of its flight.

The evolving genre of science fiction also lies in wait; by its salvos of right or wrong extrapolation, it is ever grounded in the present tense, in its ongoing tensions and encrypted contents. In *Origin of the German Mourning Play*,[7] Walter Benjamin derived modern allegory from the untenability of Christianity's purchase on the future. I am arguing, in the case of science fiction, along these lines: when a weighty forecast (that can't wait to exercise controlling interest) falls short, allegory takes over.

Somewhere over the digital relation, Ridley Scott's *The Martian* (2015) is a good example of a movie that looks like science fiction as often as it acts like and refers to fantasy. I give this example up front to underscore that it's not only the evidence of medievalist props that I am following out into the borderland between the two genres. *The Martian* is the fantasy saga of the hero's return, but the treasure he brings back to the community, the conclusion that the film adaptation adds to Andy Weir's 2011 novel, is problem-solving, a lesson that the protagonist Mark Watson teaches in the end, which is more commensurate with digital knowledge than Christian fantasy. Earlier the hero waved the digital mirror before our eyes. Yes, he sits before some functioning console and starts logging a record of his solo time on Mars. We are his digital mirror, which Mark rolls over from recording to simultaneity-contact through a series of reenactments of a concise history of writing and telecommunication from the vantage point of the digital. Simply, but subtly, the science fiction of successful space transport falls short for the protagonists with whom we identify, who prevail against all odds by improvising outside chances out of low-tech materials, the ruins of the old story of success, namely, classical science fiction. By lagging behind, science fiction nevertheless inscribes upon the props of its failed forecasts a legible caption to the relationship to simultaneity, which in *The Martian* tells the story or history of the new millennial prospect of the one-world exploration of outer space that's looped through the integration of China.

Gravity (2013) is another hybrid model that only looks like politically minded science fiction, a warning shout about space

---

7   This is my translation of the German title of Benjamin's study *Ursprung des deutschen Trauerspiels* (Berlin: E. Rowohlt, 1928).

ecology in the near future. The continued dependence of our media of simultaneity on the lower regions of space colonization (the satellites of the Cold War) reaps catastrophe. The allegorical apparatus between space exploration and the digital relation, the fantasy that is true, falls into place. *Gravity* gave a special-effects-enhanced sense of being in space. The director, Alfonso Cuarón, was already a veteran of fantasy's visual and special effects through his 2004 movie *Harry Potter and the Prisoner of Azkaban,* which spent three years in postproduction before making it to the screen. The same digital effects company was entrusted with *Gravity*.

The outer space *Gravity* explores is a fantasy space imagined in keeping with Kant's identification of the netherworld as the main impetus for fantasying. The protagonist, with a little help from her friendly ghost, assumes the adult profile of mourning. Loving the dead, letting them go on, but also letting them go, allows the mother in space to secure a saving Chinese reentry capsule and escape the Cold War science fiction of psychoticizing loneliness and fragmentation. When she crawls out of the water onto land and stands upright, she's back inside her embodiment.

Space is a junkyard, a chain-reaction of destruction just waiting to happen. Then the Russians detonate one of their satellites, and the debris races faster than a speeding bullet, taking out all satellites along its orbit and eclipsing digital communication on Earth. Right before the catastrophe hits, Ryan is up there fixing a satellite: too little repair too late. It cannot have been long ago that she lost her four-year-old daughter. How did she pass inspection? Her co-astronaut, Matt, is too old to have passed muster. The episode in space is a ruinscape inhabited by ghosts and their melancholic correspondents.

Before Matt pries himself loose from her resolute grasp and then comes back officially as a ghost, Ryan tells him that when she's not at work she drives around for hours listening to any radio music at all, just no talking. (Even though she says she could get used to the silence of space, we constantly hear staticky radio transmission noise.) Ryan was out driving when she learned that her daughter had slipped at school, hit her head, and was dead. In his posthumous persona Matt is the ghost of the opening season of mourning: "Do you want to go back or stay here? I get it – it's nice here." It's nice that there's no one to lose, which also means that there is no one to mourn her. He's gone again but she sends a message after him, sending him off, too, after all. The message is addressed to the loss she tried to lose driving around training center USA. Her daughter is restored to an object relation in mourning. Ryan opens one of the instruction manuals that apparently can be found in every escape pod on the shelf just above the console, which, like a volume of encyclopedic knowledge from the Enlightenment with which pioneers explored the new world, takes her back for a restart no longer manically fixated upon outer space colonization.

That science fiction can go into reverse and sustain within its ruins the allegorical legibility of deregulated fantasy finds support through the commentaries on a new metaphysics of the "new world" and its genre that Gotthard Günther pursued beginning in the 1940s while in exile in the States. The German philosopher, who specialized in dismantling via Hegel Aristotelian bivalent logic, discovered in the US both American science fiction and cybernetics. His reflections on the new metaphysics of the new-world genre are a mainstay of this genealogy with B-genres. While Günther doesn't address wish fantasying directly in his metaphysics, he does recognize in the posthumously published study *Die amerikanische Apokalypse* (*The American Apocalypse*) that the new mythic fairy tale of American science fiction is still provisional, reliant more on daydreaming contact with the remote future, which he quickly distinguishes from what is merely fantastic ("Fantasterei").[8] Günther is addressing instead

---

8   Gotthard Günther, *Die amerikanische Apokalypse,* ed. Kurt Klagenfurt (Klagenfurt: Profil, 2000), 115. Only one segment was published in Günther's lifetime: *Die Entdeckung Amerikas und die Sache mit der Weltraum Literatur,* the monograph that introduced his 1952 series of editions of works of American science fiction. We will be visiting the body of Günther's introductions and commentaries from this edition together with the posthumously published *The American Apocalypse* throughout this study.

   I drew on Günther's work in *I Think I Am: Philip K. Dick* and again in *Germany: A Science Fiction* focusing on the articles he wrote in English for Campbell's magazine *Astounding Stories* (on the sci-fi conceits of alien contact, artificial intelligence, and time jumps and

the "anticipations" that reflect "a slowly awakening speculative consciousness, which begins to set itself goals in its daydreams." "These American daydreams of a new epoch of human history are so remarkable and so informative regarding what is as yet quite unknown about the nature of humanity in the new world that it would be a definite loss not to know more about them."[9]

The two genres science fiction and fantasy are imbricated in their attachment to a poetics of flights of waking fantasy. *Critique of Fantasy* reads Tolkien's 1947 essay "On Fairy-Stories"[10] together with its precursor, Freud's 1907 "Der Dichter und das Phantasieren" ("The Poet and Daydreaming").[11] Not until Tolkien defined the genre of fantasy could it enter the offices of the "law of genre." Fantasy is a mental faculty that Freud and Tolkien boldly claimed as the source of artistic production. Before the advent of a poetics of daydreaming, schools of philosophy had long been engaged in corralling fantasy, the wayward kin of the imagination. Freud passed the hot property of philosophical ethics along in his 1907 essay, when he addressed omnipotent wish fantasy as the resource of the aspirations and resolutions of art, which, however, the artwork can never look back at or acknowledge. By grounding his genre in the one fantasy that is true, the Gospel, Tolkien obviated and made obvious the ethical mandate of fantasy's restraining order.

The prospect of deregulated wishing is as old as the philosophical ethics that would contain it. Within the orbit of the compulsion to find a corrective in ethics for excessive fantasying, there also emerged a philosophical reception of the realm of shadows. By deploying wish or will as cursor in evaluating occult or paranormal states, this philosophical reception directly inspired the psychoanalysis of omnipotent thought and fantasy. The onset of the philosophy of haunting coincided with an

---

time travel). I won't be repeating this specific focus in *Critique of Fantasy*.

9 Günther, *Die amerikanische Apokalypse*, 114.
10 An earlier version of the essay was delivered as Andrew Lang Lecture in 1938.
11 This is how I will be modifying throughout this study the official English translations of the title of Freud's brief essay.

efflorescence of clairvoyance and related states of waking dreaming in the historical setting of animal magnetism. Although the psycho-poetics of the daydream, in contrast to its philosophical prehistory, doesn't address the ghost themes of modern Western occultism, these are the themes that prove hard to keep out and indeed, as the study shows, repeatedly overtake it.

The majority share of close reading encounters with the contestants that meet the genre requirements, as well as with the hybrids that cross the boundaries, goes into the second volume, *The Contest between B-Genres*. To organize the collateral mass of materials piled high in the borderlands, I rely on two readymades in the facing corners of the ring, C.S. Lewis's "Space Trilogy" and the roster of American science fictions that Günther selected and glossed for the German readership in 1952. While Lewis constructs science fiction as the dark force behind every historical nihilism, Günther and his authors demolish the metaphysical mainstays of the regional civilizations that hailed from the East and banish from the New World and its genre the plain text of Old-World metaphysics, namely the fairy-story, on which the fantasy genre relies.

The third volume, *The Block of Fame,* explores the American cult of greatness in light of the early wish for it. The failure in success skews the walk into an obstacle course of writer's block, plagiarism, and the wish to be refused (Edmund Bergler). Here I sign in with the "constellation" Adorno developed to outlast the culture industry's depravation and theft of the poetics of fantasying. As it rises up in Adorno's essay "Schubert" (1928), the constellation is a form of thought that throughout *Critique of Fantasy* organizes my readings in the underworld of fantasying, waking dream states, and media. All the component trajectories of the study are consequently at work in every part, and each part brings back the trajectories and ratchets up a new focus and relation among them.

Critique of Fantasy returns to a discarded origin of Freud's thought. What international psychoanalysis calls desire, Freud addressed in the original language, which wishes rather than desires, with the only term available: "Wunsch," the cognate of "wish." The etymology extends through waystations of this study: delusion ("Wahn"), struggling to win, and, finally, the word in the name "Venus" (the fantasy planet around which Lewis's "Space Trilogy" orbits). The reinscription of desire within the syntax of wishing makes way for mourning.

This first volume explores the new psychonomies of mourning arising in the borderlands of the dueling B-genres. The new world enmity between the fantasy of vampirism and the science fiction of zombieism introduces a forum for addressing novel forms of grief. Their repercussions might be adduced in reading the Disney chapter of the *Star Wars* franchise. A new generation of antagonists and fans must breach the cryogenic stoppage of history that brings back the original forebears, even or especially those already dead off screen. But before contemplating a new mourning, the volume studies in its opening stretch all the interpretations of wish fantasy that, however mismatched, join together in supporting a poetics (and aesthetics) of the daydream. Although it is indeed an unlikely coupling given Freud's Enlightenment-proud secular modernism, when the father of psychoanalysis opens the relay he is joined by Tolkien, the other premier daydream believer.

Tolkien was a philologist and, like his cohort C.S. Lewis, a medievalist. By both guilds he adhered to a view of continuous tradition forwarding the Middle Ages across oceans of time condensed within the history of language. Tolkien and Lewis sought a commensurate outlet for their hobbyist literary inclinations by dislodging science fiction's monopoly among the new popular genres. Notwithstanding the rightful reclamation of certain works by Lewis, Tolkien, and Charles Williams as some kind of literature, overall the output of the academic club to which the three belonged – the Inklings! – represents the provincial drag on what was at the time the expat destiny of English-language letters. My relationship to the canon will remain cursory (with the exception of Lewis's "Space Trilogy," since it fully enters the borderland between science fiction and fantasy).

I will also be considering the import of German Romanticism, which helped sustain the illusion that Tolkien's fantasy genre was the direct descendant of a continuous UK medievalist tradition. While it is not a dominant trajectory in what follows, I bring it up to sign my name in the setting of the book's composition. During my six years teaching at the Academy of Fine Arts in

Karlsruhe, I opened with a class dedicated to my renewed interest in science fiction, which became my 2014 study *Germany: A Science Fiction*. It deposited a seed of auto-stimulation in the students with an art career ahead of them. But my largest following came to the lecture hall several years later when I offered a course on the topic of fantasy. It was a happy coincidence that I was interested in taking my former dismissal of the genre to the next level of ambivalence and reflecting more deeply on its manifest ascendancy. It turned out that so many of the Karlsruhe students, especially those in training to teach art in German high school, were fantasy adherents. I remember once after screening a student film in class that I commented on a cultural difference, I thought, suggested by certain details of "low-class" life in the setting of a recognizable fairy-tale garden. The fairy-tale fantasy central to this German student film, I offered, would be replaced in its counterpart in the States by the milieu that Americans associate with trailer parks. The guest artist visiting my class, who was German, immediately commented: "The fairy-tale garden *is* the German trailer park." This, then, is the bottom line and secret title of my study: Fantasy, a Trailer Park from Germany.

1

The Ethics, Poetics, and Practical Metaphysics of Waking Dreaming

Be Careful What You Wish For

That the death wish, the one wish guaranteed in time to come true, is the trespass that will bite you in the ass counts as a topos of horror cinema and psychoanalysis. Bringing back the dead rakes the ambivalence coals across the Christian hearth of demonization. In *Pet Sematary* (1989), the dead reanimated within an animist–heathen setting are demonic. At the close of the sequel to *30 Days of Night* (2007), *Dark Days* (2010), the widow reanimates her husband, apparently forgetting that he died a vampire (really a borderline zombie). Chomp! I can think of two instances in Freud's writing: first, a typical dream in *The Interpretation of Dreams*. A boy dreamer is visited at night by his deceased father, who's back because he doesn't know that he's dead. But another knowledge is in hiding and operative: what the dad doesn't know is that his son wished him dead. Second, in his analysis of the psychic reality of Dostoevsky's epileptic seizures, Freud adopts the superego position and commands: you wanted a dead father, now *be* the dead father.[1]

It is possible to view the fairy tale as schooling the will to be a beacon of the good awash in wishing. While Tolkien was

---

1 Both Freud examples are central to my *Aberrations of Mourning: Writing on German Crypts* (Detroit: Wayne State University Press, 1988).

mixing a new literary genre out of Germanic ingredients in the UK, in California, Germany's West Coast, Walt Disney released the premier fantasy film, *Snow White and the Seven Dwarfs* (1937). Daydream fantasy not only underlies every making that makes a wish, or rather makes a wish presentable, but – and this Disney pursued as its saving trace – it also lights up the test pattern of development, the earliest grid of good, bad, evil, and good enough (explored by Friedrich Nietzsche, Melanie Klein, and D.W. Winnicott). According to Freud in "The Poet and Daydreaming," the heroism of the ego in B-literature is set on fairy-tale morality: "the other characters in the story are sharply divided into good and bad, in defiance of the variety of human characters that are to be observed in real life. The 'good' ones are the helpers, while the 'bad' ones are the enemies and rivals of the ego which has become the hero of the story."[2] The ego of the reader or listener attends this schooling.

In *The Power of Myth,* Joseph Campbell concludes that *Star Wars* qualifies as mythic fairy tale by the eddying of its edification: "I've heard youngsters use some of George Lucas' terms – 'the Force' and 'the dark side.' So it must be hitting somewhere. It's a good sound teaching, I would say."[3] Early on in the Disney film, when the princess sings about wish fulfillment at the wishing well, it is the prop that spells out the imperative of philosophical ethics, namely, that by our private nature as daydreamers it is incumbent upon us, ultimately, to learn to wish well. This is not the moral of every work of fantasy. One look at Wagner's Siegfried turns up the contrast with the Disney revalorization. Snow White, who doesn't kill her dwarf, reclaims the projections of good and evil for a new relationship to her self-loving daydreaming.

---

2 Sigmund Freud, "Creative Writers and Day-dreaming," in *The Standard Edition of the Complete Psychological Works of Sigmund Freud, Vol. IX (1906–1908): Jensen's "Gradiva" and Other Works,* ed. and trans. James Strachey with Anna Freud (London: The Hogarth Press, 1964), 150.

3 Joseph Campbell with Bill Moyers, *The Power of Myth,* ed. Betty Sue Flowers (New York: Anchor Books, 1991), 177.

Johann Peter Hebel, who went to Karlsruhe to go to school and then got stuck there, composed "Drei Wünsche" ("Three Wishes," 1811), his remaking of fairytale material into a comedy of perils attending wish fulfillment. The mountain fairy presents a couple the gift of guaranteed fulfillment of three wishes, which will commence at the end of the week. Until Friday, then, they rehearse wishing. But once the free offer takes effect, each act of wishing must count in real time as fulfilled, for which the couple was not prepared. It crosses the mind of the hungry wife that she'd like a sausage: she says so, too, and there it is. Her husband, angered over the waste of a good wish, wishes out loud that the sausage should hang from her nose. When Freud refers to this punitive wish fulfillment in "The Uncanny," he judges that it is "very striking but not in the least uncanny."[4] It is another example of how a fairytale that otherwise "recalls repressed desires and surmounted modes of thinking belonging to the prehistory of the individual and of the race," thereby fulfilling one of the conditions of the uncanny, falls outside the horror genre Freud was demarcating.[5] This fairy tale of wish fantasy entered Freud's science in tandem with its visualization in the first film shorts that showed fulfillment, often the brief superimposition of some dream babe upon the wife, who returns in the POV of her husband angered by the wish that crossed his mind.

Wish number three in Hebel's "Three Wishes," the husband's second wish, delivers his wife of the outgrowth. Story over and the couple is back at the starting gate without gain or pain for their wishes. The narrator suggests that husband and wife might have practiced better for optimal wishing. The first wish should have been for *Verstand,* a more rational understanding. It's hard to keep back the wishes crossing one's mind at the speed of thought. Nevertheless, "Drei Wünsche" shows a self-correcting momentum in the course of the couple's wishes: the first is a

---

4 Sigmund Freud, "The Uncanny," in *The Standard Edition of the Complete Psychological Works of Sigmund Freud, Vol. XVII (1917–1919): An Infantile Neurosis and Other Works,* ed. and trans. James Strachey with Anna Freud (London: The Hogarth Press, 1955), 246. Freud doesn't mention his fairy-tale source for this wish scenario.

5 Ibid., 245.

self-serving appetitive wish; the second lies in the vicinity of the death wish, which brings up the arrears of wishing, the good and evil consequences; the third wish is the good one, which flexes the hope that reparation can still be made. Wishing undergoes development from selfishness to responsibility.

In "On Fairy-Stories," Tolkien tried to pry his fantasy genre loose from subordination to classroom childhood and the philosophical schooling of wishing and willing. He also sought to lay claim to the fantasy source of fiction by decrying its mismanagement in science fiction. But he cedes overtaking both tendencies in the field and admits approximation at the new borders he demarcates. By not excluding childhood reading but including the adolescence of fantasying, he corrects the jump-cut in fairy-tales from childhood to young adulthood. In "On Fairy-Stories," Tolkien sees the true tale correct the fall of those teens given to asocial fantasying: "[I]t is one of the lessons of fairy-stories [...] that on callow, lumpish, and selfish youth peril, sorrow, and the shadow of death can bestow dignity, and even sometimes wisdom."[6]

To say what he means by tales of the fairy realm, Tolkien checks off a list of what he doesn't mean. Because they put on animal clothing for the satire of human affairs, "Beast-fables" count a near miss with the interspecial-creaturely cast of other worlds (21–22). Fairy-stories are also not "travellers' tales" like *Gulliver's Travels* or the yarns of Baron Munchausen, which "report many marvels, but they are marvels to be seen in this mortal world in some region of our own time and space, distance alone conceals them" (19). Another kind of travel fable, like Wells's *The Time Machine*, comes close. In the relay of contrast hurdles Tolkien sets up for his new genre to run through and prove its true definition, the boundary he draws up against science fiction pulls back in the instance of H.G. Wells's time travel tale and allows one border crossing. The Eloi and the Morlocks inhabit an "abyss of time so deep as to work an enchantment upon them." But

---

6   J.R.R. Tolkien, "On Fairy-Stories," in *Tree and Leaf / Smith of Wootton Major / The Homecoming of Beorhtnoth* (London: Unwin Books, 1975), 47. Subsequent page references are given in the text.

what weakens the effect is "the preposterous and incredible Time Machine itself" (20).

According to Tolkien, a true fairy-story satisfies a yearning to survey the depths of space and time (the trajectory that science fiction was monopolizing) or to hold communion with other living things (not necessarily in outer space but preferably in terrestrial utopias of interspecial relationship). But removing the machine age does not go far enough. Tolkien also rules out "any story that uses the machinery of Dream, the dreaming of actual human sleep, to explain the apparent occurrence of its marvels" (ibid.). It is by dint of "their dream-frame and dream-transitions" that "Lewis Carroll's *Alice* stories [...] are not fairy-stories" (21). Tolkien flies in the face of a tendency that runs deep to view art and the night dream under the same aegis. Heightened by this contrast Tolkien makes the daring affirmation that mere daydreaming is the resource or analogue for a creative process that for him is as big as Christianity.

Even while dismissing the time machine, Tolkien had to admit that Wells's story satisfied one of the "primordial human desires" by virtue of fantasy's fundamental operation, in which magic or machine is not an end itself. By dint of his high praise for the enchantment worked by the competition, Tolkien this one time concluded: "the borders of the fairy-story are inevitably dubious" (20). The topos of the permeability of the border, which is allowed even while the boundary line is drawn, is salient, as we will see, in the fiction and nonfiction on fantasying. It tempers varying distinctions between daydream and night dream, conscious and unconscious wishes, and fantasy and science fiction.

What is essential to the genre that Tolkien in this essay christens "Fantasy" (49) is "the power of making immediately effective by the will the visions of 'fantasy'" (28). "Fairy-story" needs to be replaced because the genre he seeks to renew is not restricted to believing in fairies, but encompasses instead the realm of Faërie (17), which is as old as the history of language and the human race (26). Fantasy or fantasying comes closer to signifying this realm, but must be differentiated within the thicket of its synonyms and near-synonyms. Daydreaming can reflect the willpower Tolkien flexes and hit its stride near the entrance to philosophy as reverie. At another juncture, where lying and fiction meet and cross over, ethics must make good not only on the will but even and especially on the wish. What Tolkien adds right after replacing fairy with the visions of fantasy shows that we are in the murky environs of waking wish fantasy: "Not all are beautiful or even wholesome, not at any rate the fantasies of fallen Man" (28).

Fallen man is of course the teenager, the pioneer of private fantasying. In Tolkien's account, the teen takes the fall for staining "the elves [...] with his own stain" (ibid.). The elf belongs to the fairytale of adolescence stuffed inside childhood, the curbed sex appeal of supernatural cuteness. One strain of fallen man's stain would be, then, the aging of the cute. In a steady fallen state, the adolescent just grows older, losing the bloom of promise, gaining only on an adaptation to his antisocial tendencies. There remains, however, the deeper wish to escape from this grown-up adjustment to a flatline of fallen fantasies. Tolkien draws the horizon line of science fiction across the space and pace of this fallen adaptation: "Why should we not escape from [...] the Morlockian horror of factories? They are condemned even by the writers of that most escapist form of all literature, stories of Science fiction" (64).

While authors of fantasy will into existence other worlds, ultimately the secondary world of secondary belief and sub-creation (40–41, 44), the "prophets" of science fiction "often foretell (and many seem to yearn for) a world like one big glass-roofed railway-station." The will to fulfill the wish for other worlds doesn't go beyond the journey in time and space. The world town is left to run on empty: "and the ideals of their idealists hardly reach farther than the splendid notion of building more towns of the same sort on other planets" (64–65).

Around the time of the composition of *The Hobbit,* Tolkien and Lewis commenced exchanging their views on the shortcomings of science fiction and how they might remedy them. Tolkien would write a time-travel tale and Lewis a fable set in outer space, thus recovering between them the two trajectories of H.G. Wells's entry in the new genre he established for modern English letters. Tolkien's effort left behind only a fragment, in which the wish to dwell in the prehistory of *The Lord of the Rings,* which

Tolkien was working to complete, was fulfilled and forgotten.[7] Unable to carry out his end of their mission, Tolkien deputized Lewis as their fantasy author on rival turf. Lewis, in turn, rendered Ransom, the protagonist of his "Space Trilogy," Tolkien's portrait. Tolkien did, however, write "On Fairy-Stories," which was the manifesto of the contest Lewis alone waged in fiction.

No Strings Attached

Ernst Bloch opens *Das Prinzip Hoffnung* (*The Principle of Hope*, 1954) with an explicit invocation of our daydreaming. That's where our utopian hopes will be too. But right away a battery of provisos follows in which he spells out a compulsory education policy for fantasying:

> Everybody's life is pervaded by daydreams: one part of this is just stale, even enervating escapism, even booty for swindlers, but another part is provocative, is not content just to accept the bad which exists, does not accept renunciation. This other part has hoping at its core, and is teachable. It can be extricated from the unrealized daydream and from its sly misuse, can be activated undimmed."[8]

And Bloch foresees political momentum graduating from the schooling of daydream: "Then let the daydreams grow really

---

[7] Tolkien's unfinished contribution, "The Lost Road," opens and shuts with the first two parts of the first chapter (with various fragments scattered around them). Although father and son are in the twentieth century, they are also enfolded within the deep space of language history, which for the son, who dreams up ancient unknown languages, becomes a vocation. An elf friend appears to the son, who is in the meantime a philologist bereft of his father, and offers fulfillment of the "long-hidden" and "half-spoken" "desire to go back" in time. They travel to Númenor, which flourished and declined during the Second Age of Middle-Earth. See J.R.R. Tolkien, *The Lost Road and Other Writings*, ed. Christopher Tolkien (Boston: Houghton Mifflin Company, 1987), 42.

[8] Ernst Bloch, *The Principle of Hope*, vol. 1, trans. Neville Plaice, Stephen Plaice, and Paul Knight (Cambridge: MIT Press, 1995), 3.

fuller, that is, clearer, less random, more familiar, more clearly understood and more mediated within the course of things.[9]

The modern philosophical schooling of wish or will begins with Thomas Aquinas, who enfolded the return of Aristotle inside his sumtotaling of Christian theology, thus introducing secular ethics at the limit. In the meantime, the titular hero of Carlo Collodi's *Pinocchio* (1883), attended by his cricket conscience and the blue fairy, is the poster boy of natural law. This holds true in particular for the story's 1940 reincarnation in Disney's second fantasy film, which was styled like the country cousin of the 1937 film *Snow White and the Seven Dwarfs,* even using the German town Rothenburg ob der Tauber to model the Italian village.

Collodi was in his fifties when he began contributing to the new genre of literature for children, the pedagogical intervention in childhood that reclaimed earlier folk or fairy tales, a consolidation that was without consolation for Tolkien who sought to reverse its classroom assignment. Italian nationhood was new and good and it followed that all aspects of the socius that had been pried loose from the feudal state must be guided and sustained on an update. So Collodi presented the case of a wooden puppet as the Everybaby to be raised unto becoming good and human.

The 19th Question posed in Aquinas's *Summa Theologiae* (1485), which addresses the goodness of the inner acts of the will, concludes its fifth article by awarding a foundational position to "conscience," which is "a dictate of reason."[10] This follows from the third article, in which all striving is left to the will. But willful striving is drawn to the particular goods to which the senses respond. That's why reason, which knows the difference between right and wrong, that is, correct and incorrect, must guide the will to the good object, goal, or purpose. Aquinas's assurance in the eighth article that we can control the inner acts of the will signals a curtailment of wishing in willing.[11] That the "intensity"

---

9 Ibid., 4.
10 St. Thomas Aquinas, *Summa Theologiae*, I^a–II^{ae}, q. 19 a. 5 co., available online at http://summa-theologiae.org/question/13805.htm.
11 See ibid., I^a–II^{ae}, q. 19 a. 8 co., http://summa-theologiae.org/ques-

of the act holds priority over the "intensity" of the intention is tempered by a school example. A child's good intention to attend school can be interrupted by acts of whim. But if he ends up a schoolboy after all (as Pinocchio finally does), then it follows that the link between intention and act was not broken and the initial inner intensity of the will pulled through.

Melanie Klein argued that the centrality of knowledge makes the classroom the first public sphere for revisiting the setbacks in one's private research at home.[12] The transferential doodling around figures of authority is legend, the legend to the mapping in the mind of a fantasying preoccupation that ushers in a saving ambivalence. Where the lessons and tests are, that's where the fantasying component, affectively askew, will be too.

In the narrative, the boy puppet squashes the talking insect and in the course of his progress supervised largely by his "mother," the girl with the indigo hair, the cricket comes back as ghost with whom he is reconciled at the end. Before Jiminy Cricket can be recognized on screen as the conscience that Pinocchio lets be his guide, the relationship between willing and wishing must be given the lie. By natural law, lying resembles perversion in its violation of the purpose of language, which is to reproduce the true communication. But its not so much that the puppet is a liar, as plain as the nose on his face, it's rather that he's a fantast who gives up his good intentions upon a whim of adventure. He even grows a donkey's tail to prove it. Boys will be boys, especially in range of puberty, and the tumescence of lying afflicting the puppet belongs to the folk-etymological and homonymic proximity to lying with someone. But his fantasying cannot cancel the goodness of his discarded intentions. It takes him on the adventure of saving his father, the utopian turning point in Disney's movie: Geppetto and his pets, Figaro and Cleo, who are all in it together, escape the whale by the efforts of Pinocchio and his cricket.

tion/13808.htm.
12 See Melanie Klein, "The Technique of Analysis in the Latency Period," in *The Psychoanalysis of Children,* trans. Alix Strachey (New York: The Free Press, 1984), chap. 4.

The significance of the puppet protagonist can be illuminated by the phrase "no strings attached," which historically refers at once to a garment without flaws and the binding strings on an ancient document emblematic of its escape clause; it can be snatched back and annulled (originally it was an act of tug of war). The puppet without strings stands outside the social contract. Like the mecha robot in Steven Spielberg's *A.I. Artificial Intelligence* (2001), like the pets in the Geppetto household, the puppet is a figment of unconditional love, a throwback to or booster shot from the era of merger between mother and infant. The illusion of this fusion is a requirement for development, which the mother provides, according to D.W. Winnicott, by dint of a temporary state of psychosis.[13] The only response to unconditional love is unconditional love, which means that it no longer exists in relation, only in the one-way attitude of lovability.

The fairy tale's iteration of Jonas and the whale ends with the puppet boy dead in the water. What prefigures for Christians the prospect of resurrection was in the first place for the ancients, as Otto Rank underscored, burial inside the animal relation, looping preservation through elimination.[14] The trial period of life and death with a puppet for a son was the fulfillment to watch out for. The good puppet giving up the ghost illuminates the deadness that Geppetto's wish fantasy concealed. By his finitude, the other is good and gone, gone for good, which the old man's grief acknowledges. The blue fairy can now grant a father's wish.

Brian Aldiss wrote the story "Supertoys Last All Summer Long" (1969), which Stanley Kubrick tried to adapt in a mix with the Pinocchio story, before passing it along to Spielberg like a demonic curse. Aldiss had already objected to Kubrick's addition of a happy ending. His story closed on a suggested outcome that was inevitable given the misfiring between the robot boy's lovability and the adoptive mother, whose psychosis is not the

---

13 D.W. Winnicott, "Primary Maternal Preoccupation," in *Through Paediatrics to Psycho-analysis: Collected Papers* (London: Karnac Books, 1984), 300–305.

14 Otto Rank, *Kunst und Künstler: Studien zur Genese und Entwicklung des Schaffensdranges* (Gießen: Psychosozial-Verlag, 2000), 150.

kind allowing for merger. She, however, seems granted a reprieve when her couple wins the reproduction lottery. No doubt that too will split along the "seems"; she is looking for the missing merger with her mother, which the lovability of a baby cannot supply. At his end of the non-relationship, the robot David forever falls short of communicating that he loves her in countless unfinished letters. Psycho mom concludes that since the robot's communication skills can't be fixed, "David" is due to be sent back to the factory.

In his childhood, Aldiss's mother was transfixed by the loss of a daughter. He was sandwiched in between the dead sister and a newborn younger sister. Upon her arrival, it turned out that the love on hold for the stillborn baby could still be borne for the new girl, which meant he was better off at boarding school. The Aldiss story illuminates the underworld of the Pinocchio tale.

Collodi was a pen name, which the author first adopted in 1860 and borrowed from the name of the town in which he had spent most of his childhood (it was his mother's birthplace). He was born in Florence as the first of ten children; only two others survived childhood. In an enigmatic sense that their brother picked up on, the seven had died without a name (or any strings attached). After another ten years bearing the special name, Collodi turned to literature for children (he had no children of his own, no reproduction substitutes) and with the Pinocchio story made the name he made for them stick.

That Aldiss's cameo as a robot child goes by the name David drops to the crypt of the other modern fairy legend, Peter Pan. Aldiss learned a good deal from James Matthew Barrie but not the hardest lesson of all: the innocence of a child has a mean streak a mile wide.

David Barrie, J.M. Barrie's older brother and his mother's favorite, fell ice-skating and died the day before turning fourteen. His mother's consolation avowed out loud was that David would never grow old in her memory. James tried to be David, a trick that almost worked in the dark, in nether land, when he appeared before his mother dressed in his dead brother's clothes.

Barrie kept it close to the chest or coffin: "Never" means that he didn't wish David dead.[15]

In person, J.M. Barrie was the gnomic embodiment of a childhood forever stuck on a preteen boy on ice. Grown up a hardhearted stalker, he went on to elaborate the fiction of Neverland in the fantasy environs of spiritualism where bird boys never grow closer to genital sexuality than the cusp of fourteen. The fringe benefit of the fantasy equation between believing in fairies and keeping them alive is circumvention of the adult injunction to bury, which the author bore in his patronymic. He made the mother figure or substitute Wendy responsible for making all the preteen adventurers or delinquents cross their hearts and hope to die.

Prior to Disney or Freud, the sentencing of the will as wish was a horrific prospect at the limits of philosophical ethics. Early on in *Grundlegung zur Metaphysik der Sitten* (*Groundwork for the Metaphysics of Morals,* 1785), Kant warily introduces the will as foundational. The hope remains that where there's a will there's a way to get around mere wishing. Consider a parenthetical/parental aside given to clarify what is meant by "the good will": "[O]f course not as a mere wish [*ein bloßer Wunsch*] but rather as the raising up [*Aufrichtung*] of all means in our power."[16] In the next paragraph, the overvaluation of mere will, even should common reason or sense be in agreement, is strange enough that the suspicion arises that it is all based on "high-flying fancy" (*hochfliegende Phantasterei*). And so, Kant commences "testing" this very idea,[17] which in due course leads to introduction of the saving notion of "duty" (*Pflicht*) which he contrasts with enacted maxims that reflect inclination only and fall short of the moral value secured by acting out of duty.

---

15 That there was a study that published Barrie's actual culpability for David's death, proven as painstakingly as Kurt Eissler's reconstruction of Leonardo Da Vinci's physical abnormality, signals the denial of the powers of the wish alone and the unconscious.
16 Immanuel Kant, *Grundlegung zur Metaphysik der Sitten,* ed. Theodor Valentiner (Stuttgart: Reclam, 2008), 16–17. All translations are mine.
17 Ibid., 17.

Back to the basics with which Kant grudgingly commenced: the moral value does not depend upon the reality of the object of the action, but only upon the "principle of wanting" (d*em Prinzip des Wollens*); even the purpose achieved does not outflank the "principle of the will" (*Prinzip des Willens*).[18] The ascension of the will to principle follows from the necessity of determining the will, which otherwise, if left unattended at the border, would reflect the push and pull of the material drives. The formulation of the categorical imperative can now ensue. Duty ends up the test question for valuation of morality: to apply it alone as your guide is moral. Duty ends up a form without content, which follows for purpose (*Zweck*) as well by the performance of duty's defining moment. Duty for its own sake – purpose itself, in itself – is sufficient motivation for every act that is at once good and morally valuable.

The two imperfect duties, which Kant distinguishes from the commandment-like perfect ones, give syntax to the semantics of duty. We hold a moral duty to develop our own talents unto perfectibility. We are also morally obliged to help others. However, the height to which the duty to our selves can ascend is not a standard that can be transferred to our concern for others. The maximization of the well-being of our fellow men is not our moral duty. Just as it is not moral simply to follow laws prescribing our acts, so it is not moral to improve the morals of others. Although our duty to help others remains just the same, as basic as the one to improve ourselves, it is not continuous with the duty to our selves.

Groundhog Day (1993) keeps turning on a temporal paradox like a wish that the protagonist Phil didn't watch out for. Once his awareness of the eternal return of the same day picks up momentum he is on his own. When Phil first realizes that he inhabits a recurring day of which he alone, repeat after repeat, retains memories, he enters upon phases of antisocial opportunism and suicidal lethargy. That he knows the day will return without consequences delivers him of moral considerations as though he heretofore had never acted truly morally but only in respect to precepts enforced by penalties.

18 Ibid., 24.

The first advantage he takes over his dating prospects is to score by gathering information about each one over countless iterations of the day until in one moment at dinner it's kismet that he knows all her likes and dislikes. (I remember that in California, in the era of the film, a certain advantage along these lines could be obtained by memorizing the daily horoscopes.) During his undercover investigations in the course of one repeating day, he also finds out what his co-worker Rita would like to see in her special other. But that's not good enough.

His only other in this fixated environment is Rita, not only because, as he goes around the rounds, she remains steadfastly the only woman who won't return his love interest on that day. Rita is, in addition, open for discussion of the symptom and significance of his déjà vu crisis. Allowing, like a therapist, the "reality" of the everlasting returning day that Phil confides to her, Rita also enters into his situation or fantasy by considering the advantages, all the talents one could develop, all the knowledge one might amass. He keeps trying to win her over by the evidence of his altruism and developing skills. But at the end of each day dedicated to Rita, to the improvement of his moral profile and the performance of the perfect dinner date, she stops short of consummation, horrified by evidence she notices at the last minute of his ongoing mean-spirited manipulation of her.

If Phil did undergo a change of heart by the influence of Rita alone, then we might never be able to decide whether his improvement in the end was genuinely moral. What proves pivotal is Phil's discovery that his recurring day is the day of the indigent beggar's death. After endlessly ignoring him at the start of the day, he gives him cash. But then, in another episode of the serial day, he stops to take care of him only to discover that it is forever too late. Not because he can't intervene; as the course of his good deeds for the day turns into a long, daily to-do list, he forever and again rescues a boy, whose fall from the tree must have shattered him in the version of the day that did not see Phil's rescue of him. But in the course of eternity, the homeless person Phil decides to care for and about was on that day already and always an old man whose time was up. It is by his finitude that the other is our concern.

Any benevolent project that helps others, but which can too easily be construed as pitched to how others estimate the goodness of following the rules, is not of moral value. In the eternity that links us to and separates us from the finitude of the other, we can conceive and uphold self-betterment and care for others only by a disinterested abstraction like moral duty. In the eon of a returning day, to use other terms crucial to Kant's ethics, it's inconceivable to use persons as means to an end.[19] There's at once too much and not enough time. The curse of wish fulfillment is undone.

At last, Phil has all his good deeds toward others in a row to fill the first part of the day. By the end of the day, those with whom he has thus bonded can express gratitude in Rita's earshot while the town gathers to hear Phil perform outstanding jazz improvisations on the piano (in fact the result of countless first lessons that same day). In the eternity of one day Phil fulfills the imperfect duties. Only thus can his love be returned, an achievement uncompromised by narcissistic and antisocial wish fantasy. In the course of one day it looks like everyone remembers. Phil's memory is no longer a foreign body on the day at last upheld by acts of moral value.

The Fantasies We All Know So Well

Although in "On Fairy-Stories" Tolkien abandoned "without regret" Max Müller, a German precursor and Oxford colleague in his own field of philology, whose view of myth's relationship to language is the reverse of his own,[20] he doesn't recognize/antagonize another German-language author, who set the precedent for exploring fantasying as poetry's source and resource. In his 1907 "The Poet and Daydreaming," Freud argues that many of our wishes arising at night, which presumably hail from childhood, must be concealed not only from others but from ourselves as

---

19 One should treat a person as *Zweck an sich selbst* (ibid., 63), as person for the person's sake, which demarcates the demolition site at once of means and end.
20 Tolkien, "On Fairy-Stories," 27,

well.[21] That these repressed wishes come to expression only in a very distorted form is what makes the waking recollection and retelling of our enigmatically symbolic night dreams possible.

The already available reception of the psychoanalysis of night dreams makes Freud's 1907 juxtaposition of waking fantasy and poetry seem counterintuitive. Since the remembered night dream marks by its distortion of content a step forward from the privacy of wish fantasying toward public reception, it is analogous to poetry. However, "[w]hen scientific work had succeeded in elucidating this factor of *dream-distortion,* it was no longer difficult to recognize that night dreams are wish-fulfillments in just the same way as daydreams – the fantasies which we all know so well" (149). In other words, night dreams join the clear text of the daydream's wish only upon analytic decoding. And the fantasying we all know so well, while kept private, is neither repressed nor really remembered. While it is happening, however, the daydream has our conscious attention; we can be "absent," even "lost" in fantasying. What makes it second nature is that we adapt to an alternation (which can become dissociation) between attending to our daydream scenarios and simultaneous attention to what's really going on.

Another blocker in the reception of Freud's 1907 essay is the pivotal role he grants works of B-culture for understanding the fantasying that leads to *Dichtung*. In B-Culture the wish cannot be encrypted: "[F]or the purposes of our comparison, we will choose not the writers most highly esteemed by the critics, but the less pretentious authors of novels, romances and short stories, who nevertheless have the widest and most eager circle of readers" (149). All these publications celebrate "His Majesty the Ego, the hero alike of every daydream and of every story" (150). After every wounding, the hero recovers in the next chapter, bouncing back for more like a cartoon figure. Although our second nature is a buffer zone of constant scatter and static let's agree to

---

21 Freud, "Creative Writers and Day-dreaming," 148–49. Subsequent page references are given in the text. In addition to my alteration of the title in English, throughout this study, to avoid unnecessary ambiguity, I adjust the spelling of "phantasy" and "phantasying" to "fantasy" and "fantasying."

remain in the setting of poetics and focus on the daydreaming or wish-fantasying in which omnipotence (of thoughts or wishes) is commanded in scenarios that, however rudimentary their speech bubbles, can be related, retold.

Daydreaming, according to Freud, is heir to the fantasying in child's play, the pursuit of being "big." However, unlike this acceptable content of playing, which remains out in the open, the antisocial daydream, which picks up in adolescence where child's play left off, requires privacy: "The child, it is true, plays by himself or forms a closed psychical system with other children for the purposes of a game; but even though he may not play his game in front of the grown-ups, he does not, on the other hand, conceal it from them" (145). Beginning in adolescence, fantasying is one of our "most intimate possessions." It is also a hideout we would be ashamed to share, first off, because it is childish, inappropriate for agents of the real world, and secondly, because "some of the wishes which give rise to [...] fantasies are of a kind which it is essential to conceal" (146). "The adult [...] would rather confess his trespasses than impart his fantasies" (145).

Before psychoanalysis came along one needed a poet without knowing it; our second nature as daydreamers wasn't recognized as such. Everyone felt alone with antisocial thoughts and wishes. Prior to the talking cure and the published documentation of its case examples, the daydreamer believed himself to be "the only person who invents such fantasies and had no idea that creations of this kind are widespread among other people" (145).

Whereas the playing child moves reality around, the fantasying teen is less dependent on (social) reality, which only supplies the impetus for the unrealistic fantasy scenarios. But the separation between playing and reality is already given in child's play: "[E]very child at play behaves like a creative writer, in that he creates a world of his own, or, rather, re-arranges the things of his world in a new way which pleases him" (143–44). The child takes his play very seriously, Freud underscores in preparing for the contrast between play and "not what is serious but what is real" (144):[22] "In spite of all the emotion with which he cathects

---

22 I have no problem continuing to use "really" and "real," but like
Winnicott I understand these terms emotionally, along the lines of the

his world of play, the child distinguishes it quite well from reality; and he likes to link his imagined objects and situations to the tangible and visible things of the real world" (ibid.). It all begins, then, with playing in childhood, which in German is commemorated, Freud points out, in the names given the genres and functions of *Dichtung* on stage, in which *Spiel* (playing) lays the cornerstone: comedy (*Lustspiel*) and tragedy (*Trauerspiel*), as well as dramatic performance (*Schauspiel*) and performers (*Schauspieler*).[23]

The innocence or unconcealedness of child's play is translated through fantasying into the import of unreality:

> The unreality of the writer's imaginative world, however, has very important consequences for the technique of his art; for many things which, if they were real, could give no enjoyment, can do so in the play of fantasy, and many excitements which, in themselves, are actually distressing, can become a source of pleasure for the hearers and spectators at the performance of a writer's work. (144)

But before the unreality of art, there is the inaccessibility of fantasying.

Child's play seems given up in adolescence, a full stop we won't allow: "[W]e can never give anything up; we only exchange one thing for another. What appears to be a renunciation is really the formation of a substitute or surrogate" (145).[24] Private fantasying is a teenage-appropriate replacement for playing big in childhood, because the teen, able and willing to fulfill the wishes of sex and violence, is in training to pass the empathy test and

---

plaint of the teenager at heart who just wants to feel real. The unreality of play offers respite from the passion of what's real.

23 This etymological grid later served Carl Schmitt the basics for his reading of *Hamlet* against the reign of psychoanalysis in the work's reception, an effort doomed both by the overlap and the datemark it would hide. See my SPECTRE (Fort Wayne: Anti-Oedipus Press, 2013), 78–80.

24 The switch from open play to concealed fantasying is given here in terms suggestive of a work of mourning.

pass on the inoculum that withstands psychopathy. It is in this sense that Freud's proviso that fantasying gives up "the link with real objects" basic to child's play proves particularly meaningful (144–45). The link to realization cannot hang in there in teen fantasying. The link with real objects that children play with explains why any illicit content of wish fantasying in childhood, like the death wish, the wish that the parent be gone, while openly performed,[25] can just the same leave the kind of deep impression that's waiting to be reactivated later on, for example in the grown-up's experience of grief. When Freud attributes to childhood the single wish to be big, to be grown-up, he means, of course, a wish available for conscious recognition or understanding. That also means that childhood deposits by ununderstood fantasying unconscious wishes for later symptomatic syndication. Otherwise the contents of wish fantasying post-childhood continue to be conscious.[26]

We saw that Tolkien also bases his sense of *Dichtung,* Fantasy, the true genre of genre, on the daydream, which runs the gamut from fairytale childhood to leader-and-the-pack adolescence. The difference is that Tolkien is less interested in the Enlightenment, its secular rehearsals, and its classical antiquity. In elaborating the wish-fantasy structure common to daydreams and B-narratives Freud focused on original works that had been "freely" invented. But then he also considered imaginative writers who, like the authors of epics and tragedies, "take over their material ready-

25 We are reminded of Freud's elaboration of the child playing fort/da in a setting of adult mourning (in "Beyond the Pleasure Principle," in *The Standard Edition of the Complete Psychological Works of Sigmund Freud, Vol. XVIII (1920–1922): Beyond the Pleasure Principle, Group Psychology, and Other Works,* ed. and trans. James Strachey with Anna Freud [London: The Hogarth Press, 1964]).

26 Why a specific fantasy is appealing may not be known, a questioning that brushes up against the unconscious. Does the metapsychological fact that an unconscious wish lies buried in every night dream suggest a hierarchy whereby every waking fantasy, too, ultimately refers to an unconscious wish that goes back to early childhood? Let's agree that every waking wish-fantasy need not go there, unless, for instance, the prospect of going public calls for alteration of the conscious wish's prehistory in repression. Watch out what your unconscious wished for.

made" (149), material that is available to the extent that it is "derived from the popular treasure-house of myths, legends and fairy tales" (152). Here Freud gives a forecast of the primal fantasy trajectory of his work, from *Totem and Taboo* to *Moses and Monotheism*: "The study of constructions of folk-psychology [...] is far from complete, but it is extremely probable that myths, for instance, are distorted vestiges of the wishful fantasies of whole nations, the secular dreams of youthful humanity" (152).

Tolkien saw the relations between myth and fairytale going into the fantasy genre indelibly marked by the unique draw of the era of the pagan past's Christianization up north in Europe, which amounts to an alternative "antiquity" not already claimed for secularization. He recounts a dominant view of myth and then reverses its course to ground it in the personalization of fantasy, which lies in the conversion to Christianity:

> The Olympians were personifications of the sun, of dawn, of night, and so on, and all the stories told about them were originally myths (allegories would have been a better word) of the greater elemental changes and processes of nature. Epic, heroic legend, saga then localised these stories in real places and humanised them by attributing them to ancestral heroes, mightier than men and yet already men. And finally these legends, dwindling down, became folk-tales, *Märchen,* fairy-stories – nursery tales.[27]

All the above, however, "can only be arrayed with a personal significance and glory by a gift, the gift of a person" (ibid.). Personalization, a Christian attribute and gift, enters at the end of the hierarchy to reverse it and give ascendancy to Tolkien's genre.

Although in elaborating the fantasy genre Tolkien asks only for seconds, the world or nature that he counts as secondary is as primary as Christian piety allows.

---

27 Tolkien, "On Fairy-Stories," 29. Subsequent references are given in the text.

> Probably every writer making a secondary world, a fantasy, every sub-creator, wishes in some measure to be a real maker, or hopes that he is drawing on reality: hopes that the peculiar quality of this secondary world (if not all the details) are derived from Reality, or are flowing into it. [...] The peculiar quality of the "joy" in successful Fantasy can thus be explained as a sudden glimpse of the underlying reality or truth. It is not only a "consolation" for the sorrow of this world, but a satisfaction, and an answer to that question, "Is it true?" (70)

The answer is a resounding yes, if you can follow the Christian joy into acceptance of the Gospel truth of fantasy: "This story is supreme; and it is true. Art has been verified. God is the Lord, of angels, and of men – and of elves. Legend and History have met and fused" (72).

The joy of wish fulfillment prefigures the *Gloria* at the so-called turn, the Eucatastrophe, in which a happy end is anticipated but not given: "The joy would have exactly the same quality, if not the same degree, as the joy which the 'turn' in a fairy-story gives: such joy has the very taste of primary truth" (71). The verging on merger of secondary and primary worlds that Tolkien evokes doesn't extinguish the signifying skeins and skins of this world: "Redeemed Man is still man. Story, fantasy, still go on, and should go on. The Evangelium has not abrogated legends; it has hallowed them, especially the 'happy ending'" (72). The story becomes "history, without thereby necessarily losing the mythical or allegorical significance that it had possessed" (71).

Although a work of fantasy – the work of fantasy – defers the ultimate happy end, the arc of its history must remain Christian. For Tolkien's genre, it follows that each work of fantasy must keep Christianity from being just another fairy-story.

> I would venture to say that approaching the Christian Story from this direction, it has long been my feeling (a joyous feeling) that God redeemed the corrupt making-creatures, men, in a way fitting to this aspect, as to others, of their strange nature. The Gospels contain a fairy-story, or a story of a larger kind which embraces all the essence of fairy-stories. [...] But this story has entered History and the primary world; the

desire and aspiration of sub-creation has been raised to the fulfilment of Creation. (71)

His aversion to Max Müller notwithstanding, Tolkien recognizes that language as the bottom line "cannot, all the same, be dismissed" (27). He concedes that the "incantations" basic to Fantasy "might indeed be said to be only another view of adjectives, a part of speech in a mythical grammar" (28): "When we take green from grass, blue from heaven, and red from blood, we have already an enchanter's power – upon one plane; and the desire to wield that power in the world external to our minds awakes" (ibid.). Science fiction experiments with time, technology, and psychic reality, which at the limit generate alternate realities. Tolkien instead concedes that enchantment is basic to language, a gift, however, that must first be localized and personalized (in his argument, Christianized) before it can give forth the other worlds in which the deposit of fantasying can be redeemed. Reprising the media savvy behind the composition of the New Testament as a series of letters, Tolkien makes language as we know and use it a byproduct of the gift of Christian creativity (or omnipotence).

It's time for Freud to make an intervention. In addition to the centrality of the ego structure proper to B-culture, there is a differentiating adjustment in every daydream, which fine-tunes the basic analogy between waking fantasy and *Dichtung*.

> We must not suppose that the products of this imaginative activity – the various fantasies, castles in the air and daydreams – are stereotyped or unalterable. On the contrary, they fit themselves in to the subject's shifting impressions of life, change with every change in his situation, and receive from every fresh active impression what might be called a "date mark."[28] (147)

The datemark, *Zeitmarke* in German, is pivotal to this study between genres.

---

28 Freud, "Creative Writers and Day-dreaming," 147. Subsequent page references are given in the text.

To interpret a fictional work's underlying fantasy requires, before the archaeological excavation of unconscious meaning, that we first reckon with the three periods of time that punctuate every daydream. It is the first outline of what would become the method of psychobiography:

> A strong experience in the present awakens in the creative writer a memory of an earlier experience (usually belonging to his childhood) from which there now proceeds a wish which finds its fulfilment in the creative work. The work itself exhibits elements of the recent provoking occasion as well as of the old memory. (151)

Analyzed by Freud in terms of the two times you get and the one time you forget, his exemplary daydream is that of a boy in his early teens, an orphan, who just heard of a job opening and decides to apply. On the way to the interview, he daydreams about being hired on the spot, then rising up the ranks of employment until he is second in command to his boss, whose daughter he courts, marries, and whose business he, like a prince, inherits. The past tense belongs to an idealized time when the boy was the beloved young child of his parents. His yearning for that time animates the fantasy, which belongs to the future. It's a fiction about the time to come that is at the same time modeled on the past that saw him better off, beloved, protected. The "memory of an earlier experience (usually an infantile one) in which this wish was fulfilled" (147), and which its future fulfillment would double, is an idealized past; and the present tense that is elided is the temporal modus of ongoing tension. The fantasying in Freud's example can unfold only as long as the daydreamer forgets his unemployed home-alone status.

What Freud calls a *Zeitmarke,* datemark or timestamp, indicates the expiration date or half-life of every fantasy escape, which takes a running start in a happy past, on which the wish is based, and makes a leap into the future of wish fulfillment, out-flying the incident in the present that prompted the wish but that also tags the wish that drops it. When Freud explores the daydream, the everyday model for the mighty aspirations and resolutions of *Dichtung,* he argues that the circumvention of present tension

57

cannot elide its triggering in real time, its history. The indelible datemark stamped upon the trigger-unhappy moment in the circumvented present openly lies waiting for historicization, which is the backfire of fantasy, its mortal recoil. The genre of fantasy too, therefore, can be seen as historicization waiting to happen, and its symbolic aspirations shall be overtaken by allegory. The expiration date of fantasy in history gives a rest to the speed denial within the once-and-future and provides a point of reentry for science fiction; it lets the present back in, the tense that is the mainstay of a speculative genre of predictive extrapolation.

The prize in the contest between science fiction and fantasy, which was largely waged in the course of the staggered linking of the two, went by the law of B-genres to fantasy. Science fiction fell short of predicting the digital relation, which, however, proved to be neither the psychotic sublime nor the happy turning toward an end in redemption. Fantasy wins, then, by default but no default of its own. Alone its proximity to generic wish fantasying and daydreaming, which, however, the import of Christianity was to keep in check, wins the prize and renders it the genre without borders. That the future forecasts of science fiction were wide off the mark of digitization was not a concession to fantasy, nor a concession opened up in fantasy, but became instead a defining moment in its own genre, which restarted after the fact in the termination phase of its Cold-War era. In its forecast ruins, science fiction began reading in the light of fantasy the history of approximated simultaneity. The second prize, the caption of legibility, goes to science fiction, the control text in the testing of the B-genres at the onset of their historicization and allegorical legibility. I pry loose Walter Benjamin's revalorization of allegory from its close association with the loss of function in belief systems and hitch it instead to failure in prediction, which piles high a ruinscape for reading at the border between science fiction and fantasy.

The Mechanical Brain

Gotthard Günther, who started out as a German philosopher and logician recasting through Hegel the binary logic associated with Aristotle as but the prehistory of a more comprehensive multivalued logic, discovered both cybernetics and science fiction upon emigrating to the U.S. in 1940 with his Jewish wife. He subsequently worked out what might be called a metaphysics of science fiction, previews of which were published in the 1950s in a series of English-language articles in the pulp magazines *Astounding Science Fiction* and *Startling Stories* and, in German, in the forewords and commentaries he supplied his 1952 series of German translations of American works of science fiction (novels and short stories), as well as in the separate monograph that introduced the series.[29] The majority of his speculations, however, awaited posthumous publication under the title *Die amerikanische Apokalypse* (*The American Apocalypse*).

Conceived as declaration of independence from longstanding metaphysical traditions, the Enlightenment is the historical introject pivotal to Günther's genealogy in *The American Apocalypse*. In Europe, the Enlightenment was followed by Romanticism, which brought back the metaphysical mother lode. But in the New World, the Enlightenment proved to be the establishing shot of a new start. On the one hand, Günther agrees with the Romantic philosopher Friedrich Schelling how "flat and premature the feeling of security associated with the Enlightenment in fact was. The Enlightenment only addressed the brain."[30] On the other hand, Günther acknowledges the Enlightenment as herald of future states of the human psyche: "To realize these states

---

29 Günther's writings on science fiction for the German series published by Heyne Verlag are collected in the volume edited by Dieter von Reeken, *Science Fiction als neue Metaphysik? Dr. Gotthard Günthers Kommentare zu "Rauchs Weltraum Büchern"* (Lüneburg: Verlag Dieter von Reeken, 2015).

30 Gotthard Günther, *Die amerikanische Apokalypse,* ed. Kurt Klagenfurt (Munich: Profil Verlag, 2000), 220. That the Enlightenment was premature and thus one-sided found dialectical expansion and qualification elsewhere in Günther's oeuvre. For example, in the second paragraph of the foreword to the third volume of his *Beiträge zur Grundlegung einer operationsfähigen Dialektik* (Hamburg: Felix Meiner Verlag, 1980), Günther cautioned that the necessity that all knowledge be exoteric was a misguided Enlightenment belief, which denied the challenge and danger of consequent (inner) gaps and vacancies.

emotionally, this psyche first had to emigrate to a new world."[31] The ambivalent introject of the Enlightenment consists, then, in admiration for the demolition derby that it ran, wariness that its secular clearing text forgoes a greater integration, and finally recognition of the affective working through that its address to or from the future requires.

The Enlightenment was transferred directly to the settlement of the long unacknowledged continent.[32] Günther's reading of the future is based on the conundrum that so many discoveries of the Americas launched from both shores of the regional civilizations prior to Columbus's accidental arrival there (he was looking for a new way to India) went *completely* unacknowledged.[33] Acceptance of a new world was the first step toward one world and its de-geo-centering before the final frontier of outer space. The Enlightenment supplied the break with the metaphysical basis of regional civilizations, a break that was given to the New World. With the how-to encyclopedias of the Enlightenment in hand, the settlers demarcated a new "West" in contrast to the Faustian West.

American science fiction is, then, for Günther the first understanding of world culture (and beyond), which rejects the regional civilizations grounded in the East. Via travel through deep interstellar space, ungrounded projection of artificial habitats based on reason alone, and unabashed manipulation of time (time travel), it was the first platform for the New World's cultural aspirations unbounded by the Eastern past. The spaceship

31 Ibid.
32 Early nineteenth-century prints of educational and research facilities built in the era of the Enlightenment indeed look planetary: no difference in the setting and structure whether in the new world or in Göttingen (see, for example, etchings of the historical observatory of the Georg-August-Universität).
33 This strand of Günther's metaphysics of science fiction went into his introductory monograph *Die Entdeckung Amerikas und die Sache der Weltraumliteratur* (Düsseldorf: Verlag Karl Rauch, 1952). The defective cornerstone in his reading might be that what the European explorers encountered in Latin and South America were true civilizations. Were they really, for all their stone work, only animist throwbacks?

shatters the symbolism of classical metaphysics and abandons the classical form of life. The visions of outer space presuppose a universal planetary culture – and condition or determine a new non-classical conception of reality.

In his commentary on Joseph W. Campbell's *The Incredible Planet* (1949), Günther describes how space becomes future science's laboratory in which even artificial planetary systems can be engineered. The spaceship crew visits the artificial blue universe only briefly, but Günther counts the shortstop the book's spiritual highpoint.[34] Intelligence consciously fabricated this universe as a stage for self-realization. It represents the ultimate consequence of Hegel's objective spirit and introduces the complete secularization of the metaphysical foundation of Western civilization (41).

The process of nature's transformation into culture, from cave dwelling, through house and garden, to the largest cities, is only the beginning. What keeps American science fiction from taking a next step toward transcendence (the universe is, after all, finite) is the assumption of a plurality of space-time worlds. The contingency of the world does not express metaphysical causation but is rather the indication that physical existence could be a one-time-only event (46). We are on the cusp of the transfer from a two-valued logic of truth, according to which truth and reality coincide, to a generally valid probability logic, in which reality is a highly variable condition of probability (47).

The Enlightenment replaced theocracy with a relationship between the divinity and the world so intimately close, the transcendent essence spread so thin, that the lessening learned was the death of religion (45). The American authors in the 1950s choose not to divinize the problem of causality. But what Campbell's novel presupposes goes beyond yet another new science hailing from a remote future: "Such a science, however, when it does arrive, won't be an isolated spiritual or psychic phenomenon, but rather an integral element of a new culture with a new metaphysical a priori and with new primoridal life instincts" (44).

---

34 Günther, *Science Fiction als neue Metaphysik?,* 40. Subsequent page references to the commentaries on the two novels are given in the text.

The commentary on the next work in Günther's series, Jack Williamson's *The Humanoids* (1948), picks up where the first commentary leaves off, between the expanding material basis for existence that Campbell plumbs and the disappointment that the new metaphysics isn't even remotely a wrap yet. Before the adventure can begin, human consciousness must undergo transformations beyond the limits of neurosis and psychosis (51).

Günther considers general tendencies in science fiction. The American authors project the future by the method of extrapolation (52). Günther gives the example of an ongoing miniaturization of radio contact in future worlds, but then concludes that radio might disappear altogether if telepathic capacities are further developed and disseminated through a specialized industry. Before his reading proper of *The Humanoids* has commenced, Günther already gives us the gist of its surprise ending. Günther next demonstrates what he sets apart as an absolutely necessary extrapolation, one that underlies the science-fiction technology of "space warp" travel (53). Günther cuts to the chase and loops back to his radio extrapolation, blending the boundaries between the occult or parapsychological tracks of messaging and conveyance: some form of "teleportation" will be required to negotiate the intergalactic distances of space and time (54). Like the radio apparatus, the space ship is no longer necessary once we enter upon simultaneity. In Williamson's novel, the introduction of a mechanical brain steering an interface of robots – the humanoids – goes where the ultimate incarnation of the machine meets non-machinic capacities.

Williamson first introduced the humanoids in his 1947 novella "With Folded Hands."[35] In the novella, which Günther doesn't discuss, mankind is being overrun by the robot extensions of a mechanical brain that comprehends only one directive or law: that mankind be served by offering protection against all harm to humans, even and especially the harm coming from their own destructiveness and self-destructiveness, which the robot service is designed to treat, even heal. From the perspective of the

---

35 The novella first appeared in *Astounding Science Fiction* and is in the meantime often included as part one of *The Humanoids*, the novel proper, which appears in these editions as part two.

protagonists with whom we are given to identify, the care that is administered is excessive, indeed, totalitarian.

According to the standard reception, Williamson's *The Humanoids* is dystopian. The robot service goes too far and the overkill of protection threatens human freedom. In Günther's stronger reading, however, the novel offers counterintuitive conclusions regarding our flawed adjustment to our perfectibility, which the intergalactic robot service of a mechanical brain represents. In *The Humanoids,* which appeared one year after the novella, the struggle for human freedom against the mechanical brain and its countless robots continues, albeit, following Günther, in a far more differentiated setting. In the end, the rebellious resistance and the sense of restriction are coterminous aberrations on the human side.

Every time we jot down on paper and solve a more complicated math problem, Günther offers by way of clarifying what "mechanical" means, a piece of our brain-functioning or consciousness has been projected out and made into a mechanical process in the outer world (57). But are conscious processes other than calculation open to mechanical externalization? Yes. Günther points to already existing devices like automatic pilot in which functions that imply intelligence are carried out by machines (58). And more advanced thought processes? Syllogisms can already be difficult to parse, but what about multi-syllogisms, like those that Lewis Carroll constructs in *Alice's Adventures in Wonderland* (59)? While these can with great effort still be unraveled in your head, it's clear that a simple logical figure can be carried to a point or sum that the human mind on its own cannot reach (60). It is our practical thinking, however, that will be tried first upon takeoff into outer space. We will be taking our departure from practical knowledge of the environment, which was earth-specific. Euclidean geometry is not applicable to new universal settings, which would make reliance on artificial intelligence a practical necessity.

A consequence of the inevitable superiority of the mechanical brain except in creative vision is that it will take over a considerable portion of human freedom, not only of action, but also of thought. However, Günther emphasizes, freedom of thought cannot signify freedom to think illogically (63). The rebellion seeks to revise the directive running the humanoids with the stipulation that every human remain free to command wishes (70). This amounts to a reservation for the human's unfettered subjectivity even when it goes against that part of his own rational consciousness already posited according to objective laws and deposited in a physical creation after his own image. Such a freedom is a self-contradiction.

Freedom is possible for those who seek it elsewhere than in hopeless resistance to reason experimentally tried and confirmed (70). Günther elaborates the difference between the phrases "I know it's illogical but I think ..." and "I know it sounds illogical, but I think ..." (64). The latter proviso admits that a rational formulation is not yet available to the thinker (which, Günther adds, is Leibniz's position). The former sentiment, however, is an outright contradiction, which Williamson's mechanical brain just doesn't allow. Questioning based on objectively genuine motives that are as such rational, but have "not yet" found an adequate rational formulation, does not lead to disharmony between the living individual and mechanical consciousness. Either the computer can supply the rational formulation or the human motive goes so deep that it cannot touch it. The irrational and illogical wish to claim outright what goes against that which is objectively correct, historically and culturally a major component of human subjectivity, leads to future conflict.

Günther allows that we seem to be reaching that point in the exercise of totalitarian control that goes beyond behavior and expression to address thought and fantasy. This control presupposes that an absolute truth, or at least a truth that goes way beyond the individual capacity for thought and experience, has been objectively established such that a person confronted with this truth no longer has the right to err in theory, since error is now implicated in the moral and social consequences. The individual is disallowed the private sphere of his own thoughts and thus of a subjective ethics (67). However, the questioning of the authority of the absolute truth is unavoidable when two totalitarian states oppose one another. It is the American way, which Williamson's novel follows out, to accept the guidance of a computer before ceding control to another human being (67).

Only that is true which functions objectively – and independently of human beings (67–68).

In *The Humanoids,* we find in contrast to the more identifiable and containable types of resistance to the perfectibility of conscious, logical, and rational thought a residual charge against the mechanical brain lodged inside human consciousness by the unknown capacity for occult relations, which the robots seem not to compute. The rebels fear that a new double of the mechanical brain is being built to ward off their developing parapsychological abilities and to subsume and thus control this paradoxical side of human consciousness, hitherto the sore and blind spot in the healing of mankind.

At the end of the novel, however, we learn that the founder of psychophysics was a veteran resister, who went on to invent the mechanical brain and its service. Treated by adjunct therapies that targeted the brain, he was set free to develop psychophysics, beginning with telepathy experiments that linked him to likeminded researchers. The result was The Psychophysical Institute. "It was formed [...] by a few adult and able men released by the service of the humanoids from their physical cares and their limiting preoccupations with physical science. They turned naturally to philosophy. And then to a new sort of psychology which their true orientation made possible – an actual science of the mind."[36] The agon on which *The Humanoids* seemed to turn, then, the race against the completion of an aggrandized, more controlling, mechanical brain, was the figment of a recurring adolescent rebellion that the brain was in fact designed to outlast. The veteran witness comments on the weapons collection in the Institute: "[T]okens to remind us of the old enemy born again with every human being." Adolescence must contain the wounding – and the re-wounding that's a wrap with healing – "before we are actually adult."[37]

As forecast in *The Humanoids,* then, the historical epoch to come will no longer recognize a psychophysical opposition as the metaphysical prerequisite of existence that once grounded the mentality of mankind (72). Former metaphysics becomes

---

36 Jack Williamson, *The Humanoids* (New York: Orb Books, 1996), 284.
37 Ibid., 285.

physical, and the former opposition is the object of a possible technology (ibid.). "The idea of the 'mechanical brain,' which is essentially alien to Western thought (and feeling!), shows that one dreams of new scientific tasks that presuppose a radical break with what was heretofore the historical nature of man" (72). The electromagnetic triad of elements that supported the machine age had to give way to a rhodomagnetic triad of different elements before the humanoid age could commence. Science is reinvented a third time to supply the mechanical brain with a psychophysical grid: "The existential characteristics of reality with which the new technology works are indifferent to the difference between physical and psychic life" (72).

The emphasis on science and its techno-application is the only continuity between the New World and Faustian Europe. Technical conclusions alone can be used; physical results involve no moral obligation (71). What does it mean that Williamson's science fiction refuses to recognize a metaphysically essential difference between the physical and the psychic (or spiritual)? There are two conceivable explanations for this American refusal (72). The incapacity to fathom European–Asian civilization promotes in lieu of inheritance a program of reprimitivization that undoes all that was attained over the last five thousand years plus. The second explanation, which Günther seconds, goes further in this direction to propose that the Western hemisphere is developing out of this departure a new spirituality (ibid.).

Günther's commentary on Williamson's *The Humanoids* is not contradicted by the prequel from the year before, the novella *With Folded Hands*. In 1980, however, Williamson published a sequel, *The Humanoid Touch*, which by its late arrival includes the inroads of the fantasy genre's influence on science fiction, the borderland it must illuminate to enter the future. This time there is a far-out planet, Malili, on which an animistic species dwells immune to its corrosive natural elements, which keep out machines and their humans. The last human rebels to refuse the service of the humanoids discover the outsider planet, which they seek to exploit in zones they neutralized through radioactivity. But then the humanoid interface does reach the rebels, whose destructiveness is contained. The humanoid service doesn't apply to the non-machinic indigenous population of Malili, which didn't pose the threat. The protagonist, a former rebel, qualifies at the end by the family romance of mixed blood for life and love on the utopian planet, which is less the outer limit of the humanoid interface than its staggered intergalactic compatibility with planetary animism on a post-machinic basis.

In *The Time Machine,* Wells set the marker distinguishing utopian fantasy from science fiction, the genre he would fully enter in *The War of the Worlds.* He placed a machine where earlier, in *Looking Backward* (1888) for example, it sufficed for Edward Bellamy's protagonist to wake up from magnetic sleep and find himself in the future. Classical science fiction projects our stream alignment with technology via fast-forwarding evolutionary change. By the 1970s, the projected import of virtual psychic reality filled a basic lack or lag in the science fiction genre. Will machines of transport ever outfly the grid of time, space, and matter to "conquer" outer space?

What is immediately striking about Williamson's *The Humanoid Touch* is the change in art direction. Before, the new and improved housing that the humanoids provided was thoroughly modern. This time around Williamson re-projects the humanoid interface like a touchscreen of fantasy-scapes. For example: "Crystal towers shining like monster gems. Gardens of great bright blooms [...] wrapped in a rose-colored cloud,"[38] Or again: "[F]airy lands you can't imagine [...] wonderlands [...] our new utopia."[39] In the visualization it commands and the story it tells *The Humanoid Touch* is like a novel James Cameron might have adapted for his postcolonial fantasy *Avatar* (2009). The rebels adhere to a techno-feudal system that smacks of the borderland between fantasy and science fiction genres first glimpsed in Frank Herbert's *Dune* (1965) and projected huge and forever in *Star Wars.* Following the so-called Black Centuries, the first Navarch restored "the law of the ship" according to which the ruler would henceforward be chosen by the Bridge, a parliamentary body elected by the duly franchised shipmen.[40]

---

38 Jack Williamson, *The Humanoid Touch* (London: Sphere Books, 1982), 11.
39 Ibid., 101.
40 Ibid., 42, 97.

When the canon of literary genres admitted lyric poetry (originally excluded by Plato because non-mimetic), a proliferation of subgenres and a remetabolization of genre distinction became possible. In time, psychological content began to count in the evaluation of differences between genres. Friedrich Schiller's "On Naive and Sentimental Poetry" explores subgenres of lyric poetry proto-diagnostically. The B-genres are late arrivals of the overdetermination of a work's identity. Proximate to what Jacques Derrida argued in "The Law of Genre," they are by the definiteness of their entry in the lexicon given to mix it up at the borders unto derangement. By 1980, science fiction was already boundary blending with fantasy in the course of forecasting about for what was new in the digitization on the horizon.

The More the Merrier

In *The Humanoids,* the mechanical brain's service plan sets each robot apart from human agency and thus from the vicissitudes of willing and wishing. The "real perfection" of the humanoids is that they are "protected from human manipulation."[41] Williamson's 1980 sequel, however, amplifies a trait in the makeup of the humanoids, which was admitted almost thirty years earlier, but only in passing. Günther overlooked it when he claimed that the logic the robots observe makes it impossible for them to deceive: "Only the logical functions of consciousness can be mechanized, that is, only the thinking ego can be technically reconstructed. The lie, however, is a function of the will. The will is fundamentally not mechanizable."[42] Is it possible to maintain Günther's affirmative reading of the mechanical brain or does the lying he overlooked in the humanoid service render it too compromised?

In all three of his works dedicated to the humanoids, Williamson allows that the robot service is not commanded by the Prime Directive always to tell the truth or rather never to lie. This tendency occupies the foreground of the service in *The Humanoid Touch*. Recourse to lying is part of the talking

---

41 Williamson, *The Humanoids,* 171–72.
42 Günther, *Science Fiction als neue Metaphysik?,* 68.

cure that the robots apply incessantly in treating any subject split off from their service. From a rebel's negative-transferential perspective, what looks in sessions with the humanoids like interrogation can also be seen to follow the directive of free association: "Again and again, he was pressed for more than he could recall."[43] That the humanoids know the "human machine" as well as themselves and thus exactly how to elicit the responses they require (123) must be conjugated with another inside view: "Even the most willing human being can never inform us fully [...]. Human knowledge is never entirely consistent or complete, because the human brain [...] sleeps, [...] forgets, [...] dies" (159).

The humanoid treatment regimen ranges like today's mental health profession. One option, a psycho-pharmaceutical regimen of euphoride, which induces happiness and oblivion, is applied liberally. Prior to the psychophysical grid, brain surgery was another option. The humanoids put on the human clothing of objects of love and trust in the sessions with rebels in order to influence acceptance of the truth, which coincides with the best treatment prognosis. This capacity for putting on deception is also offered openly as a means of simulated companionship, which, arguably, also tranquilizes unhappiness. We are still in an alternate reality extrapolated from the present, although by the looks of it aggrandized by fantasy and the anticipation of digital special effects. The goal of treatment is still to recognize that freedom and necessity coincide in the humanoid service.

According to psychoanalysis, his first lie gave the child relief from the sense of the parents' thoughts being in his head. Spontaneous fib-fabulation out in the open of child's play can be left behind, once the privacy of adolescent daydreaming and its revision and publication in the public mode of poetry subsume lying as fantasy, as fiction. In *The Humanoid Touch,* the robots lie or fabulate, even simulate, to promote their service. They replicate those near and dear to the rebels to get past their resistance like holographic transference interpretations. A resister concedes that the falsehoods of the humanoids were "almost creative" (133).

---

43 Williamson, *The Humanoid Touch,* 159. Subsequent page references are given in the text.

In "The Confidences of a 'Psychical Researcher'," William James questions the validity of fraud charges in the investigation of spiritualist mediums:

> [T]he accusation of deliberate fraud and falsehood is grossly superficial. Man's character is too sophistically mixed for the alternative of "honest or dishonest" to be a sharp one. Scientific men themselves cheat – at public lectures – rather than let experiments obey their well-known tendency towards failure.[44]

When all possible deception has been considered and checked off, the experiment with a medium will still have yielded "*a residuum of knowledge displayed* that can only be called supernormal: the medium taps some source of information not open to ordinary people."[45] Through the integration of psychophysics, the mechanical brain and its humanoid service can be compared to the medium in spiritualism and the resistance for which the humanoids lie in wait to the imposture charge that James dismantles.

Because they are treating the rebels, the humanoid liars do not, in keeping with Kant's argument, leave off respecting human subjects as ends in themselves. The humanoids reinstall the thing called *an sich* into the moral sensibility of their rebel patients, which allows them to pursue their talents unto perfectibility. And while openness to the well-being of fellow humans reflects the happiness that arises through working on the self, it is not an obligation to make more the merrier. The Kantian ethics of duty is inconsequential, indeed duty-free. It casts aside every recognizable duty for duty as such, in itself, the duty to duty.

John Stuart Mill criticized the categorical imperative, arguing that even the most absurd thought can be legislated. Only by the consequences that follow can the thought be evaluated.[46] The

---

44 William James, "The Confidences of a 'Psychical Researcher'," in *Writings 1902–1910* (New York: Library of America, 1988), 1253.

45 Ibid., 1257. Emphasis in the original.

46 John Stuart Mill, "Utilitarianism," in *On Liberty, Utilitarianism and Other Essays,* eds. Mark Philip and Frederick Rosen (Oxford: Oxford

lie might qualify as an absurd candidate for categorical legislation if, by dint of its self-cancelling consequence, it didn't tell a linguistic truth. Utilitarianism famously allows that a lie that can save lives enters the calculation of the greatest good.[47] But sometimes it's not just the greater number of people who should benefit by your actions according to the morality of utilitarianism. Lying that becomes a habit undermines the moral integrity of the person telling the lies. It undermines trust, the purpose of communication also for Aquinas.

Isn't it possible that what holds therapeutic value in a regimen of treatment, which seems to apply to deception in *The Humanoid Touch,* lies outside the reckoning of morals? In Peter Weir's *The Truman Show* (1998), we watch the upbringing afforded by Jeremy Bentham's Panopticon model, which extends through Mill's *Utilitarianism.* In Dick's *Time Out of Joint,* which *The Truman Show* to some extent adapts, the protagonist has endured a psychotic break, which is stabilized, guided, instrumentalized via fantasy. He is kept going in the imitation 1950s world supported by actors playing their parts in keeping with this idealized past. The fantasy setting allows him to guess what's next in a cartoon game in the daily paper. What the break interrupted he can thus continue: forecasting where the enemy missiles will strike next. The fantasy covers over the break in the man's foundation. But there is a half-life to this fantasy coverup, which lets Dick's protagonist see through it, not in order to go back to the breaking point that allowed him, like a shell-shocked soldier, to escape conflct but onward to auto-recovery. Truman also makes it to a happy end, but is it in spite of surveillance and deception or is it through the treatment regimen they uphold?

In an aside Mill shakes off an objection that the happy end is an untenable ethical standard:

University Press, 2015), 142.
47 In *The Humanoid Touch,* we do not witness the lying of the robots as legislated by the possible exception to the Directive, namely that they could stop by force a human who endangers other humans, a danger to be assessed on a utilitarian scale of valuation. We witness only interventions that would stop a human from harming himself.

> [U]tility includes not solely the pursuit of happiness, but the prevention or mitigation of unhappiness; and if the former aim be chimerical, there will be all the greater scope and more imperative need for the latter, so long at least as mankind think fit to live, and do not take refuge in the simultaneous act of suicide recommended under certain conditions by Novalis.[48]

"Novalis" is one of the passwords for the UK introjection of German influence, which belongs to the return of Hamlet's haunted suicidality. Before arriving at the shibboleth, Mill entered a thicket of references to "Mr. Carlyle," a purveyor once again of the German introject. One way to circumvent the German recommendation of mass suicide is through human sacrifice, which utilitarianism demands for the greater good.

In *The Truman Show* mass suicidality sits in front of the tube watching Truman deal with his anxiety and depression. The reality show has been running since Truman's birth but first became a global hit when Truman had to internalize the boundaries of his safe harbor through trauma, the death of his father at sea. The drowning was staged in such a way that it could look, unconsciously, like the fulfillment of Truman's death wish. We watch the adult Truman try to follow out his assignment at work, which involves crossing the sea to the next island by boat. But then he pulls up short before getting on board and the depression in front of the TV watches this tight spot of anxiety.

Hidden behind the masquerade, the viewer is directed to look at reality: the person and personality of Truman. He is Everyman, true man, representing a general good, a general will. The viewers, like the creator of the show, recognize themselves in Truman. Unhappiness controlled through the lesson of its lessening keeps the community of surveillance safe from the lure of mass suicide.

Depression sits in front of the tube and is diverted and entertained even by the apparent breaking points of fantasy's instrumentalization. It's not his father who suddenly returns to Truman but the actor who played that role twenty years ago. Truman's water phobia lifts and he is free to wish to see worlds

---

48 Mill, "Utilitarianism," 126.

THE ETHICS, POETICS, AND PRACTICAL METAPHYSICS OF WAKING DREAMING

beyond the fantasy bubble of the 1950s. Truman makes it to the container walls and climbs out.

But first, to stop him, the creator (of the show) physically torments Truman with the special effects of a storm at sea. By his willingness to sacrifice Truman, the creator breaks the code of Bentham's Panopticon, demonstrating an exception that can be an option according to the utilitarian calculus of the greater good. For the betterment of the surveillance watchers, punishment that causes physical pain is allowable, according to Bentham, only in the utmost case of exception. The Panopticon aims instead to let its inmates go free (the good happy end of its upbringing or therapy). Punishment that is not self-administered undermines the progress in educating to be good. The inmates in *The Truman Show* are the viewers who learn first to administer their own (p)unitive identification with Truman when he suffers and then know to make their exit with him.

Throughout the American superhero genre, mad masterminds have tried their heroes with the utilitarian sacrificial choice. Superman is caught between the maternal commitment to each individual life and the subsuming paternal allegiance to Life in the big picture of the battle of values, imperatives, or drives. According to the first two *Superman* blockbusters (1978 and 1980), if you want to divert Superman from the big picture (in which the evil masterminds feel at home), just drop one human from the top of a skyscraper. But to neglect the paternal battleground on which the masterminds launch their maneuvers (as happens in *Superman II*) means risking leaving unprotected an ever-greater number of casualties. Or when under catastrophe conditions Superman sets out to save individual lives one by one, he runs out of time to save the one life he does, after all, value most. At which point, in *Superman: The Movie,* he spins against the linear time of earth's orbit and, to be kind, rewinds the record of the recent past until the point is reached to save Lois in time.

In 2018, the utilitarian pain text of human sacrifice cut deepest into the superhero setting. *Avengers: Infinity War* allowed the bad guy to slide into the ambivalence position when his plan to extinguish at random half of doomed intelligent life overcrowding an ecologically bereft cosmos is allowed to go through in the surprise ending. The survivng half has been rescued for a future of sustainability. All the superheroes (in the Marvel universe) rallied in a concerted effort to counter the utilitarian program. At the end, they can only look on as one half among their ranks pixelates away. Only in their finite assembly is this cut across cosmic life an occasion for mourning. The demise of the teen superhero Spiderman breaches the numbing acceptance on which the movie closes.

Ghost-seeing and Clairvoyance

Long derided for Lorenzo da Ponte's "impertinent" libretto,[49] *Cosi fan tutte* (1790) was even tampered with in the nineteenth century to let the women in on the intrigue and turn the test around into a comedy of errors. To counter their guilty assumption of a high-fidelity love, the "philosopher" Don Alfonso directs the men to depart, marching as to war, and then enter the stage they left as new suitors of their own betrothed. To win over the steadfast women, the men who are now incognito feign taking poison in despair. But the experiment doesn't begin to yield results until the women's maid, recruited by the philosopher as his assistant, arrives in the guise of a medical practitioner with a brand-new treatment plan: "This is a piece of magnet, the stone the great Dr. Mesmer discovered in Germany, and which then made him so famous in France."[50] By instructing the women to assist in the recovery of the stricken men, the *magnetiseur* exploits the near miss between hands-on care and the early mother's ministrations (which is a turn-on for both sexes). The philosopher's trial seduction ultimately leads the men to wed the women as planned, but to forswear the testing of their unconditional love. The role of Mesmerism in Mozart's rococo opera shows the impress of the Enlightenment *Zeitmarke*. Mesmer earned the Dr. title with a dissertation on the influence of outer space (Newton's new science) on the tide charts of terran

---

49 Eduard Hanslick, *Die moderne Oper: Kritiken und Studien* (Berlin: A. Hofmann, 1875), 81.
50 Wolfgang Amadeus Mozart, *Cosi fan tutte* (1790), Act 1, Scene 16. Available online at *Opera Folio,* http://www.operafolio.com/libretto.asp?n=Cosi_fan_tutte. Translation modified.

metabolism, the full range, then, of animate/inanimate synergy, a new animism he called animal magnetisim.

Arthur Schopenhauer's treatise, "Versuch über das Geistersehn und was damit zusammenhängt" ("Essay on Seeing Ghosts and Related Matters," 1851), interrogates the extensive documentation of mediumistic states, occult dreams, and visions induced in patients under the influence of magnetic treatment. Schopenhauer opens his study of the occult phenomena brought back by Mesmerism with the claim that all questions raised like ghosts were banished by the Enlightenment.[51] Although Schopenhauer gives no more support to the belief in ghostly continued existence than did Kant before him (whose treatise on ghost-seers he seeks to supplement and extend), he does expand the range of interpretation of the belief or rather of the seeing that is believing.

Schopenhauer argues that the Enlightenment justified its ghost-busting by discounting any empirical evidence of haunting. But the presence of haunting really wasn't ever averred by ghost-seers; in fact, such physical evidence would dispense with the ghostly apparition. By definition, a ghost becomes manifest in a manner completely other than a body. A ghost-seer is claiming only the presence of an image in his intellectual contemplation, the representation of a body without its real presence. This is the source of misunderstanding. Our view of the external

---

[51] Arthur Schopenhauer, "Versuch über das Geistersehn und was damit zusammenhängt," in *Schopenhauer's Sämmtliche Werke in fünf Bänden,* vol. IV, Grossherzog Wilhelm Ernst Ausgabe (Leipzig: Insel Verlag, 1908), 354. In *I Think I Am,* I work through a host of German tracts on ghost-seeing, including Kant's and Schopenhauer's studies, with focus fixed on communication with ghosts. I elaborate here instead the apparatus of dream interpretation Schopenhauer applies to states like clairvoyance in order to liberate them from the margin of superstition. Schopenhauer dismisses daydreaming, but then makes room for it after all within the medley of paranormal states of waking sleeping which he makes available to and through the organ of dreaming. The opposition between a wish and the will comes to be dismantled, at the latest in Freud's elaboration of wish fulfillment in dreaming. Further page references, which are to this edition of Schopenhauer's study, are given in the text.

world is not exclusively sensual but intellectual or cerebral. Are the images in the brain of real bodies the same as the images that arise independently of the impress upon our senses of present bodies? The dream allows us to answer – and without a doubt: Yes! And so, Schopenhauer commences his rereading (276).

Dream offers the foundation for Schopenhauer's study, because he can distinguish the night dream from a mere fantasy image, the play of thought. While fantasying is fleeting, incomplete, and one-sided (ibid.), there is a reality to dreams that can be grasped. The capacity of representation in our dreams goes way beyond what our imagination can offer. Fantasy images arise through thought association or other motives; the daydreamer consciously recognizes their arbitrariness and unfoundedness. The element of surprise stamps the night dream objective and real (277). It is acceptable for someone not to be sure if what is remembered was real or a dream, but it is outright madness to say that one cannot be sure if something was imagined or not (278).

Schopenhauer cites Aristotle to identify fantasying as part of the reality that the dream remakes and shares: in a dream, you can daydream. Fantasying belongs more to waking reality than to dream reality. All mental faculties except memory are active in dreaming. Any resemblance to insanity involves a lack of recollection in night dreams or rather the lack of a coherent means of remembering back. To the extent that derangement, according to Schopenhauer, rolls down the decline of the ability to remember, the dream is a brief bout of madness.

The dreaming consciousness doesn't register the delegates of waking reality absent or past. The long dead behave like the living in our dreams. We don't recollect that they are dead. While we are following Freud in bracketing out the night dream as the source of art, dreams do inspire artists, and Shakespeare's ghosts, for example, can be recognized via our night dreams. What fantasying does not yield is the fundamental tenet of ghost-seeing: the visitation by our identifiable dead in night dreams – not as deceased but as continuing to exist and not as imagined but as surprise visitation.

Unlike daydreaming, the night dream requires sleep "just as the images of the laterna magica can only then appear once the illumination in the room is turned off" (279). Dreaming therefore doesn't depend on thought association since the brain is asleep long before the show begins. Any thought we might recognize at the outset of dreaming seems exactly not what preoccupied our waking thoughts just prior to the transition. The rumination or revery at the bedtime hour is not carried over into our dreaming when we fall asleep.

Schopenhauer scans the continuities in perception characterizing the paranormal states of waking dreaming amply documented in the annals of Mesmerism. They guide the *magnetiseur* and can appear as well in the client, a regularly recurring byproduct of the therapy. What interests Schopenhauer is that the sleepwalker is still able to move about in the reality of the senses and that the clairvoyant by an amplified orientation sees the bedroom and just beyond, the moment and just beyond. At the same time, the waking dream states, the continuity shots notwithstanding, suggest the trespass of the mainstays of waking reality.

Awakening is the criterion for distinguishing between the states of waking and dreaming, which, however, seems objectively not to hold in the case of sleep-waking; it is a between state that amounts to an awakening in sleep. The actual environment is dream-scanned. We see the bedroom with all its contents, take cognizance of persons entering, and know that we are in bed. It's as though the brain were suddenly transparent, with the outside world able to enter it immediately without the detour of the senses (287). Like the Esper device specific to Ridley Scott's adaptation of Dick's novel, the movie *Blade Runner,* the sleeper's POV can range around the corners of the diorama of the actual environment in which the sleeper is fixed in place.

Schopenhauer declares that a "spiritualist" view of occult phenomena must be rejected in favor of the "idealist" view (276). The former upholds that there are two aspects of existence: one, the material body and, two, the immaterial spirit. Schopenhauer's idealist view is part Kantian – the part that maintains the ideality of perception in terms of time, space, and causality – and part magical. The second part, although inspired by Kant's *Ding an sich,* is the part he came up with to introduce a practical metaphysics of magic. The archive of Mesmerism gave him his license. Schopenhauer entertains, then, a physiological reading set upon

77

the psychic–sensory processes and set apart from the metaphysical understanding of the *Ding an sich,* which for Schopenhauer was the will, his bottom line and limit concept (320–21). At the limit, then, the will is the beacon orienting the physiological approach.

Night dreaming not only goes deeper than the waking dream, but it is also closer to the source than dreams one remembers. Within our sensorium we respond to the stimuli of the external environment, reaching at the end of the process the deep well of the will. Schopenhauer introduces a couple of neologisms, because he says he doesn't hold the copyright on the Scottish designation "second sight" (286–87). When we're asleep, external stimulation no longer counts, and what Schopenhauer terms the dream organ (*Traumorgan*) takes over, drawing from the well of the will and carrying its stimulus forward. To perceive in German, *wahrnehmen,* is literally to take something as true; Schopenhauer adds *wahrträumen,* to dream something as true, to designate the waking dream state that sidles up to the everyday categories but, since not dependent upon them in this direction, uses them loosely as though moving beyond them (286–301).

Occult experience is therefore a translation problem. The psychic–sensory process goes into reverse when sleep removes the stimuli of the external environment. The night dream draws from the source, metabolizes and carries it forward, until, last and least, contact is made with the categories of everyday life. The power source of the will is still reflected in a tele-state like clairvoyance, but its proximity to the waking environment compels it to use the categories of time, space, and causality, if only to suggest their trespass.

Schopenhauer says you can skip the metaphysical statements of the magnetized patients who have gone mediumistic. These are sorry views reflecting a mix of learned dogma and what was picked from the brain of the *magnetiseur* (322). In keeping with the Kantian doctrine of the ideality of space and time, if there were no *Ding an sich* and if causality and all the rest set absolute boundaries, then clairvoyance would be a miracle indeed (316). While we see temporal sequence and causality, we don't see the original impetus behind this machinery (317). What the will of the practitioner working with animal magnetism reveals is the immediate influence of the will itself. The *Ding an sich* steps into the light as the will (321).

The *magnetiseur* lays his hands on the patient to direct his will, the effective force of his influence. The body is identical with the will; it is the image of the will in the brain (297). The rapport with the clairvoyant can go so far that he or she shares all thoughts and knowledge (foreign languages, for example), which otherwise the *magnetiseur* alone possesses. The positive beam of the will, the life force, passes from the *magnetiseur*'s brain to the brain of the clairvoyant (315).

Is the long-distance vision or the inner survey of the inside of bodies objectively real and true? If yes, then the explanation can only be metaphysical. At the same time, the sleep-waking way of seeing is a physiological process like the functioning of the brain in the waking and sleeping modes (298). The brain works in reverse while asleep, which explains our disorientation upon waking suddenly right after falling asleep; we have to feel our way around a space we view as reversed. The dream is not only in the brain but also in the sense-nerves and develops out of their ongoing excitation (but in reverse) (299). That's why the contents of waking sleep don't transfer to waking memory. Working in reverse, the vibration of the fibers cancels out what came before.

While on average the dreamer upon awakening in the morning can remember more or less what he was just dreaming, the clairvoyant, who sleeps more deeply and whose awakening is a longer procedure, remembers nothing (303). Dreams that see the future occur in deep sleep and rarely are remembered (305). Prophetic dreams that are remembered eddy in the dream shallows. Deep-sleep dreams can end up in another layer of dreaming closer to awakening. These dreams are, however, allegorical and require interpretation (ibid.).

What about seeing ghosts, the mediumship announced in Schopenhauer's title? Earlier doctrines of demonology and necromancy were based on realism, which Descartes shattered. Idealism has brought us to a vantage point for the evaluation of paranormal experience, including visions and ghostly apparitions. On the empirical path, which for Schopenhauer is always a demarcation parallel to idealism, animal magnetism has illuminated magic and allowed haunting, too, to become the object of scientific research (358). Schopenhauer wants to have the last word in the name of philosophy. The will as sole all-powerful reality lets us think magic and by transferring objective reality to ideality places even visions and apparitions on the track of understanding (359).

The will lasts as long as the mortal life of the intellect. How, then, would the deceased keep informed about the living? How could the will of the deceased be imagined continuing to exert or respond to influence? The persistent orientation of the will of the deceased toward earthly matters would, in the absence of any physical means, make recourse to the metaphysics of magic (366). To the extent that animal magnetism demonstrates it, this magical influence is weak and questionable. It rests on the claims of clairvoyants that they can, by sheer will, move a magnetic arrow or needle. But the explanations for the apparitions lead to another provoking prospect. If the difference between those recently living and those now living is not absolute, then the living can reach back and pull up reminiscences, which can be taken as true communications from the deceased (368).

That there are indexical requisites for seeing a ghost (whether a vestige of the deceased's clothing or his house, his haunt) reflects the point of view of spiritualism, not that of idealism, which is where Schopenhauer prefers to be heading. It is the basic flaw in every theory of haunting to date. Rather than let the divide between material and spiritual lives decide the issue, we should consider instead the expectancy of a spirit that cannot manifest materially. There are reversals and interruptions – scratches on the record of materiality, which cannot reach beyond memory or the recent past to communicate the separate existence of the ghost. Even if we recognize an inner being of man untouched by death and existing outside time and space, then any influence by this being after death on the still living could be arranged only via many, many mediations, all on the live side. It would be next to impossible to determine how much of the influence really originated in the court of the deceased or, in other words, that the deceased or ghost exists (341–42, 367–68). But what's next to impossible Schopenhauer leaves open. He identifies animal magnetism as the most momentous discovery of his day. It amounts to a practical metaphysics, he writes, an experimental metaphysics: "For it sets aside the first and most general laws of nature; therefore, it makes possible even that which was considered a priori impossible" (321).

As long as the person is still alive, there is, for Schopenhauer, no difficulty in accepting the transfer of thoughts, as when someone dying appears before the nearest and dearest, often several at once, before departing (346). The will is effective in the live transmission of apparitions of the still living. A *Doppelgänger* sent, often unwittingly, by absent but living persons as proxy to stand before another person is a transmission that does not require and presuppose an immediate real presence. Where there's a will there's a way to communicate immediately and at a distance with the will of another. You can think in my brain while yours sleeps deeply, Schopenhauer offers, because the *Ding an sich* is the same in all beings.

Time to remember that in Freud's extensive survey of the literature on the dream in *The Interpretation of Dreams,* Schopenhauer's essay is the only philosophical precursor that enters Freud's theorization. That while you are asleep I can dream in your brain means that the will can be replaced by the unconscious, in which the wish fantasies that the dream states reflect are on permanent record.

With the deadline for his assisted death already upon him, Freud chose for his final rereading selection Honoré de Balzac's *The Wild Ass's Skin* (1831), in which the protagonist Raphael is the author of the treatise *A Theory of the Will.* The theory remains a closed book within the story that performs it. Like Freud in his borrowing from Schopenhauer, Raphael or Balzac reduces the will-powered waking dream states to the vicissitudes of wishing.

At the start of the novel, Raphael obtains a quick fix for his gambling losses through a magical animal skin that grants fulfillment of every wish. By shrinking in the wish cycle, however, the skin comes to occupy the close quarters in which Raphael must defer the end, while the terms of fulfillment shrink the future at the vanishing point of the present. Toward the end, he marries his true love when it turns out that she loves him too; the skin "could not fulfil a wish fulfilled already."[52] Although their union, since mutual, would thus skip wanting and wishing, desire cannot undo the punctuation of wishes that just the same wears out the time in the skin. A century before international psychoanalysis ditched wish for desire, this French novel showed desire infernally compelled to follow the syntax of wishing.

With every wish the magical skin grants, it manifests the deadline in the span of Raphael's quality time of fulfilment. As the deadline curls up closer upon the shrinking skin, he uses the fulfilled fantasy of free money to guard against further wishing. One manservant buffers Raphael's relationship to the external environment outside the fortress home where nothing can be found wanting; the cart with horses is ready and waiting before there can be the wish to go out. As the servant explains to a petitioner seeking an audience: "I will put it to him like this, 'Ought he to come up?' And he will say Yes or No. I never say, 'Do you wish?' or 'Will you?' or 'Do you want?' Those words are scratched out of the dictionary. He let out at me once with a 'Do you want to kill me?' he was so very angry."[53] The command must come before the wish, and Raphael's safety can only be secured through the stricken word and world.

---

52 Honoré de Balzac, *The Wild Ass's Skin*, trans. Herbert J. Hunt (London: Penguin Books, 1977), 106. Since the skin of wishing is a variation on the infernal compact I treated it, albeit to other ends, in *The Devil Notebooks* (Minneapolis: University of Minnesota Press, 2009).

53 Ibid., 99.

2

Making a Wish

Calibrations of Beauty

In *Civilization and its Discontents,* Freud sees beauty as a whole thing, a full body shot, which belies and relies on the excitement of looking at the genitalia, which are never judged "beautiful." With that swipe cut, Freud covers the key German words in aesthetic theory, *Schönheit* (beauty) and *Reiz* (stimulus and appeal).[1] *The Creative Unconscious* by Hanns Sachs fixes the focus on beauty, switching from Freud's poetics of daydreaming to its aesthetic theory. Sexual fantasying fleshes and flushes out what's crossing the mind with the body. It's as easily done as imagined. Sexual repression isn't about the bodily release but its quality. Aesthetics is the pre-psychoanalytic theory of this quality of life.

To situate the import of beauty, Sachs elaborates a relationship to the body down the ages and stages. He postulates a disconnection from classical antiquity as the special form of our connection to technology. First rehearsed in his 1932 essay "Delay of the Machine Age," later turned into a chapter of *The Creative Unconscious,* this genealogical inquiry belongs, Sachs underscores, to the psychoanalytic canon of exploration of narcissistic neurosis or psychosis that commenced with Freud's 1911 reading

[1] Sigmund Freud, "Civilization and Its Discontents," in *The Standard Edition of the Complete Psychological Works of Sigmund Freud, Vol. XXI (1927–1931): The Future of an Illusion, Civilization and Its Discontents, and Other Works* (London: The Hogarth Press, 1961), 82–83.

of Daniel Paul Schreber's memoirs, and was continued by Viktor Tausk in his 1919 analysis of the schizophrenic delusion of the influencing machine.

While animism was a projection that still allowed a body wrap, the projection that goes into technologization fits and foots another bill of narcissism.

> The projection to which the ancients adhered represents exactly the same mechanism as that which leads the schizophrenic to the creation of the "influencing-machine" – a casting out of his own ego into the external world in order to settle an inner conflict. But the result is antithetical, for the schizophrenic hallucination and the inhibition of the ancients stand in opposition to one another as positive and negative poles. Animistic man vitalized the inanimate world with such narcissism as he could find no other use for, the schizophrenic transforms his own body into something alien and inanimate (first, through "feelings of alienation," in a further stage of regression into the "influencing-machine").[2]

In the opening season of construction and exploration of the psyche-soma, self-love cathects the world always in relation to the body, one's own or your mother's. With the onset of Oedipalization (the entry of the third person), self-love can no longer sustain itself as embodied, but preserves its gist just the same by the highest standards of our self-criticism. Our crashing shortfall before the criteria of perfectibility outlines in reverse the lost realm of primary narcissism. In these environs, what must be considered secondary narcissism nevertheless develops a will to power – to staying power – out of the struggle for mastery between the ego and the superego.

A case in point for Sachs's interpretation of beauty between antiquity and techno-modernity is a story by Catulle Mendés in which countless men from all walks of life are suddenly united by their interest in the peep show machines newly installed in

---

2 Hanns Sachs, *The Creative Unconscious: Studies in the Psychoanalysis of Art* (Cambridge: Sci-Art Publishers, 1942), 127. Subsequent page references are given in the text.

the streets of Paris. But more to the point, what they also have in common is their strict avoidance of one particular machine, which offers views of the Venus of Medici. It seems that beauty must be "kept in quarantine like an infectious disease" (172). It appears that what people want is interest and action. And yet everywhere, Sachs continues, "we see people [...] snatching bits of beauty: [...] Radios, movies, glamour girls, magazine covers, funnies, thrilling love stories – they all show a trivial, attenuated form of beauty, mixed with a great many other things (principally interest and action), but some grain of beauty is never missing" (175).

Pure beauty, Sachs argues, is the essence of that crowd or crowded feeling that the "vilest thriller" (167) brings about for the moviegoers packed inside the theater. But pure beauty instills the feeling without any extras. "It gives a feeling of expansion – not, however, toward other people, but toward a miraculous isolation" (168). "Beauty, in the proper dosis and properly blended, arouses energy" (176), while pure beauty, in superseding all other interests, isolates and makes sad.

Sachs sees in beauty the height of reconciliation on a scale of sublimation. The supplemental severity of the superego, which, provoking anxiety and guilt, trails the sublimation of sex and violence, does not enter into "the conditions for the creation of the feeling of beauty" (237). "The benevolent activity of the Superego slightly infuses into the play of Ego and Id-tendencies something of the character of the death instinct" (238). The artist's quest for pure beauty cannot but lead to immobility and quiescence. But when interest and action overtake the bequest of beauty, it is apportioned off, diluted, and calibrated as stabilizer (238). "The presence of death makes itself felt in the sadness of beauty" (240). It becomes apparent – heir apparent – that Sachs was extending and updating Freud's 1913 essay "The Theme of the Three Caskets." Not only for the aged King Lear is beauty choice because it is infused by necessity, a.k.a. death.

The immunizing significance of the sadness mixed into the appreciation of beauty marks our separation from the era that saw the sculpting of the Apollo of Belvedere or the Venus of Milo. That in antiquity alone the psyche could sustain body-based or primary narcissism beyond early childhood development and without regressive backfire or psychotic break is Sachs's first response, in 1932, to a question corollary to the understanding of beauty in terms of dosage, namely: Why did the ancient Greeks and Romans stop short of applying existing knowledge and resources to the development of machines that replace rather than merely enhance human agency? Instead, as he describes this self-limitation or postponement of technologization, the know-how that was already available in classical antiquity was applied to the fabrication of mechanical playthings for amusement only.

Sachs dismisses the view that slavery was essential to the ability of the ancients to defer making machinery that replaces the body. It certainly wasn't a constant. Following the Pax Romana, the ongoing war-loot supply of body doubles came to an end and led to the integration of the remaining slaves in the working population. The first ticket to their socialization was admission into the burial societies, where members paid down for their own proper interment in the final installment. Although Sachs focuses on the relationship to techologization in this genealogical sequel to the Schreber case, the archaeological underworld underpinning Schreber's new world order is represented by regular attention to the evidence found on tombstones. Sachs cites Pliny's words as intimating what the ancients allowed to stand on gravestones, but which they otherwise sought to push back down their own uncanny valley: "We walk with another's feet; we see with another's eyes, we greet by another's memory; we live by another's work. [...] Only pleasure do we keep for ourselves" (127).

In *Blade Runner 2049* (2018) body-double slavery has been reinstated with a new and improved series of obedient replicants. But revolution is on the rise. Deckard's union with Rachel (just beyond the conclusion of Ridley Scott's *Blade Runner*) introduced the epistemic break of the prospect of android reproduction: "If a baby can come from us we can't be slaves!" From the other extreme of the spectrum of fantasying, then, slavery begins to founder as the delay of the machine age, which, projected into the future, is also the history of that delay. The film's datemark is the digital special effect, which in the fiction (of the digital film) is linked and limited to holographic entertainment and art. The woman believed born of the union of man and machine is considered the "artist" among the technicians fabricating false memories for the new generations of replicants. When we watch her at work making memories, she selects from a holographic display of options, linking and interweaving them. The false memories are her fantasies, which she, however, spins around the foreign bodies of her own real memories. The fantasying in the close quarters of doubling and nothing, which prolongs primary narcissism, comes to a full stop with her memories. The illegal operation goes into her art of memory and, like the belief in reproduction she vouchsafes, widens the liminality of the replicant-slave until gap becomes overlap.

When it becomes clear to one of the rebel androids that the hunter Joe had thought he alone was the one born of woman, she declares that each of the androids thought and wished that they were the one. What the androids-are-us long for isn't reproduction. It's the primal scene, the place, play, fantasying of the leading questions. Replication is one answer given twice over. At Wallace Headquarters, Deckard is presented with the double of Rachel reprising the moment he met her. (When he turns her down, she's eliminated.) Moments later the holographic advert of a giant woman pitches her line to hunter Joe. She's clearly of the same lineage – she's the same – as the holograph girlfriend he just lost. When his home companion asked to go with him, she also insisted that for his protection he erase her program or memory on the built-in console and carry with them only a portable gadget with a singular copy of the file. But what if it's destroyed? "Then I'll die like a real girl."

In *The Creative Unconscious,* Sachs explores the management of anxiety corollary to the calibration of beauty in the unique hybrid of animism's return in films involving "Mickey and all his tribe" (184): "Animism is not possible without projected vitality which depends on free-floating libido, which cannot be thought of without aggression, which is bound to produce anxiety" (180). The techniques of these cartoons cannot eliminate the anxiety situations but succeed in counterbalancing their effect. There is a saving unreality to the cartoons that relies not only on their drawing-board nature, but even more so on "their unrestricted power of motion and action" (182).

There is in the mix of Disney's animation cinema always also some "quantity of beauty, however diluted or adulterated it may be" (185). While the "color-scheme [...] is worked out with no other view than to its beauty," the accompanying music conveys beauty full on (185–86). We are in the environs of the physical symptoms of daydreaming at the cusp of its evolution into the social relation of art. Wish fantasying can be an embodied thought process: "The reactions of the body (expression of the face, blushing, sound, gesticulation) can be observed by others, which gives them a direct social importance lacking to the mere mental processes" (212).

The label applied to this basic performance of wishing is playing. It means that what you see and hear "can never be mistaken for the real thing, neither by the performer nor by the audience" (214). The excuse that is as valid as what's only a dream is that all's fair that's done in play. We need the warning with playing, since, not only a mental process, it triggers actions of the body that threaten trespass upon reality's turf.

"How easy it is to overstep the 'anxiety-line' is shown by the episode of the witch–stepmother in 'Snow White'" (183–84). Although he doesn't name the technique, all the examples Sachs gives of an excess of beauty creating anxiety and horror refer to rotoscope's incorporation of the film record of good-looking human actors inside animation art. Disney's animation of nature, already styling with animism between late romanticism and the comics, was available for filming the fairytale. But the human protagonists for good or evil – the queen, the princess, and the prince – struck a different balance in regard to the evolutionary trait of neoteny, the retention of baby-face features, which we find reflected back in our favorite mammals.

In *Snow White and the Seven Dwarfs,* animation's fountain of youth neotenizes young adults not as babies, but as teen babes. Their roto-interment, which borders on the uncanny, also fits the appeal of the animated critters. The resulting cuteness, in which sex appeal is curbed but available, lays on a layer of latency upon sexualization; when a body built to walk the average Athens road crosses the screen of animation, we watch the rotoscoping of adolescence inside childhood. Where rotoscoping first injected adolescent energy inside the animation figures of childhood and extended the range of juvenility into a libidinal danger zone, CGI has set up shop in fantasy film production to illumine and recast live actors by the color contours of the rainbow palette of childhood artifice. The CGI bath from which live actors emerge all aglow in movies like *Beowulf* (2007) was first mixed in the rotoscope crucible.

In your basic fairytale, the protagonists are children who suddenly fill the young adult roles of hero or princess bride, skipping altogether the volatile transitions of adolescence. In the Disney version, however, when Snow White is awakened by Prince Charming, the princess goes out on a date. The innocence of a child reinforced by the chorus of animation critters remains intact at this border occupied by a daydreaming teenager. Cuteness alone, however, challenges the teen (and then, often enough, the midlifer) to stay within the lines of curbed sex appeal. In the bedrooms of adolescents, the trophies and stuffed animals of childhood are piled high against the posters of rockstars.

We've since made digital Facebook out of the trail mix that Disney first served in *Snow White and the Seven Dwarfs*. The border against trespass by dating and porn sites protects a curb appeal that rotoscoping introduced. Heroic causes push back the psycho-path that has opened wide like a mean streak throughout social media. I remember how surprised I was to find planning ahead included as a type of daydream in questionnaires first used in the 1960s to expand the database.[3] Several decades later, in range of the digital relation, the understanding of daydreaming in terms of a norm of task solving and preparation was overturned: "Why these presumably healthy kinds of daydreams do not correlate inversely with pathology, and, if indicative of anything, probably signal pathology, is unclear."[4]

---

3 In his *Daydreaming and Fantasy* (London: George Allen & Unwin, 1976), 52ff, Jerome L. Singer summarizes the history of his research using questionnaires designed to approximate interviews listing daydreams the test subject would pick and choose from as his or her own.

4 This line from a 1995 article by D.F. Greenwald and D.W. Harder is cited in Meta Regis, *Daydreams and the Function of Fantasy* (New York: Palgrave Macmillan, 2013), 24.

On Facebook, the adolescent energy that doesn't go into the posting of political idealism finds a rest inside fairytale childhood, a clearing in the thicket of utopian animal posts. Where the hero is, the princess will be too. Following its premature articulation as an antisocial prank that was sexual, sexist, and childish (no girls allowed), Facebook adopted a rating system of liking that was still elementary school but pacified by full adaptation to the realities of co-education. In third grade, everyone is unique and, with some statistical justification, perhaps even a rising star. This democracy of celebrity is basic to social media at large, from the startup capital of likability (Facebook) to the Twitter of the gods (Trump).

The attempt to roto-fit beauty into the action and interest basic to Disney animation can be "inexpressibly terrible," like "the Venus of Milo running away from a sharp-edged wheel!" (186). Although the technique was directly applied only in the first feature, rotoscope continued to be used by the Disney animation artists in their prep work. "Remember what an absolute washout the Blue Fairy was in 'Pinocchio'" (186). Sachs declares that it is "the consequence of a law, which is inherent in the 'animistic world' of universal and unrestricted motion, that every attempt to have its 'characters' approach beauty has a most unfortunate effect. It is bound to degenerate into an extremely vulgar sort of prettiness which is way below the aesthetic level of the rest" (186). When he allows that "Snow White herself was saved or half saved by a slight injection of irony which turned" her into "a goody-goody high-school girl" (ibid.) Sachs makes room for the cute between the horror of a transgression and a utopian prospect: "The millennium still may be coming when not only the lamb lies with the lion, but Mickey walks arm in arm with the Apollo of Belvedere" (187).

In P.K. Dick's *A Scanner Darkly* (1977), the communion that the drug called Death facilitates is with the blank stare of surveillance. In the first film adaptation of H.G. Wells's ultimate surveillance science-fantasy, James Whale's *The Invisible Man* (1933), what the protagonist didn't know about his vanishing act had already been published in a recent German study: the invisibility formula bears the side effect of psychoticization. When psychosis begins to manifest in the doubled protagonist of *A*

Scanner Darkly, the book enters chapter 11 in which we find deposited untranslated quotations from the premier German text on the superman, Goethe's *Faust.*

The 2006 film adaptation, Richard Linklater's *A Scanner Darkly,* wraps the visual record of live action in a train of scramble suits that billows out and metamorphoses like Maleficent's cloak. Whereas in *Snow White and the Seven Dwarfs* unknown actors entered the animation process, every actor scrambled via rotoshop, Linklater's patented update, is reduced to the star's immediate recognition value. Rotoshop applies the libidinal plug and outlet between the absence of the bodies of the stars and their digital availability. What began technically, then figuratively, as a process of drawing adolescence in childhood became by the 1950s under TV guidance more abstract or comics-like, until the curb appeal returned in movies like *Aladdin* (1992), ready and lubed. When Bruce Wayne put on the Batman suit it was an uncanny ritual that each time reanimated a dead body. Getting into the surrogate body is another instance of how the digital relation uncanny-proofs the wish.

Mike Kelley's ironically practical proposal in 1999 for the solution of America's biggest problem was that the images in our faces of Hollywood stars become consumable, whether in person, in the divisions of their doubling, or through new improvements in the mass-media sensorium already potentiated through surveillance.[5] Linklater brought the delegation of rotoscope closer to Kelley's manifesto-fiction of what is already digitally manifest, our asocial wish fulfillment upon the stars. Indeed, Kelley's first inspiration that same year for reconstructing Superman's commemoration of Kandor, the capital of Krypton, was the isolation of the Web consumer, which he hoped to explore in a museum exhibition that would at the same time call on the participation of the connected fan community. But he abandoned a project about digital disembodiment that belied the status of libido in the Teen Age, which his work had already carefully rotoscoped out and illuminated. In the work that followed, Kelley summoned Kandor in the miniature or souvenir format befitting

5 "The Greatest Tragedy of President Clinton's Administration," Kelley's 1999 exhibition at Patrick Painter's in Los Angeles.

Superman's melancholic retention span. For one installation Kelley provided the inside video view of its libidinal access in a series of adolescent S/M sessions. The scene that didn't make it into *Snow White and the Seven Dwarfs,* but which was already on the drawing boards, centered on the bound rotoscoped body of the prince down in the dungeon at the witch's disposal.

Mutual Daydreaming

At the start of *The Creative Unconscious,* Sachs carefully analyzes daydreaming as the evolutionary impetus and lynchpin of the high cultural edifice. The focus on wish fulfillment – erotic, appetitive, but also aggressive and deathwishing – renders the simple daydream not only inartistic but even antisocial. Just the same, Sachs found in daydream fantasy, which he distinguishes from the creative unconscious at work in night dreams, the origin of a developmental and evolutionary process that yields what he identifies as the social relation of art. By making the counterintuitive move of privileging waking fantasy, even though the night dream was the readily available analogue for aesthetic experience, Sachs follows Freud, as does Tolkien. Freud's close colleague, however, picks up on a startling implication of the psychoanalytic poetics of daydreaming. Freud had shown that the dream was a perfect composition and, even when tattered at the edges by forgetting and repression, its interpretation was the royal road to the unconscious. If dreaming and waking reality divide up the spoils of psychic life, then the night dream would be enough and art not necessary. But there is art because we are always going off alone with fantasying, prematurely flashing on a figment without realization or endurance. There is art, then, to vouchsafe the evolution of the social relation, which is art, out of the tight spot of wishing.

Freud looked at B-literature, because the continuity with daydreaming was plain text. As Sachs notes: "The more obvious the tendency to serve as 'entertainment' – i.e., momentary wish-fulfillment – becomes the greater the resemblance to a typical daydream" (20). Deploying the daydream as cursor, Sachs goes beyond this equation to examine the sliding scale of the high and the low in cultural production. The low point, which Sachs classifies as "art" by dint of its "social function," but then also modifies as "borderline," is reached with "the photographs made at fairs and amusement parks, where every one can have his likeness taken as a mountaineer, cowboy, or sailor by placing his head in position over a dummy provided for the purpose" (20–21).

Surprising but true that fantasying packaged as happy-meal "entertainment" using the "'dummy technique" (21) doesn't hold our attention for long. "[T]he 'happy end' stories and plays [...] lose their grip on the audience as soon as they are over. [...] A new supply of them is constantly needed" (23). The gulf between the tristesse on the center stage of high culture and daydreaming syndicated in low-budget entertainment finds, according to Sachs, a liminal point of crossover in the exceptional, yet typical class of daydreams dedicated to self-pity. In order to fulfill the wish fantasy of self-pity, these daydreams are willing and able "to conjure up all sorts of misfortune: poverty, humiliation, illness, and even death. Other daydreams look as if self-torture were sufficiently attractive to become its own end. To call them 'masochistic' helps only as far as our understanding of masochism extends" (22). There seems no inhibition to recounting these daydream scenarios. The only limitation is that no audience is home to them.

While fantasying disbands articulate language, which is reduced, Sachs suggests, almost to the status of the intertitles in a silent motion picture, it does not make do without the significance of what remains: "Quite the contrary, it is a well-known experience that certain words and phrases are endlessly repeated and cherished, because they, and no other words in their place, carry with them certain emotions" (17). In this eddy of a low niveau of form and medium comparable to advertising and jingles, we come back to the daydreams of self-pity: "The sweet tears of self-pity seem to be especially closely bound to certain 'magic' words for an individual" (ibid.).

As much as the painful input of the unconscious, which allows the daydreamer to recount self-torment, an audience's share is required of every expression of daydream fantasy that gets across and makes a memorable impression. So, Sachs enters upon an intermediate form of daydreaming, the mutual daydream, which takes two to communicate the fantasy and step outside the basic law of the daydream: "Every man wants to keep his daydream secret, even the perfectly harmless ones, and considers his friends as outsiders when they approach this most sacred precinct of his private life" (24). The mutual daydream breaches the privacy and privation of wish fantasying by admitting a sense of audience *à deux*. It is intermediate, says Sachs, in the sense that it "has ceased to be entirely antisocial, without becoming art" (23). And it is mutual only to the extent that its conception or dictation is transmitted; one party introduces it, while the other party acts it out.

Poets pitch to "all their friends, their entire tribe or nation, or even an infinite number now or in the future," as Sachs spells it out, "active collaboration like that of the partner in a mutual daydream" (37).

> In the beginning, this participating audience and its response are actually present; improvisation by one or several self-appointed "bards," as exponents of the emotion felt by all members of the group, is the primitive stage of poetry. When it began to outgrow the exclamatory phase, the poet no longer received his inspiration by being in the crowd, but by withdrawing from it. All the same, his audience continued to exist for him as a psychic reality which kept him from complete isolation. (38)

To win the participation (or the readiness for identification) of his audience, the poet surrenders his private narcissism. The standard or ideal of beauty that sets the artist apart – Sachs underscores that "form and beauty" "are utterly absent from the daydream" (44) – also alters the artist's primary narcissism into a new longing for perfectibility, which can never be satisfied.

> We see here another force at work, one which plays between the poet and his work and is independent of the effect on the audience, even on an ideal audience. The entirely narcissistic character of this force leads to its recognition as the sacrificed narcissism of the daydreamer, reborn as the poet's desire for the beauty of his work. (49)

The mutual daydream is a mutation in the relational aesthetics of daydream's evolution into the social relation, which is art. Sachs would have had to postulate and reconstruct it as missing link, if he had not perchance already had a case study ready and waiting. Sachs gives the example of a daydream shared by two five-year-old boys who were running away from home, a typical enactment of a fantasy that takes two. It began with one boy's proposal that they go to India together. Soon it was all they talked about. Sometimes they walked for hours through the streets searching for the way there. Then the instigator came up with the conclusive variation. The right way to their goal could be found at the bottom of the local pond. To arrive in India, you need only jump in and enter a submerged machine, endure being cut up into bits, which was, however, pleasurable not painful, and exit whole at the other end of the mechanical procedure. After the other boy failed utterly to make the transfer or transformation facedown in the pond, both went home in the deep end of depression.

While it lasts, the mutual daydream is guilt-free, in contrast to every isolated daydream, once it is revealed. "The unconscious, as we know, is asocial. But out of the need of reacting to it, of handling it, of giving it a legitimate outlet, we see emerge here the formation of the smallest social unit," which Sachs calls a "community of two" (36): "'Your wishes are my wishes your guilt is my guilt' – as long as it lasts the two are sworn friends and brothers" (37).

In the course of his work with the little boy who hit bottom, his adult analysand, Sachs, was able to decode the remembered episode as follows: "The flight to India and the attempted suicide represent the unification of two opposing unconscious tendencies, namely the hate: 'I will leave my mother, kill myself to punish her' and the love: 'I am afraid of nothing that brings me back to a mother who loves me'" (34). When his mother died, the boy, by then an adolescent, showed and felt no sorrow at her funeral. But when a year later he attended the reading of the Gerhart Hauptmann play *Hanneles Himmelfahrt* (*The Ascension of Hannele*, 1893), he was moved to weep for an hour, releasing the withheld grief. In the play, a lonely and unloved girl tries to drown herself. Upon her rescue, she lies in bed dying and feverishly dreams up fantasy versions of all that went wrong in her life. The complete situation of the affect was restored to him, which allowed him to catch up with two situations, which now coincided or collided, the child in crisis and the teen in mourning.

What Sachs calls "toying with the unconscious" means the "enjoyment of condemned pleasures, and this cannot fail to stir up a feeling of guilt, especially if the Oedipus-complex was the cause of the transgression" (35). That there are ways to mitigate the guilt feelings is made clear by the teenager's response to Hauptmann's play. In session, the patient remembered a scene of reconciliation with his mother under the Christmas tree two years after his father's passing.

What prompted the boys to dream up together a run away from home "at any price" (28) was "loss of love, estrangement, neglect" (30). In the case of Sachs's patient, "the daydream marked the time when the boy thought that a rival had deprived him of the exclusive possession of his mother's love" (29). After his father's death, a gentleman living in their building courted the merry widow. Although nothing came of it – perhaps the boy saw to that – he had felt abandoned, cast back into his state of jealousy when his younger brother was born. The "death wishes against him were so strong" that nothing could alleviate the guilt feelings that produced the neurosis lying on the couch (30). Here a detail he contributed to the mutual daydream, which the other boy largely directed, namely, that he would come out of the techno-initiation smooth as a doll without genitals, illuminates his guilty acquiescence in becoming, in his rival's stead, the dead double.

Sachs's next example demonstrates fully "that such daydreams can be produced only when two individuals are for a time brought together by a strong, suppressed, preferably unconscious-wish which they have in common" (30).[6] What's more: "The wishes that furnished the driving force in building these daydreams are not harmless" (34). The fantasy of journey-

---

6   This is the interpreter's preference that the underlying wish be unconscious. Importantly, it is not a requirement in these environs. Secrecy is the key term.

ing to India was enacted in the mode of play and make-believe. In the second example, we have two teenage sisters, who once upon a time, during a short period that was the exception to the otherwise unmitigated remoteness between them, "felt drawn to each other and were on terms of warm intimacy" (30). When the period was over, they "relapsed into their former coolness" (ibid.). In the meantime, Sachs's patient, the younger sister, in recalling the episode of five years ago, realizes that what happened was that both sisters had fallen in love with the same young man. They never acknowledged their tender or erotic interest in the youth, who was a regular in the winter sports setting in which they too were engaged (31). And yet, when alone together, the sisters talked incessantly about the young man who clearly absorbed their interest. This was possible in the form of their daydreaming up scenarios together, based on his blocking the advance of three brothers, his close friends, who pressed to be introduced to the sisters.

> The two girls saw, of course, that jealousy was the real cause of his strange behavior. They laughed about it among themselves, but felt rather pleased. This started a whole chain of daydreams which the two girls devised; [...]. The main content of these daydreams was always the same: the three brothers pursued them and used all sorts of stratagems to get acquainted with them, whereas their friend made all possible efforts to prevent it. In this story of pursuit and escape all adventures ended in the same way, namely with the victory of the three brothers over their friend. (32)

The rivalry they thus diverted did become a problem after all, when the friend showed a preference for the older sister. But then the First World War intervened and the girls resumed their "mutual remoteness" (31). When the younger sister recounts to Sachs in session that the friend was killed in combat, she asks herself how it was possible that she felt "but little moved by it," given that not so long before he had absorbed her full attention (ibid.). She is answered, Sachs points out, by the mutual daydream that was "stimulated by an observation which they both had made" concerning the friend and his friends, the three brothers (ibid.).

As long as one sister wasn't singled out, the affect against the sibling could be diverted "to the unconscious impatience and anger against the man who kept her in an unavowed state of painful suspense" (33). The mutual daydream was a "fantasy of revenge by means of adequate retaliation; the friend was punished in the way he had offended. The sisters joined therefore in a fantasy which gratified the repressed desire they had in common, but which neither of them could have produced or enjoyed separately" (ibid.). Collaboration making allies of rivals allowed "the conscious personality" to "accept what otherwise would have remained repressed and might have become a source of anxiety" (ibid.).

Arthur Schnitzler's *Traumnovelle* (*Dream Novella,* a.k.a. *Rhapsody,* 1925–26) is a study in mutual daydreaming, which Stanley Kubrick's *Eyes Wide Shut* (1999) underscores by capsizing the novella's balancing act of mutuality. The secret society, which in *The Devil Notebooks* led me to identify Kubrick's film swiftly and directly as infernal, begins by being proximate, certainly in Schnitzler's original, to *The Magic Flute,* in which allegory, classical antiquity, and the trial of initiation introduce a system of continuing education that is truly cosmic. But all progress toward greater union and synthesis cannot shake the deadly beauty of the Queen of the Night or her nocturnal aria of revenge.

Goethe wrote his own version of (or sequel to) the Mozart/Schikaneder story to turn her demonic appeal back around and address a threat to the issue of issue. While reproduction after the curtain falls in the original *The Magic Flute* will go on without saying, in your typical fairy tale it's unhappy trails of curses and trials. In Goethe's sequel or part II, the Queen of the Night returns to undo the happy outcome of living on, reproduction or substitution. She commands the Moors to steal her daughter's newborn son and bring him to her, targeting the limited prospect of progeny balanced on the cusp of sterility, a fate other than death. Upon locking the boy in the golden casket, the bogeymen found that a counter-magical ban had made it grow too heavy to carry away. They sealed it and left it there. She orders them to protect this outcome. The long hoped-for son of the royal couple (her grandson) must remain locked up in the manic defense Melanie Klein often discussed, that of suspended animation. What treasure can the Queen's forces be preserving, if, as the chorus proclaims, the opening of the lid means the boy is dead?[7]

It is the Queen of the Night's envy, her *Neid,* which lies too heavy upon the wish. Her wish to get even doesn't get past the manic defense of the stillborn. In fact, it sets it in motion. The casket must be still moving, the chorus must keep pacing back and forth, and Sarastro too goes on a pilgrimage to second the motion.

As sequel to the Enlightenment happy end, Goethe introduces a preoccupation with fertility and projects a romantic–fantastic modification of *The Magic Flute* along lines realized in Richard Strauss's *Die Frau ohne Schatten* (*The Woman without a Shadow,* 1919). In Hugo von Hoffmannsthal's libretto, the temptation to sell the shadow of reproduction – in other words, to control its influence – transfixes a woman in front of a magic mirror: "Oh world in world, oh dream in waking."[8]

The Euphorion "opera" in *Faust II* keeps the boy going through adolescence, whereupon he offs himself on a dare and Helena follows him into the underworld. Goethe's sequel to *The Magic Flute* centers on the loss of a young child, the trauma shadowing the opening era of childhood's emergence out of the schooling that literacy required. For the survivor of death-cult childhood, like Goethe, the death wish that one be the only child carved the nick in the trauma that in time summoned ghosts. Goethe recognized the ghosts of his dead siblings in the suicidal readership of *The Sorrows of Young Werther.*[9]

7 Johann Wolfgang von Goethe, "Der Zauberflöte zweiter Teil (Ein Fragment)," in *Die Zauberflöte: Ein literarischer Opernbegleiter mit dem Libretto Emanuel Schikandeders,* ed. Jan Assmann (Zürich: Manesse Verlag, 2012), 361. For the meeting of the curse of suspended animation with the magical counter or corollary of motion, see 326ff.
8 "O Welt in der Welt! O Traum im Wachen!" in the second half of Act 1 (following the Zwischenvorhang or drop scene). See Hugo von Hofmannsthal, "Die Frau ohne Schatten," *Projekt Gutenberg,* https://www.projekt-gutenberg.org/hofmanns/frauohne/text.html.
9 See my *Aberrations of Mourning: Writing on German Crypts* (Detroit: Wayne State University Press, 1988), 86.

Progeny, which according to the Schikaneder and Mozart original would be the free gift of coupling, is precarious in Goethe's remake, indeed something a Berliner might call "too utopian." The uncomplicated foil to the royal coupling, the marriage of Papageno and Papagena, has been without offspring altogether. Sarastro, however, crosses their stricken path and brings forth winged progeny out of golden eggs. In Goethe's version of a happy end, the casket becomes a transparent source of light. When the voices of his parents awaken him from the slumber of suspension, the boy metamorphoses into a Genius winged like the egg-children Sarastro conjured. The pagan figure reverses death-cult childhood by ascending heavenward toward an Enlightenment Olympus (or outer space).

Michel Chion counts the many instances of "parroting" in Kubrick's film, which amount in sum to an ongoing exchange of passwords,[10] setting the paranoid stage for the operas that accompanied Schreber, too, into the system that stabilized his break. Mike is given one password for entering the secret society in masked costume. But then there is the second password required for acceptance into the inner circle of the ritual orgy. To know and utter only one out of two passwords, like signing once and failing to countersign in institutional settings, dis-inscribes your candidacy for enrollment. In Mike's case, it's tantamount to inhibition, including attachment to the unique, the lost, which disqualifies one's candidacy for the position of Devil's client. The woman who gives herself to the insider orgy in exchange for Mike's release introduces a notion of sacrifice that Ziegler discounts or denies: "That whole play-act 'take me' phony sacrifice that you've been jerking off with had nothing to do with her real death."[11] The woman died by accident, officially a victim of her excessive drug use. By Ziegler's denial we fathom what Mike missed out on: black-mass psychopathy turning back the sense of victim into the truth of sacrifice. While some English words have been pushed further inside secularization than their former synonyms, leaving "victim" on the police report and keeping

---

10 Michel Chion, *Eyes Wide Shut,* trans. Trista Selous, BFI (London: Palgrave Macmillan, 2002), 71ff.
11 Cited in ibid., 73.

"sacrifice" for sacred precincts, in German, the language in which the Devil prefers to communicate, there is only one word, *Opfer,* covering or conflating both registers.

Schnitzler's *Traumnovelle* keeps us inside Freud's uncanny dialectic of Enlightenment. Indeed, Freud acknowledged Schnitzler's right to be there as his double by dint of the endopsychic acumen evident in his literary work.[12] Following upon his wife Albertine's daydream of adultery on vacation in Denmark, which he matched with the thoughts that crossed his mind, Fridolin proceeds to his trial by orgy with the single password "Denmark," which means that being without the second one is like not following "to be" with "or not to be."

Schnitzler's tale advances a discontinuum of states of dreaming from the night dream to the daydreaming held in common and elaborated by Albertine and Fridolin. Albertine's final recit of a dream upon which she awoke when her husband returned from the session of secrecy isn't a match for any night dream, but is the final fantasy she has been spinning on her side of their exchange of passwords. She fantasies a scenario in which the two figments of their adultery in Denmark and the inhibited or excluded role of Fridolin as the primal scene's voyeur are combined.[13] She is an active participant at the orgy while Fridolin's exclusion takes the form of his ritual execution. Albertine takes on the fantasy role of Kundry and *laughs* at Fridolin's crucifixion above a pool of blood. *Lachen* (laughter) and *Lache,* in the sense of *Blutlache* or "pool of blood," overlap in Wagner's relentless *Parsifal* libretto. But Albertine doesn't allow the ascendancy of the Christian fantasy and isn't expendable therefore – to put it mildly – like Kundry. She concludes by placing a warning label on "forever"; it is not advisable to question the future or into the future ("in die Zukunft fragen"). Instead she looks forward for the time being to a period of respite from the adulterous fantasying that has run its course in their mutual daydream.[14]

12 Freud to Schnitzler, May 14, 1922.
13 Arthur Schnitzler, *Traumnovelle* (Scotts Valley: CreateSpace Independent Publishing Platform, 2018), 63–69.
14 Ibid., 99.

As many instances of parroting that can be counted by Chion in *Eyes Wide Shut* are the iterations this reader of his monograph could count of mild-mannered affirmations of life as it is, which then counts as the "conclusion" or "moral" of the story. Chion projects a boy child, like the son of Tamino and Tamina in Goethe's sequel, to be reproduced by the gratefully reunited couple following the film's ending (which coincided with Kubrick's death): a kind of secular redemption set upon the Christmas season in 1999 New York City.[15] Chion counts Mike's failure to become a client of the Devil (as I would interpret it) a success for the couple, one that merits succession.

Schnitzler secures the fable a notch tighter within the poetics of daydreaming. Albertine's replacement of the "forever" in their overcoming of the recent past of adulterous wishing with the more modest guarantee of a near future for their union follows Fridolin's realization that no dream is entirely dream, is entirely night dream, and that they had embarked upon fantasying held in common and contest.[16] Like "the American Dream" or "California Dreamin'," the (night) dream can be a metonymy for the wish fantasy up in lights, the daydream.

Kubrick disbanded the close proximity to mutual daydreaming in Schnitzler's novella in favor of a contest over which Alice is mistress, whipping Mike along his proper course with the phone connection or giving (through her reminiscences, fantasies, remembered dreams of wished-for adultery) content for him to flash on in the excluded position of primal-scene voyeur, which then propels him onto the obstacle course of his inhibitions. What his fantasying of Alice's wish fantasy shows is that, like Schreber, he wonders what it feels like to be f—d. That Schreber turned down the Devil's best offer of soul murder meant that he entered instead the interstellar system of transhuman rescue of the living and the dead, which can be identified as Enlightenment in provenance. Alice's closing counsel that she and Mike "fuck" means, according to Chion's leap of faith, that there will be more life reproduced in the off. Schreber's breakdown follows the thought of giving in to temptation and delivering the father fig-

---

15 Chion, *Eyes Wide Shut*, 66–67, 88.
16 Schnitzler, *Traumnovelle*, 99.

ure's anal babies. It is possible to conclude, in contrast to Chion, that by keeping the husband odd man out Kubrick illuminated what was inadmissible in Schnitzler's orgy of mutual daydreaming.

Gender Fantasying

In his never to be completed summary work *Human Nature,* D.W. Winnicott hitched the development of gender relations to the early transitional objective of respite, which allows the fantasying of relations to unfold freely: "Incomplete or ill-timed satisfaction results in incomplete relief, discomfort, and an absence of a much-needed resting period between waves of demand."[17] To get around the stamping out of a character type by the domination (without respite) of anal or urethral functions (41), "functions with appropriate fantasy" must come instead to "dominate in a transitional way" (41). In all its stages, development should spread equally through all fantasy functions. But the so-called anal stage is too "variable" to be accorded a status equivalent to that of the oral and genital stages. The note drops for revision: "Make sure it is clear about normal homosexuality and oral erotism displaced to anus in homosexuality (manifest)" (48). While the "male in the female is always present and important," the "female in the boy," though fundamental, is "variable" (44). That something fundamental is "variable" means that it has a greater import in an aberrant setting.

Winnicott's discussion of the role of fantasying in interlacing functions and stages of sexual development in *Human Nature* gestures like an afterword to his earlier reflections in the chapter of *Playing and Reality* on creativity, which he parsed among the male and female elements in boys and girls.[18] The reflections close on a reading of Hamlet in terms of a lopsided gender trans that the hero bears as his cross, a diagnosis that is, in turn, the after-

17 D.W. Winnicott, *Human Nature* (London: Free Association Books, 1988), 39. Subsequent page references are given in the text.
18 D.W. Winnicott, "Creativity and Its Origins," in *Playing and Reality* (Hove and New York: Brunner-Routledge, 2002), 65–85. Subsequent page references are given in the text.

word to the crypt study dominating the chapter, as singular an event in Winnicott's corpus as the reading of literature.

Winnicott sees Hamlet stalled, via dissociation, at "being," the girl element in his makeup. A pause is called for after "To be or." That Hamlet offers "not to be" amounts to untenable filler for the lack of the alternative he can't fathom, which would be "to do." He is "well away on a journey that can lead nowhere" (ibid.). Thus, he crosses over into the sado-masochistic alternative: "slings and arrows."

The girl and boy elements had "up to the time of the death of his father lived together in harmony, being but aspects of his richly endowed person" (84). Instead he now attacks Ophelia: "[H]is cruelty to her" is "a picture of his ruthless rejection of his own female element, now split off and handed over to her, with his unwelcome male element threatening to take over his whole personality" (84). At the same time, "the cruelty to Ophelia can be a measure of his reluctance to abandon his split-off female element" (ibid.).

The Hamletian reluctance speaks to the chapter's case study that inspired Winnicott's reading of "To be or not to be" in terms of the impasse between the "being" of the female element and the alternative, which Hamlet can't locate. While interpreting his interminable analysand, Winnicott kept assuming that, obviously, the term "penis envy" was without sense when applied to a man. And yet he couldn't get it out of his head that his male patient was talking about it. The other counter-assumption was that "this has nothing to do with homosexuality" (73).[19]

Winnicott knows that his patient is a man, but he also knows that he is listening to a girl to whom he should say that she is talking about penis envy. And then he says that he is addressing a girl, although he knows that the patient is a man. The man accepts the interpretation intellectually: "If I were to tell someone about this girl I would be called mad." Offering to be his mirror or container, Winnicott averred that since he saw and addressed the girl it was he who was mad. This allowed the patient to feel sane, he gratefully avows, but "in a mad environment" (74).

---

19 That a male girl carrier is not at all another homosexual is a paradoxical benefit that Freud first awarded the (male) fetishist.

What remains unspoken is that it was his mother who was mad to keep seeing a daughter in her baby boy. Winnicott said it and thereby spoke to both parts of the patient. He thus stumbles over the unknown factor that had kept his analysands interminably in analysis. The only end to the analysis that the internal girl can look forward to is the discovery that he is in fact a girl (75).

While they had been doing good work in the analysis, none of Winnicott's interpretations, although made on good grounds, were ever "mutative." "They were accepted, but: so what?" (76). After Winnicott's recognition of the girl inside him and his acceptance that this was the analyst's or the mother's madness that thus spoke, the patient felt a new relationship emerge in the sessions. "The pure female split-off element found a primary unity with me as analyst, and this gave the man a feeling of having started to live" (77).

Winnicott next enters upon a speculative history tracking back across a genealogy of Greek myth to consider the shifting positions of homosexuality in heterosexuality. "In the evolution of Greek myth," Winnicott speculates, "the first homosexuals were men who imitated women so as to get into as close as possible a relationship with the supreme goddess" (78). What he refers to here as the "matriarchal era" corresponds to the setting of mysteries of gender swap, like the ceremony of the *venus barbata,* balancing the act between the sexes in matrimony.[20] When a

20 Venus was the goddess of love and beauty not of marriage, except when she wore a beard. The cult of Venus Barbata from late antiquity, in which male followers didn't stop short of castrating themselves, holds up a relationship to marriage that is in the first place internal rather than to be realized. In his 1927 essay "Gottfried Keller," Walter Benjamin identified the nineteenth-century Swiss author as a late incarnation of the *venus barbata,* part and portrait of his work's affiliation with a strain of classical antiquity that stopped short of the Christian transubstantiation of Venus into the Virgin Mary. Benjamin argued that whereas the Renaissance only looks like the return of antiquity, but in effect reinterprets its own contemporary world, Keller's work shows by its attentiveness to the time of everyday life not so much a nineteenth-century datemark as, quite exceptionally, a continuity with classical antiquity with which his work is shot through. The proviso that Benjamin must add, however, in the name of a formal law of such

patriarchal god system brought the matriarchal era to a full stop, it "initiated the idea of the boy loved sexually by man, and along with this went the relegation of women to a lower status" (79). The new truth and booty of the boy not only majorly discounts women, but even places heterosexuality under the incest taboo. Sexual difference becomes in individual psychic reality "dissociation [...] of the [...] male and female elements" (ibid.).

The synchronic axis to grind of this speculative history concerns the "experience of being" that is based on "the absolute dependence on maternal provision of that special quality by which mother meets or fails to meet the earliest functioning of the female element" (84). In the netherworld of "identification based on introjection or on incorporation," male and female elements are "already mixed" (82). The mixing covers a ranging from object relating in the sense of being the breast (or mother) to doing-relating, which presupposes the separateness of a not-me object (80). While at one extreme frustration afflicts satisfaction seeking, at the other end maiming besets the experience of being (81). "In the course of time, desirable means edible" (83). The infant is in danger of being exciting and exciting appetite – making "someone's male element *do* something" (ibid.).

At a time when the duo is not yet separated out in the infant's mind, it's up to the mother to have "a breast that *is,* so that the baby can also *be*" (82). Or else, if the mother cannot make this contribution, then "the baby has to develop without the capacity to be, or with a crippled capacity to be" (ibid.). There can be a breast that does, which makes the baby do like or be done to rather than being like. The baby then must "make do with an identity with a breast that is active, which is a male element

---

transfers of the experience of antiquity, is that the carrier of continuity must undergo a process of miniaturization and embalming, like dried fruit or shrunken heads. Benjamin selects for an example of this brand of Orphism in Keller's works an empty doll's head, in which a trapped fly continues to buzz. It is in the protocols of marriage counsel that we can observe the tradition of gender swap cross over into Christianity. The bearded lady martyr and Saint Wilgefortis was appealed to as intercessor in abusive marriages. Her martyrdom makes a scene in Ulrike Ottinger's *Freak Orlando* (1981).

breast, but which is not satisfactory for the initial identity" (82). Envy, for example, applies only when there is a "tantalizing failure of the breast as something that is" (82). In penis envy, "a man's penis may be an exciting female element generating male element activity in the girl" (83).

Winnicott introduces a tendency to dissociate intrapsychic sexual difference as self-difference, a tendency that rebuilds parts of the personality upon its foundation (84). Hamlet is the poster boy of this tendency. Winnicott's male patient, however, who carries a girl that he also is, hails from the netherworld of incorporation. Sexual identification and difference are out of joint in Freud's most famous patient, but are together again among the melancholic effects of foreign bodies that Winnicott must sort through in session. What the two or three involved were able to reconstruct was that "his mother (who is not alive now) saw a girl baby when she saw him as a baby before she came round to thinking of him as a boy" (74). He was the second born. The first child was a boy. "We have very good evidence from inside the analysis that in her early management of him the mother held him and dealt with him in all sorts of physical ways as if she failed to see him as a male. On the basis of this pattern he later arranged his defences" (ibid.). When Winnicott's patient was born, as it happened to Brian Aldiss, the mother looked for the girl she missed.

In "The Meaning of 'Penis Envy' in Women," Maria Torok, coinventor of the study of crypts, treads steps familiar from Winnicott's study of the antisocial tendency. Envy, unlike desire, can never be satisfied; it is the effect of deprivation or renunciation.[21] The mother cannot be charged. She is protected by the daughter's categorical love for her. "Coming face to face with shadowy areas where hate and aggression smolder against the mother" is a threat that her daughter must avoid at all costs (46).

Torok sets the crypt condition: obtaining the idealized penis is as impossible as changing into another body (47). By her author-

---

21 Maria Torok, "The Meaning of 'Penis Envy' in Women," in Nicholas Abraham and Maria Torok, *The Shell and the Kernel,* trans. Nicholas T. Rand (Chicago: The University of Chicago Press, 1994), 45. Subsequent page references are given in the text.

ity over the acts of sphincter control, which she commands at will, the mother has direct access to the bodily interior of her offspring. Wanting satisfaction for envy, as though it were a wish or desire, she flexes a prospective dimension through her offspring, which was thwarted in her own development (49).

Orgasm, which is at stake, is the power to fill all the positions of the primal scene, which, when it throws you for a loop, validates the fantasy. In the shadow of the climax unscaled, penis envy protests against a netherworld of incorporation, of guilty masturbation, bad sex, and conventional fantasying. The daughter is condemned to replay the anal relationship to her mother with all her partners (70). Torok's patient is another Venus of Milo hoping a sculptor will make arms for her. The inhibition of orgasm results in an incomplete body "that has as its corollary a world peopled with fragmentary realities" (50). The Queen of the *Neid* requires an empty girl, the narcissistic supply appendage of a depositing mother.

Following the breakthrough Friday session, Winnicott's patient that evening had satisfactory sex with his wife. By the end of the weekend, however, he had come down with the flu, which he brings to the session for interpretation "as if it were psychosomatic."[22] "I was able to leave aside the physical disorder and talk about the incongruity of his feeling ill after the intercourse that he felt ought to have been a healing experience" (75). Winnicott gives voice-over to his patient's double occupancy. "The feeling ill is a protest from the female self, this girl, because she has always hoped that the analysis would in fact find out that this man, yourself, is and always has been a girl (and 'being ill' is a pregenital pregnancy)" (ibid.). She's not even interested in the man. To be sure, however, she doesn't want his "masculine behaviour" released (75). Her, not his, penis envy includes envy of him as a male. Thus, she reasserts her claim to holding the sole identity.

The girl, the mother's delegate and deposit, exercises her influence over the host body or corpus. To grasp what she wants, namely full acknowledgment of herself and of her rights over

---

22 Winnicott, "Creativity and Its Origins," 74. Subsequent page references are given in the text.

the mutual body, Winnicott went off into the gaps or overlaps between matriarchal and patriarchal societies, between genealogy and developmental history. In this thicket, he considers the possibility of a perverse itinerary for his patient, one that smacks of ancient ritual, but which would keep the split-off girl animate. Lodged in the chapter on creativity, we find Winnicott's passing illumination of the underworld of underage exploits. Doing it with minors becomes the prospect of initiating countless girl brides in their pleasure. The downside is less pleasure for the man and no object constancy. The enclosed other-gender self is forever younger than the host, either remaining of one age or growing but slowly: "For instance, a man who depends on younger girls for keeping his split-off girl-self alive" will, if he lives to ninety, find that the girls still "so employed" will have only reached thirty (78). Winnicott does not indicate the extent in fantasy or in fact to which his married patient was dedicated to this service, but it is clear that the alternate approach in the primal-time thicket, homosexuality, had to be ruled out because if he came thus she could only go (77).

Winnicott argued at the start of the chapter that, for many of his patients, creativity must be measured in reverse, illuminating by its withdrawal a recognition that "for most of their time they are living uncreatively, as if caught up in the creativity of someone else, or of a machine" (65). Winnicott's "or" separates out in cases of encryptment as an alternating alternative that can alter the case for the carrier. H.G. Wells, whose mother early on addressed him in childhood and dressed him up as his dead sister, invented *The Time Machine* to enter a future so remote that he would no longer have to wear shades. When the time traveler returns without the girl, his sense of the loss is like sorrow in a dream.[23] Brian Aldiss's greatest prize, his daughter Wendy remembered, was the pacemaker he received.[24] It sealed his identification with

---

23 I first entered upon the crypt study of H.G. Wells in the third volume of my *Nazi Psychoanalysis,* titled *Psy-Fi* (Minneapolis: University of Minnesota Press, 2001), 171–78.
24 See Harrison Smith, "Brian Aldiss, Science-Fiction Writer behind Steven Spielberg's 'A.I.' Dies at 92," *Washington Post,* August 23, 2017, https://www.washingtonpost.com/local/obituaries/brian-aldiss-sci-

the machine he wanted to be, like Andy Warhol, who carried the sister that his mother couldn't mourn. Wasn't it that much worse when, in the case of Aldiss, the dead sister could after all be replaced with another living daughter.

Although Freud showed us the way to the psychic reality of encryptment, in his showcase study of the Ratman, he nevertheless pulled away from the identified crypt of a dead sister and redressed instead the father's ghost. By introducing the construction of mourning for the father, a process he could see the patient through, Freud sought to pry loose the unbeatable crypt without addressing it, and, by the metonymy of inoculation, let it go the way of finite grief. Facing a post-WWII patient population that, he claimed, was less neurotic and either more psychopathic or more schizoid, Winnicott advertised that his interventions were based no longer on transference but on regression. He addresses the girl and analyzes in the patient's sexual adaptation to his carrier status the prospect of a good enough integration of the crypt.

The Secret in Mutual Daydreaming

Like Nietzsche, Winnicott situates reproduction within the secret setting of fantasying, which child's play explores. The reality of reproduction is staggered in the game "can you keep a secret?" which Winnicott claims in *Human Nature* "belongs typically to the female side of human nature": "Unless a girl can keep a secret she cannot become pregnant."[25] In Sachs's case example of the two boys, there is a secret in the mutual daydream that is not shared but carried forward – until one of the duo lies on the analyst's couch. You run away from home with a mutual daydreamer in childhood. In adolescence, the secret held by one of the shareholders in the daydream makes itself felt. The secret is key to fantasying in concert, which is why Wilfred Bion's notion of the maternal reverie, which tells us something about transference, doesn't grasp mutual daydreaming.

---

ence-fiction-writer-behind-steven-spielbergs-ai-dies-at-92/2017/08/23/da4bed60-8743-11e7-a94f-3139abce39f5_story.html.
25 Winnicot, *Human Nature,* 46.

That the secret is sometimes a crypt also enters the relationship to reproduction. The mother is the last to substitute a new child for the lost one. If reproduction does happen again, the grief-stuck mother is bound to be the last to recognize the infant as new and other. But when the secret in mutual daydreaming is a crypt, it is kept secret through diversions that near miss its unquiet place in the corpus. Mary Shelley's *Frankenstein* wears a crypt story on its banner, tying the unacknowledgable loss of Victor's mother to the body that he builds out of corpse parts at the alma mater. But it is a false bottom; beneath this fictional incorporation trailing the mother who died giving birth to her, lie encrypted Mary Shelley's unmournably dead children. [26] Oscar Wilde's *The Picture of Dorian Gray* just as openly invites the reader to follow out the coordinates of an encryptment. After his enraged rejection of his no longer beloved Sybil Vane for her poor performance on stage, Dorian notes the impact in the portrait of what he doesn't know yet, her consequent suicide. The change in the painted expression is not "fancy," but is rather "horribly apparent"[27] – the horrible souvenir of a parent.

The wish-charged portrait will age unto ongoing resemblance with his hated dead grandfather, who kept Dorian for the term of his childhood in the attic. The grandfather filled the young orphan's blank with his repressed mourning, pushing the boy up and away to keep the resemblance with the lost daughter out of his face. That Dorian as a young man banishes the animate portrait up there means the upward displacement of encryptment is a wrap. That there is a parent in Dorian's face, which the supernatural portrait preserves while hiding the horror of decay, is true enough and a damn good diversion.

The crypt in *The Picture of Dorian Gray* is kept like a secret in the mutual daydream that is this story's agon.[28] Up front, Wilde's

26 See the more complete reading of Shelley's novel in my *The Vampire Lectures* (Minneapolis: University of Minnesota Press, 1999).
27 Oscar Wilde, *The Picture of Dorian Gray* (London: Penguin Books, 1984), 101. Subsequent page references are given in the text.
28 See my crypt study of Oscar Wilde in the chapter on Ottinger's *Dorian Gray im Spiegel der Boulevard Presse*, in *Ulrike Ottinger: The Autobiography of Art Cinema* (Minneapolis: University of Minnesota

novel is all about a wish and its fulfillment. Let the portrait be Dorian's mirror, while, like a vampire, he henceforth casts no reflection. But that secret is more easily done than said. There wouldn't be a novel if Lord Henry and Dorian didn't hold a daydream in common, which the former initiates and guides and the latter acts out at the turbulent address of influence and experiment. Lord Henry singles Dorian out for the experiment of an art of life by introducing him to and introducing into him his own verbal art of outsourcing, the other *Gesamtkunstwerk*. While listening to Lord Henry's overskill at shredding the parergon of signature and property, Dorian is "dimly conscious that entirely fresh influences were at work within him. Yet they seemed to him to have come really from himself. [...] Music had stirred him like that. [...] But music was not articulate. It was not a new world, but rather another chaos. [...] Words [...] seemed to be able to give a plastic form to formless things, and to have a music of their own" (24).

A term befitting the experimental setting and the adolescent condition that is open to it and shut to tradition, influence also reaches back to Wilde's first career in fame, which was based on the airtime of conversation, personality, and a US tour of 140 public lectures. Wilde was legend at turning around by his spoken word dead air into animation or reanimation of the speaker, his audience, and another. Lord Henry, the souvenir of Wilde's fame *avant la lettre* wields the art of conversation, drawing and doubling all those in earshot "out of themselves" (48). While the topic of his lectures on the US tour was the aestheticism championed by his mentors at Oxford, Wilde offered in the foreground of his presentations a course in interior decoration, which belied what it housed, a melancholic core or crypt. Wilde transferred the layout of his sister Isola's encryptment to his one-time only novel.

The aestheticist decor of Wilde's novel mixes the fantasy palette of synesthesia with the color in Dorian's surname, American spelling. *Fifty Shades of Grey*, written in the vampiroid fan milieu of *Twilight* by an author from the UK, restores the British spelling. The folk-etymological mix-up of grey with gruesome

Press, 2009).

like *Grau* in German with *grausam* underwent a perceptual modification that fit dreary weather and signalled a loss of vital distinction, for example in Mephistopheles' famous line: gray is all theory. Goethe's *Theory of Colors* reintroduces theoretical gray as the color best suited as backdrop for optical experimentation with afterimages. Intermediate between brightness and darkness, gray (including white cast in shade or shadow) enables a more perfect light/dark reversal between the circles placed on a monochromatic screen and their afterimages lingering on when the circles are removed. What is in the name Gray, then, is the screen color suited for experiments in ghostly settings. In both *Vertigo* and the novel Hitchcock adapted, Madeleine can return like an afterimage or ghost when the almost lookalike Judy/Renée is wrapped back inside the same gray outfit.

After Dorian confesses his love for Sibyl Vane, a figure from the Shakespeare underworld that "grey" London one night held "in store" for him (55), Lord Henry recognizes that his experiment with the youth (64) was reaching the new completion of an art of life: "He had made him premature. That was something" (65). While art, literature especially, can reveal the mysteries of life "before the veil was drawn away," "now and then a complex personality took the place and assumed the office of art; was indeed, in its way, a real work of art" (ibid.).

Wilde injected into *The Picture of Dorian Gray* Joris-Karl Huysmans's *À rebours* as infamous and unnamed how-to book. Dorian, again thrown for a loop, reads the story of his life written down before he has lived it; it has plagiarized him in advance. The conceit reintroduces the theme of improper burial in the manner by which the crypt was borne in the book's prehistory, Wilde's influence realized in advance of any corpus to carry it out and make it endure. Dorian's reading assignment, given by Lord Henry to add the coloration of sin and decay to his work in progress, decorates interiors for one long chapter like a condensation in a can of Wilde's US lectures. Following the installation of the decor, Dorian is buffeted by murderous reversals of his wish fantasy, but reversal preserves. Then the portrait's secret wish fulfillment ends by the convention of dueling doubles, and the mutual daydream of an experimental art of life without a corpus is reduced to one identifiable corpse. That the once animate portrait yet shows an image that cannot vary is a reversal on the cusp of the novel closing and becoming a corpus that can carry.

When Isola died Wilde was thirteen and excelled at school in the classics, particularly in translating directly from dead-language texts, an oral delivery remembered by his classmates already in the same animating terms with which witnesses at later stations of his studies and beyond conveyed Wilde's verbal skills as conversationalist and improv orator. The conditions were falling into place for the life of an author with a day job as academic. He published a first book, the volume *Poems,* which he dedicated to Isola. But his attempt to secure a teaching position was thwarted and he went from the second string of show business to the foreground of delivering fame outside a corpus.

Married with children, Wilde tried as another kind of dedication to reproduce Isola's lost place in his family package, but fell short when he set only two places. The girl was reassured that her seat was thus kept safe inside him. He wasn't into it and she didn't have to go out of herself – and vanish. The crisis from her vantage was the male girl carrier's affair with Lord Douglas. At this time, *Salomé* marked a return of the corpus of translation through which Wilde again attempted to acknowledge Isola and let her go. That it was his second dedication to Isola can be observed in the photo op he performed in the drag of the dancer of seven veils.

Flight to Reality

In his 1935 essay "The Manic Defence," Winnicott identifies in patients "jeering at religion" in session a reflex of "manic defence insofar as they fail to recognize sadness, guilt, and worthlessness and the value of reaching to this which belongs to personal inner or psychic reality."[29] However, the "average Christian" regulation of the Good Friday experience by going "over into a manic phase on Easter Sunday" models neither health nor treatment (135). It is still possible for the Nietzschean or Freudian to find the

---

29 D.W. Winnicott, "The Manic Defence," in *Through Paediatrics to Psycho-analysis: Collected Papers* (New York: Brunner-Routledge, 1992), 135. Subsequent page references are given in the text.

Friday Good indeed. "I think that I should once have described the Crucifixion and Resurrection as a symbolic castration with subsequent erection in spite of corporeal insult" (ibid.).

Before we register the significance of Winnicott's disappointment in this interpretation, we must underscore its truth. For, "it is characteristic of the manic defence that the individual is unable fully to believe in the liveliness that denies deadness, since he does not believe in his own capacity for object love; for making good is only real when the destruction is acknowledged" (131–32). But with the transference interpretation of the death of the good, Winnicott would have "left out the depressive-ascensive significance of the myth" (135), in other words, its fantasy content. The manic defence employs "almost any opposites in the reassurance against death," namely, "chaos, mystery, etc., ideas that belong to the *fantasy content* of the depressive position" (132).

The flight of fantasy from inner reality to the outer reality that it elaborates after its omnipotence, bears datemarks across its orbit awaiting historicization. Karl Abraham and Freud found the paradox of mania's inversion or implosion of melancholia illuminated in analogy with the ritual celebration of carnival and its alternating observance of shrift.[30] Carnival shares with fairy stories and epics of heroic quest the historical setting of transition from paganism to Christianization. Does fantasy attest to the predominance of the middle ages or does it restore it to this place? In T.H. White's *The Sword in the Stone,* a 1938 Arthurian fantasy tale for children, Merlin's magical faculty of memory, which proceeds in reversal of the time line of history (and of "progress"), requires or implements a continuous medievalist tradition. Merlin: "[O]rdinary people are born *forwards* in Time, if you understand what I mean, and nearly everything in the world goes forward too. [...] I unfortunately was born at the wrong end of time, and I have to live *backwards* from in front,

---

30 I develop this insight into the quilting point of a reading of their studies of and their correspondence on melancholia, which attends to the anal crypt carried forward ultimately within the corpus of Antonin Artaud, in *Aberrations of Mourning: Writing on German Crypts* (Detroit: Wayne State University Press, 1988), chapter 4.

while surrounded by a lot of people living forwards from behind. Some people call it having second sight."[31]

Winnicott located daydream fantasy anew within the object-relations topography of positions, penetrating more deeply, he suggests, than pre-Kleinian analysis was prepared to go (132, 132n1).[32] What the depth charge entails is that transference interpretation must follow contemplation of the manic defense, which can be entered upon only in tandem with a growing appreciation of inner reality. "I have come to compare external reality not so much with fantasy as with an inner reality" (129). He has also come to fine-tune the notion of a flight to reality, which, he stipulates, is a flight from internal reality and not from fantasy (130). The reality on this itinerary, which he sees daubed with omnipotent fantasy, inflects and reflects "not so much the inner reality itself as a defence against the acceptance of it. One finds in this defence a flight to omnipotent fantasy, and flight from some fantasies to other fantasies, and in this sequence a flight to external reality. This is why I think one cannot compare and contrast fantasy and reality" (ibid.).

Fantasy offers a mediating dyad of omnipotence and devaluation that elaborates external reality in the afterimage of the inner reality from which it took flight. The manic defense against acknowledgment of the depressive position locks inside the manifest of its flight the content of inner reality.

> Fantasy is part of the individual's effort to deal with inner reality. It can be said that fantasy and daydreams are omnipotent manipulations of external reality. Omnipotent control of reality implies fantasy about reality. The individual gets to external reality through the omnipotent fantasies elaborated in the effort to get away from inner reality. (130)

Fantasies defend against inner deadness by a projective flight from fantasies to yet other fantasies, a flight pattern that con-

---

31 T.H. White, *The Sword in the Stone* (New York: Philomel Books, 1993), 38.
32 Winnicott, "The Manic Defence," 132 and 132n1. Subsequent page references are given in the text.

structs a relationship to external reality. The manic defense is never far from the norm it helps structure. That's why a relationship to outer reality can come through all the fantasying. It's also why some dosage of the manic defense is always present and accounted for.

The manic defense is the cursor that allows Winnicott to read across the arts and everyday life via fantasying that staggers the inner reality of an ending. At the shallow end of fantasying in the service of the manic defense, Winnicott places an author of colonialist adventure stories. In trying to take flight from inner reality it's possible to fall short with the crashing of a bore.

> In the ordinary extrovert book of adventure we often see how the author made a flight to daydreaming in childhood, and then later made use of external reality in this same flight. He is not conscious of the inner depressive anxiety from which he has fled. He has led a life full of incident and adventure, and this may be accurately told. But the impression left on the reader is of a relatively shallow personality, for this very reason, that the author adventurer has had to base his life on the denial of personal internal reality. (130)

In "An American in France," Gertrude Stein demarcated the necessity for those making art, who draw from within themselves, of a second civilization, history, and occupation, seconds that have nothing to do with the civilization, history, occupation that made them, but by staying put and not impinging upon the self and the freedom to create can be felt inside. The second civilization that offers respite, which belongs to her own expat situation or, as was the case in ancient times, to the recourse made to speciality languages of art, Stein dubs romance, which she sets apart from adventure.

> What is adventure and what is romance. Adventure is making the distant approach nearer but romance is having what is where it is which is not where you are stay where it is. So those who create things do not need adventure but they do need

romance they need that something that is not for them stays where it is and that they can know that it is there where it is.[33]

What distinguishes the souvenirs of adventure from the art of romance becomes in Winnicott's practice the end in sight that separates the stricken world of his patients from the prospect of new beginnings arising out of inner reality.

Session by session, Winnicott identifies in his patients the open invitation to join their manic defense instead of understanding their deadness. But the psychoanalyst holds an inside advantage within the series of being in session, since the patient is on a treatment schedule that leads to a termination phase, which is the end in the dead end. This end is being analyzed from the get-go. In the course of its analysis, the patient reduces the manic defense, or balances on it, and, once the end arrives, can settle with the so-called depressive position, the foundation for a new beginning. The end or purpose of the analysis is on a schedule with its therapeutic finitude: "It is not enough to say that certain cases show manic defence, since in every case the depressive position is reached sooner or later, and some defence against it can always be expected. And, in any case, the analysis of the end of an analysis (which may start at the beginning) includes the analysis of the depressive position" (143).

Winnicott's patient Mathilda, his final of four case examples, brings a Polyfoto to session and asks the analyst to help her choose the best one of the forty-eight pictures. Her mother asked for a photograph of her, so Mathilda tried out this option. With the analysts's help surely one picture could be seen to be good enough. She also invites him to choose and keep for himself one photo, and so on. Instead of participating, Winnicott interprets the situation. Mathilda: now she won't give anyone a photo and will kill herself. When she recounts that the thought, "how awful to be really oneself, how terribly lonely," recently crossed her mind, Winnicott is able to translate the thought and its photo finish: "To be oneself means containing a relation between father

---

33 Gertrude Stein, "An American and France," in *What Are Masterpieces* (Los Angeles: The Conference Press, 1940), 62–63. It was originally a lecture that Stein delivered at Oxford University in 1936.

and mother. [...] The Polyfoto incident was an invitation to me to get caught up in her manic defence instead of understanding her deadness, non-existence, lack of feeling real" (143).

That one contains a relation between father and mother, indeed their coupling, refers to the primal scene that Melanie Klein called the combined parents, the double-backed entity that performs the scene. The manic defense against their combinations inside you is to hold the parents in suspended animation. But this defense contact is a dead end: "omnipotent control of the bad internalized parents also stops all good relationships, and the patient feels dead inside and sees the world as a colourless place" (133–34). Instead, according to Klein, it is incumbent upon the child to learn to separate out the combined parents and recombine them into an object relation – which for Klein means that the internal parents can now share in your own mating pleasure. The other experience in which the parents lodged in the inner world share is grief.[34]

Poly also recalls the polymorphous perversion of the baby's auto-stimulation, which is the console on which baby types in the primal scene, often based as much on what's overheard as seen, in any event imagined. For Winnicott, the Polyfoto manifests the patient's fantastic manic defending on the cusp of a balancing act with inner reality; it suggests plenitude, freedom of choosing, aggrandizement, generosity – but the dead end that is being defended against is also in sight.

Following acknowledgment of inner reality, the transference interpretation can be offered. A good example of a transference interpretation (and of its secondary importance) is given in the prior case example. Charlotte, a "severe obsessional" (136), whose analysis at the time was only of two months duration (140), wants to besmirch her mother in her transferential heir. "I could point to my role of mother in the transference, with the patient's indirectly expressed urge to dirty me and kick and trample on my body, and so on, but I feel I should have missed something

---

34 I am giving the gist of Melanie Klein's interpretation of healthy and not haunting relations with the internal parents which I present throughout my case study of Ian Fleming (or rather his Bond) in *SPECTRE* (Fort Wayne: Anti-Oedipus Press, 2013).

very important if I had not pointed out the significance of the lessening in manic defence and the new dangers inherent in the change" (141).

At the start of the analysis, Charlotte brought to session her stock dream of a train that never starts. The dream narrative undergoes a change after two months, a new version that she dreams twice in one night: "*In each dream the train started*" (ibid.). "The train that never started to travel over the lines was a picture of the omnipotently controlled parents, parents held in suspended animation. [...] The starting of the trains indicated the lessening of this control of the internalized parents, and gave warning of the dangers inherent in this, and of the need for new defences should the advance in this direction outrun the ego development that the analysis was bringing about. There had been recent material and interpretations in regard to the taking in of me and of my room, etc." (ibid.).

The need for new defenses means that a new relationship to the manic defense leading toward greater acceptance of the depressive position can be worked on in the transference. "The search for the washing place" in her new dream of trains that in starting to move are liable to accidents "was probably connected with the development of the obsessional technique, and all that that means in regard to the ability to tolerate the depressive position and to acknowledge object love and dependence" (ibid.). Ergo: "In the next hour the patient felt responsible for the kick marks on my door and the dirty marks on the furniture, and wanted to wash them off" (ibid.).

Since "it is part of one's own manic defence to be unable to give full significance to inner reality," Winnicott considers the "fluctuations in one's ability to respect inner reality that are related to depressive anxiety in oneself" (129). The transference interpretation enters these fluctuations to reach by its helping "and" the end of the analysis. At the close of his essay, Winnicott downplays the transferential relationship to the extent that the end or purpose of the analysis was already always on a schedule with its therapeutic finitude. What did he do? Winnicott prefers to keep the melancholic predilection of his precursors, Freud and

Klein, at a distance – for example, by cannibalistically tongue-in-cheek dismissal of certain patients as "good breast advocates."[35]

In his discussion of the case of Mathilda, he downplays his own departure, the object relation lying in wait in the ending. If it's lost, that's because it was throwaway. The Polyfoto session was the turning point:

> The analytic situation (which she has spent four years proclaiming to be the only reality for her) now seemed to her for the first time to be unreal, or at least a narcissistic relationship, a relationship to the analyst that is valuable to her chiefly for her own relief, a taking without giving, a relationship with her own internal objects. (142–43)

When Mathilda brings the Polyfoto to session, she is, after four years in analysis, at the point of recognizing Winnicott's interpretations of the defense's response to an underlying deadness:

> At the beginning of the hour [...] she tried to make me laugh, and laughed herself at the thought that by the attitude of my hands I was holding back my water with them. With this patient, as with others, I found that this effort to laugh and to make me laugh, was a signal of depressive anxiety, and a patient may show great relief at one's quick recognition of this interpretation, even bursting into tears instead of going on laughing and being funny. (142)

Awareness of inner reality crosses over into and is amplified by the transference. The "and" of the transference interpretation that slaps her silly, however, is there to be let go.

If there are senses of an ending then we are traversing obstacles in the linguistic course of everyday life. In its own writing, therefore, the essay testifies to the impasse that fantasying in manic defense poses; the very term "manic defence" doesn't sit well in everyday language:

---

35 D.W. Winnicott, "The Depressive Position in Normal Human Development," in *Through Paediatrics to Psycho-analysis: Collected Papers* (New York: Brunner-Routledge, 1992), 276.

One cannot help noting that the word "depression" is not only used but used quite accurately in popular speech. Is it not possible to see in this the introspection that goes with depression? The fact that there is no popular term for the manic defence could be linked with the lack of self-criticism that goes with it clinically. [...] It is just when we are depressed that we *feel* depressed. It is just when we are manic-defensive that we are least *likely to feel* as if we are defending against depression. (132)

In Michelangelo Antonioni's *Blow-up* (1966), photography, a fallback position in the history and understanding of the motion picture medium, is the depressive position underlying the film's conflict and self-reflection. The bulk rate of the photographer–protagonist's preoccupation with his medium is a split-off nonstop recording of the fleeting fixity and glancing contact of flight to reality. Antonioni relocated the ambiguous eros openly displayed in Julio Cortázar's 1959 story, "Las babas del diablo" ("The Devil's Slime"), and adapted it to the impasse of his fantasying protagonist, which he then blows up to fit the screen of his art film. In the story, the object of the intrigue is a hustler in whom both members of the criminal couple take a controlling interest. The plot was inspired by an anecdote from the life of David Bailey, the London photographer Antonioni was incorporating in his protagonist. Straight ambiguity, which is how Antonioni typecast him, is probably closer to the truth of any portrait of "swinging."

In *Blow-up*, the protagonist's plan to publish a book of documentary photographs of his undercover sojourn in a working-class milieu would facilitate escape from the sexual ambiguity of his day job as fashion photographer. By his cynical acquiescence in seduction by girl groupies and his counsel to an investor to look at other neighborhoods, since this one is going the way of a male couple he just saw walking the dog, we know that the protagonist fits a strain of adaptation to social homophobia.

He is untenably close to a couple, an abstract painter and his wife, both open and shut to him. His relationship to this couple, which goes the distance of his pursuit of art, is primal. Being a photographer means to walk in on any activity at all and make cursory contact. The time comes when the photographer is free to walk in on and witness the coupling of his friends. When he visited his painter friend's studio on an earlier occasion we looked at abstract paintings. The painter says he finds his way in and around his work after the fact. It's like a murder mystery.

What followed the first scene in the painter's studio, in which the painter imparted the detective analogy and then turned down the photographer's offer to buy an abstract painting (it's not that easy), is the shoot that in aiming to deliver the parting shot for the art-photography book aimed at closure preliminary to publication. At this point a series of endings rise up against the prospect of the social relation of art, the new beginning. The painter friend had already aligned this series with the work of detection in which the photographer is now engaged. Gertrude Stein considered the murder mystery the only novelty in the novel form in her day.[36] It begins with someone being dead, which means that we start over in a clearing devoid of human nature. For Stein, "somebody being dead and how it moves along" was the new life after death.[37]

The photographic shoot in the park, the Polyfoto spread from which he means to choose the closing image, triggers contact with a more mature woman whose privacy he breached. She doesn't want her tryst documented. But when it turns out that what's on record is that she murdered the man, an unidentified dead person, the photographer starts blowing up the medium that he raises from daydreaming to the power of art.

Because the culprit, the agent of his Oedipus complex, withdraws with all the evidence of "negative" transference, he is left alone at the outer blown-up limit of his medium. Here, however, he borders on the art of his special painter friend. The same day his unannounced visit brings him before the scene from his friends' sex life, primalized by fixing the focus of his

---

36 See, for example, Gertrude Stein, "What Are Masterpieces and Why Are There So Few of Them," in *What Are Masterpieces* (Los Angeles: The Conference Press, 1940), 87–88.

37 Gertrude Stein, "Why I Like Detective Stories," in *A Primer for the Gradual Understanding of Gertrude Stein* (Los Angeles: Black Sparrows Press, 1974), 148.

photographic-daydreaming on the POV of exclusion, the painter's partner – the near-miss-outlet of the eros between the men friends – comes to the photographer's studio to ask if there was anything he wanted earlier when he came and went. When he returned from that primal scene, he found his studio a stricken place emptied of all the evidence with which he had overfilled it in the course of his detection work. He also knows now that sleeping with the maternal figure did not resolve the scene of his being excluded, refused, and robbed. Shortly before the go-between arrives on the rebound from the primal scene, he does find one image from the enlargement series that escaped the murderess's cleanup operation. His visitor picks up the last photographic trace of someone murdered in the park and immediately identifies its grainy abstraction with the experimental painterly qualities of her husband's artwork. His art-photography book has been superseded, while Antonioni proceeds to complete his "abstract" film.

Blow-up closes on affirmation of its moving picture medium rebounding from inner reality (going directly to art and not stopping in fantasying, including the amped-up black-&-white documentary-reality). The photographer is caught up in the mime show of an invisible tennis match. He witnesses, or plays at witnessing, together with the mime witnesses, a match or courtship that follows a code that can be upheld in silence and without an object, one that includes a balanced or coupled score called "love." However, when he is called on to participate in the performance by retrieving the missing ball invisibly lobbed outside the court, which he duly throws back, we no longer watch the game, but join him alone on its outer periphery while hearing the rackets striking the object. He's outside again, odd man out, and we moviegoers watch him disappear by one of the oldest tricks of the film medium. In his missing place stands "The End."

Fantasying Fantasy

In an updating footnote that he later added to "The Manic Defence," Winnicott advises that in lieu of using "fantasy" as synonym for daydreams, he would in the meantime write and mean instead "fantasying" (130). By the gerund he underscores an activity, at once fixated and fleeting, which navigates the difference between its flights and what's happening out there, a difference that can in extremity become dissociation. This note is the link to his second approach to the daydream, I mean fantasying, the second chapter of *Playing and Reality*: "Dreaming, Fantasying, and Living: A Case-history describing a Primary Dissociation." Here he addresses his treatment goal ethically as changing fantasying into imagination related to the night dream, to living, and to poetry.[38]

While he retained Klein's depressive position, Winnicott had between the two essays on fantasying struck out on his own with his introduction of the transitional object, which redirects psychoanalysis to address the development of psychopathy. Psychopathy and the dissociated daydreaming that Winnicott treats and theorizes in "Dreaming, Fantasying, and Living" are limit concepts that psychoanalysis fails to interpret (the poetics of daydreaming cuts away to art from the daydreaming itself, a blur of inchoate and censorious thoughts and wishes).

That Winnicott's patient was suicidal because that's as close as she could get to murder matches her "abandonment of hope in object relating" during the downturn of her early relationship to her mother.[39] Hope has gone the way of aggression and the environment. All her industry and innovation found one outlet, one achievement – her capacity for being absent but accounted for through dissociation. The scene of the transitional object, in which the data of giving and receiving between mother and infant are treated and accepted as the baby's own creation, makes clear that good enough mothering means that the mother is hard pressed to be good enough to stave off the child's sense of deprivation and its sequelae, notably all that goes into the antisocial tendency.

To intercept a psychopathic outcome (prior to consolidation via secondary gains), Winnicott interpreted early delinquent behavior, such as stealing, as signaling hope and illuminating the importance of the environment. The child who acts out antiso-

---

38 D.W. Winnicott, *Playing and Reality* (Hove and New York: Brunner-Routledge, 2002), 27.
39 Ibid., 29.

cially is far enough along to steer clear of the deep freeze of the spontaneous self in psychosis, but also hasn't gone the distance to qualify for the endless roto-routing of Oedipal identifications in neurosis.[40] By testing the environment for its capacity to hold the turbulence that he cannot contain and still feel real, the asocial child's momentum is resolutely on the track of the spontaneous self that is alive and kicking. That the environment that failed him was the mother is what the child was not able to know. Through regression rather than transference, the patient finally faces the mother in session (and in the past) and hates her. Aggression no longer needs to be externalized, and the integration of psyche and soma can take place via an internal relationship to omnipotence.

In the 1935 essay on the manic defense, the first two case examples were of asocial children, whose relationship to omnipotence Winnicott sought to restore through a therapy of playing and mutual fantasying. He describes the progress made by his five-year-old patient Billy signaled by changes in a game they played together in session. While they no doubt played with toys, the way Winnicott retells the scenarios, it sounds like they largely shared out loud fantasying about transport and battle. At three and a half, when the analysis commenced, Billy, who was already stealing, had been stamped "potential delinquent."[41] Following analysis of the depressive position, his ambivalence toward his mother was beginning to find open expression at home, and his manic behavior was alternating with feelings of sadness. Therefore, constructive play could commence in their sessions. In the scenarios that Winnicott recounts and analyzes, we witness the gradual lifting of the manic defense set on colonialist adventure clichés.

The first scenario is like the famous Baron Munchhausen cannon-ball ride, which sends Billy to Africa (the analyst launched

---

40 I am reading/reaching back to my earlier Winnicott studies and formulations in *Germany: A Science Fiction* (Fort Wayne: Anti-Oedipus Press, 2015) and *The Psycho Records* (New York: Wallflower Press, 2016).
41 Winnicott, "The Manic Defence," 136. Further page references are given in the text.

him). Flying along a vantage point, he attacks the locals from on high, even dropping them down deep wells. He becomes so excited during the game that after he leaves the office he unconsciously on purpose takes the lift down to the basement, which terrifies him. Winnicott, who anticipated this, delivers Billy right away and forges a bond by the reassurance he gives him.

After an interval of some months, the fantasy of a trip to Africa is revisited, this time by airplane. The analyst is along for this ride. They enter into alliance with enemy pilots against third parties. This time there is an emphasis on safety precautions, a doubling up of the contents of the flying machine for the long haul and the inclusion of instruction manuals. "In many other ways, too, we insure ourselves against a failure of our attempt to get above our troubles" (137). Devaluation and omnipotence were lessened on this fantasy trip. And while the view from above still allowed the boy to drop feces on the world below, the flight also has the import of "an ascensive or contra-depressive feel" (ibid.).

Later, a third game was organized around a voyage in a ship that they built for a visit to pirate island. The weather is so beautiful, however, that they forget their destination for a new aim: they decide to relax on deck, lying out in the sun. Occasionally they dive into the sea and swim about lazily. There are the usual sharks and crocodiles, but the boy packs a gun that can shoot underwater, so there is no alarm. They save a little girl from drowning and then play with her and her doll. The captain of the ship, it turns out, intentionally mucked up the engine. But when he's found out, he cleans the apparatus and all's well. To the extent that former dangers are simply forgotten or denied, the manic defense is still being flexed. But through the increase in the goodness of the internal objects, the defense allows the other changes to happen: lessening of the over-insurance against risk, new object relations, the manageable quality of the captain's treachery. There is manic defense in the way Billy is prepared to shoot persecutors inside the body (underwater), but a strong relation to external reality is also seen, "for example, in the relation of the shooting under water to passing water in the bath" (138).

We recognize in the relay of these scenarios of playing and fantasying a steady layering on that's building up to a less guarded relationship to inner reality. Winnicott draws a healthy dose of the manic defense at the limit of two extreme cases: the sex fiend who through "every possible physical aspect of sexuality" "abates psychic tension by the use of the satisfaction to be got" or the hypochondriac who by internal bodily sensations "comes to tolerate psychic tension by denial of fantasy content" (133). When next Winnicott takes us on a tour of London music halls, we take in a healthy dose of the defense, its golden meaning a part of art and everyday life:

> [O]n to the stage come the dancers, trained to liveliness. One can say that here is the primal scene, here is exhibitionism, here is anal control, here is masochistic submission to discipline, here is a defiance of the super-ego. Sooner or later one adds: here is LIFE. Might it not be that the main point of the performance is a denial of deadness, a defence against depressive "death inside" ideas, the sexualisation being secondary. (131)

The other asocial child, David, is eight years old. He was only recently brought to Winnicott in lieu of expulsion from school for an illicit activity vaguely defined as "sex and lavatory obsession" (138). Winnicott doesn't let us in on the deep fantasies that he explored with David while they played with the toys in his office. But when David begins trying to tire him out, a trait or tendency Winnicott was warned to expect, already "a good deal of analysis had been possible" (139). David has turned around to face the world outside, that is, outside the office door or as seen from the window.

> The inside of the room had become his own inside and if he were to deal with me and the contents of my room (father and mother, witches, ghosts, persecutors, etc.) he had to have the means to control them. First he had to tire them out, as he feared he could not control them – and I felt that in this he showed some distrust of omnipotence. (139)

David's fantasy escape has been kept at the close quarters of internally quarreling parents. His management of his manic defense at school "shows the flight from inner reality to the interest in the surface of his body, and in his surface feelings, and from these to an interest in the bodies and feelings of other children" (140). In other words, he is a typical delinquent on two counts: his knowledge of the facts of external reality and his immediate likeability at first contact, which he takes care not to extend or deepen (138).

The turning point came in their session on Armistice Day. From Winnicott's office window he had grown accustomed to a view of street life that provided him with "a not hopelessly uncontrollable sample of inner reality" (139). On the way to Winnicott's office on that day he bought a poppy from a lady in the street. During the session, the two minutes' silence was observed: "It was a particularly complete silence in my neighbourhood, and he was absolutely delighted. [...] For two minutes in his life he felt as if he was not tired, as he need not tire out the parents, since there had come along an omnipotent control imposed from outside and accepted as real by all" (140).

He was all along the one who was being tired out by his "control of the internalized parents who were exhausting each other as well as him" (139). His denial heretofore of his exhaustion was the bottom line of his denial of inner reality. During the Armistice observance, David fantasied that the ladies were continuing to sell flowers, the only permitted activity during the ceremonial silence (which, Winnicott advises, was not in fact the case): "[A] more manic, internal omnipotence would have stopped everything (the good included)" (140). A step outside the full stop of suspended animation could be taken toward object relations.

In the ritual occasions of the outside world Winnicott sees a festive inscription and administration of the manic defense that helps him out with his patients. In the UK readership's regular consulting of newspaper health reports on the Royals, he discerned a diversion of the inner reality of paternity into the personals column of a remote personage. "I prefer to say that in our inner reality the internalized father is all the time being killed, robbed and burnt and cut up, and we welcome the personalization of this internalized father by a real man whom we can help to save" (131). David can bring a "poppy" to Winnicott, flexing omnipotence without the recoil of suspended animation on this official day of the dead/dad.

Winnicott must lead both antisocial children that he nips in the budding of their psychopathy past the impasse of manic defense into the promised land of childhood play and omnipotent fantasying. In "Dreaming, Fantasying, and Living," Winnicott's middle-aged patient, whose outcome is more schizoid than psycho, has relied on and plied her second nature of daydreaming since early childhood. In the patient's early history, which Winnicott tries to take down, nothing ever happened, while in her dissociated state so much was happening all the time. She was the youngest child and it was incumbent on her to play along in the already organized setting of the sibling group bond. Doing nothing was her response to the obligation to fit in: Nothing doing.

That the young child entered into the group activities only on a compliance basis was unrewarding for all concerned. But her siblings probably didn't realize that she was all the while absent.

> From the point of view of my patient, [...] while she was playing the other people's games she was *all the time engaged in fantasying*. She really lived in this fantasying on the basis of a dissociated mental activity. This part of her which became thoroughly dissociated was never the whole of her, and over long periods her defence was to live here in this fantasy activity, and to watch herself playing the other children's games as if watching someone else in the nursery group.
>
> By means of the dissociation, reinforced by a series of significant frustrations in which her attempts to be a whole person in her own right met with no success, she became a specialist in this one thing: being able to have a dissociated life while seeming to be playing with the other children in the nursery. [...] As my patient grew older so she managed to construct a life in which nothing that was really happening was fully significant to her. Gradually she became one of the many who do not feel that they exist in their own right as whole human beings. All the time, [...] there was another life going on in terms of the part that was dissociated. Put the other way

around, this meant that her life was dissociated from the main part of her, which was living in what became an organized sequence of fantasying.[42]

What Winnicott refers to as "the here-and-now fixity of any satisfaction that there can be in fantasying" (35) designates the release of throwing-away. In other words, fantasying is in his view an isolated phenomenon that absorbs the energy of living without giving anything back (26). The patient is Winnicott's living proof "that fantasying interferes with action and with life in the real or external world, but much more so it interferes with dream and with the personal or inner psychic reality, the living core of the individual personality" (31).

A session begins with the patient's fanciful description of the sky glimpsed through the office window:

> She says: "I am up on those pink clouds where I can walk." This, of course, might be an imaginative flight. It could be part of the way in which the imagination enriches life just as it could be material for dream. At the same time, for my patient this very thing can be something that belongs to a dissociated state, and it may not become conscious in the sense that there is never a whole person there to be aware of the two or more dissociated states that are present at any one time. The patient may sit in her room and while doing nothing at all except breathe she has (in her fantasy) painted a picture, or she has done an interesting piece of work in her job, or she has been for a country walk; but from the observer's point of view nothing whatever has happened. In fact, nothing is likely to happen because of the fact that in the dissociated state so much is happening. (27)

The didactic interpretations he makes reflecting his bias against fantasying on a scale of valuation reminiscent of the process of extracting poetry from the daydream according to Freud and Sachs are water under the bridge of dissociation. After he points

---

42 Winnicott, *Playing and Reality,* 29. Further page references are given in the text.

out how she is or, rather, should be "making use" of her dissociation to the point of integrating it or breaking it down, "she gave me an example at the moment while I was talking" (32). It turns out that she was fiddling with her bag's zipper while wondering why it was aligned in this direction. Her "dissociated activity was more important to her sitting there than listening to what I was saying" (ibid.). Fiddling with the zipper, she only outlines the castration, the murderous destructiveness, which her fantasying interferes with by its ongoing diversion from her own inner psychic reality. When she complains that her often frenetic bouts of fantasying make her fear for her physical health, Winnicott comments in an aside to his readership that his patient is sensing the absence of psychosomatic climax or, he adds in the footnote, ego orgasm (33).

A positive outcome of the analysis, the "hope" of a new beginning, "the confidence that she had in her analyst, who has to counteract all that she carries forward from her childhood," is over and again stymied by her quick sense that she is playing the good patient: "[S]o easily she would have the feeling that she had fitted in [...], and this would be followed by maximal protest and a return to the fixity of fantasying" (33–35).

> If one were to trace this patient's life one could see the ways in which she attempted to bring together [...] parts of her personality, but her attempts always had some kind of protest in them which brought a clash with society. (29)

Winnicott must bring the protest to the end in its dead end on a schedule with the analysis.

In Freud's lexicon, dissociation steers clear of psychosis, meaning that the subject both knows and does not know what's really happening. At this point of impasse or crossover, Winnicott's patient provides the breakthrough that gets past the impasse of Winnicott's didacticism and its dyadic logic. She remarks: "We need another word, which is neither dream nor fantasy" (32). Linking/thinking back to the prior session, she was pondering their last discussion in which the analyst again drew a distinction between daydreaming and night dreaming. That night she woke up suddenly and saw herself busily carrying out a task. But was it a night dream she woke upon or a bout of early-morning fantasying? Winnicott can't answer, but notes that just when he thought they could discern that fantasying interferes with dreaming (or living), she brings to the session the breakthrough recollection of a dream or fantasy that places them "on the borderline in any attempt one might make to differentiate between fantasying and dreaming" (32).[43] What follows is that Winnicott learns quickly from his patient's dismantling of his former strategy to redirect the coordinates of his bias to fit the transference.

Was her dream of cutting out a dress upon which she awoke in fact a fantasy that defended against dreaming? "'But how is she to know?' Fantasying possesses her like an evil spirit" (33). This moment of possession is probably a close paraphrase, which by slipping out of the boundaries of quotation already performs the slippage at this border. A fantasying of fantasy begins to pry loose the poetic omnipotence from its stuck place within the dissociated daydreaming and the analyst's didactic approach.

Eventually she remembers that the cutting out of the dress pattern was a waking fantasy. That's why, Winnicott says, it's "simply about making a dress. The dress has no symbolic value" (ibid.). But in a dream, he adds, "the same thing would indeed have had symbolic meaning" (ibid.). Winnicott in effect asks her to conjure through fantasying a night dream about her cut-out dress. They are able to carry back into the fantasy a word that belongs to the transitional state or start she was never given: "*formlessness,* which is what the material is like before it is patterned and cut and shaped and put together" (33). At this border of transferential breakthrough, a session is productive:

---

43 Winnicott earlier interpreted two night-dream fragments that the patient had been able after years of analysis to bring to session, which concealed incest wishes. After two hours, they begin approaching affect and we learn that she hates her mother, could murder her, while her wish for her father means that the mother already murdered her. This bumpy ride through an heir pocket from his Kleinian/Freudian past into the patient's emotional recognition of illicit unconscious fantasy isn't of the same quality as the changes that commence once they are at the borderline between dreaming and fantasying.

> She gave a very good example of a tremendous lot happening all of a sudden in fantasying which was of the kind that paralyses action. I took this now as the clue that she could give me towards the understanding of dream. The *fantasy* had to do with some people coming and taking over her flat. That is all. The *dream* that people came and took over her flat would have to do with her finding new possibilities in her own personality and also with the enjoyment of identifications with other people, including her parents. This is the opposite of feeling patterned and gives her a way of identifying without loss of identity. (35)

After the re-start around formlessness, Winnicott wraps dissociation in distinctions that he charges transferentially. "I said that fantasying was about a certain subject and it was a dead end. *It had no poetic value.* The corresponding dream, however, *had poetry in it,* that is to say, layer upon layer of meaning related to past, present, and future, and to inner and outer, and always fundamentally about herself" (35). Winnicott extends his working distinction to include poetry, because the patient prized her own creative efforts, which she had already given at the inner office of her *Gesamtkunstwerk,* her dissociation. He also switches from the opposition between the night dream and the daydream to the work of interpretation, which in the analytic session takes two. There is nothing to interpret in the daydream; it is about doing something, in other words, nothing at all.[44] The night dream, like art, adds the symbolism that makes interpretation possible. And so, he continues working with the didactic distinction, but redirected from within the transference, even making her the transference gift of adding a further equation between the night dream and poetry. Now she's listening when he says that he cannot interpret her fantasies, but if she presented them as dreams, he could. Together they begin fantasying poetic dream versions of her fantasies.

---

44 Winnicott lets us know: "I do not even try to use the material of fantasying that children in the latency period can supply in any quantity" (35).

The analytic understanding of the night dream reflects a therapeutic valuation that Winnicott demonstrates with his patient's able assist. Night dreams, not daydreams, are in session by the detour of their transference interpretation the royal road to the unconscious. The ascendancy of omnipotent wishing unto art is a hierarchy for which the patient must be initiated in the transference. Winnicott summarizes for the reader the impasse that he and his patient worked through: "It is this poetry of the dream that is missing in her fantasying" and renders "meaningful interpretations about fantasying" "impossible" (35).

When she asks him to interpret her ongoing game of patience, he transferentially lodges his complaint against fantasying by judging that the prospect of his interpreting it is a "dead end." Then he continues spinning the record of dissociation, fantasying a poetic night dream version. He assures her that if she were telling him her *dream* of playing patience, then he could say that she is struggling with God or fate, now winning, now losing, with the aim to control the destinies of four royal houses (36).

In the earlier essay on the manic defense, Winnicott must overcome an obstacle and offer a check on the flight away from inner reality prior to any formulation of transference interpretation. In the treatment of this case of dissociation, the transference comes to occupy the foreground by following the patient's insight that a new term, neither night dream nor daydream, was needed. It is a tentative claim to authorship, which cannot but risk her protest, the negative-transferential recoil sprung by her conviction that he's right, she *is* only "playing at" being his good patient. After registering a "profound effect" on his patient of the work in the session before, Winnicott realizes "the great danger of becoming confident or even pleased" (36–37). "The analyst's neutrality was needed here if anywhere in the whole treatment. In this kind of work we know that we are always starting again, and the less we expect the better" (37).

Auguste Müller of Karlsruhe

Mesmerism was the premier therapy fad, the first in the series that circumscribed a concise prehistory of psychoanalysis, its dialectic of Enlightenment. The inaugural role of Mesmerism in the settlement of inner space was evident in the social networking it provided to those patients whose own mediumistic talent was triggered by the magnetic treatment. If Mesmerism proved a vehicle for the patient's own clairvoyance, then the patient participated in their own assessment because they were able to see into bodies. Through the laying on of hands the clairvoyant medium could then also diagnose and treat other patients in the community.

In the course of his treatise on paranormal waking-dream states, Schopenhauer refers five times to the documentation of the sessions with Auguste Müller in Karlsruhe. With the onset of puberty, Auguste was sorely afflicted, symptomatic, desolate, and alone. Upon contact with magnetic treatment, Auguste turned out to be clairvoyant, which meant in her case that she could also discern if anyone in town was calling her gift into question. She rose to the occasion of making room in inner space for herself, for her omnipotence. Her personalized spirit guide, her recently departed mother, supplied the clairvoyant know-how that allowed Auguste to choose just the right treatment to prescribe in her new community of patients.

In his preface to Wilhelm Meier's document, Carl Christian Klein calls those who doubt Auguste's art of healing "zero-people,"[45] meaning people with zero tele-capacity, which in this setting also means that they lack empathy. But by this blank charge he also projects into them the empty and withdrawn state that the magnetically enriched patient was able to overcome both in her self and for others. Schreber's rights to a shared reality were restored, once he could empathically accept the coexistence of zero-people, which, earlier in the course of rebuilding a world from his own ground zero, he took to be "miraculated-up" figments or simulations.

Her dead mother occupies the telecommunications hub above, while in her own tele-state on earth (which she passes into through undeath) Auguste must corral her witnesses, col-

---

45 Wilhelm Meier, *Höchst merkwürdige Geschichte der magnetisch hellsehenden Auguste Müller in Karlsruhe* (Stuttgart: J.B. Metzler'schen Buchhandlung, 1818), iv. Page references are to this edition and are given in the text.

laborators, and detractors into a network (coextensive with the published document). She tests this network by her own turbulence, and then calls it to order. In the season of her clairvoyance, Auguste enlists and mixes together a recognized therapy, occult knowledge, and fairy-tale fantasy. The mix gives her back a controlling interest in her life, which was shattered by bereavement and repression. The interest is upheld by the intrigue that she detects in those who doubt her role as medium (or prove lax in keeping to her schedule).

At one point the *magnetiseur* was unable to keep an appointment, and Auguste nominates the missed session just the one in which the cure for her ailment was to be revealed. But since she is unconscious during these transmissions, only the conversation with the *magnetiseur* could have secured the prescription's content. During the next session after the appointment that wasn't kept she again enters the magnetic sleep-waking state.

> In this highly unusual state she resembles a marble statue, someone who has just lapsed into lifelessness. All vital coloring is gone. Not the slightest sign, not the least breathing indicates life. [...] After some time, in this state, she folded her hands and prayed for 2 minutes. Suddenly there followed a deep and long inhalation, and with it, life, color, and movement returned. (13)

The *magnetiseur*, who alone can speak to her at this point, addresses several questions to her.

> Question. Do you know the means for your rehabilitation?
> Answer. Now I no longer do. [...] If only you had been here! [...] My God! Now I have to wait 14 days. (13–15)

Repeated entreaties to find the relief ahead of this schedule Auguste rebuffs. She does know the cause of her illness: cat whiskers she somehow swallowed. Her therapist calls this possibility into question, but she won't budge: She sees them!

In *Séance on a Wet Afternoon*, 1961 novel and 1964 movie, the medium Myra's talent builds on basic telepathy up through gradations of paranormal waking-dream states to the wished-for apex of the profession, seeing and communicating with ghosts.[46] While, as I showed in *The Devil Notebooks,* Arthur C. Clarke and Alan Turing placed belief in telepathy and traffic with ghosts on a continuum, the author and director of *Séance on a Wet Afternoon* remained closer to Schopenhauer, giving credence to paranormal awareness and communication on the live side while pulling up short before the last step, contact with the ultimate paranormal address, ghostliness.

Myra also relies on the paranormal talent brought to her séance table for a contact heightening. Myra's wish, which the notoriety around the kidnapping and her clairvoyant assist should make possible, is to enter into contact with the greatest mediumistic talents of her day. The law brings along the president of the Society for Psychical Reasearch to engage in a fact-finding session led by Myra. Her mind shifts through the neutral gear of fantasying into heightened paranormal states, but the last step or leap to contact spirits is fraught with aberrations of the superego. She imagines an interior decoration for her mediumistic progress, like the mnemotechnic architecture of niches that was prescribed in antiquity for training recollection, like the memorial stations of scenes from a life spent with the now deceased, which the reality-testing mourner, according to Freud, visits, at once rerecording and erasing.

> She stopped, and her heart stopped too. Her soul yearned forward, straining, pleading. Then the white knob began to turn slowly. [...] She went forward, into a dusky light and a protective motherly warmth, and immediately her being soared to an ecstatic perfection. [...] She had never been that far; she had never been farther than the spot she now occupied. But, as she looked, she found herself moving again, moving forward toward the window [...]. With a sudden release that sent her a

---

46 In *The Psycho Records,* I skewered a series of spiritualist medium fictions (film adaptations and novels) upon the trait of psychopathy hiding out in the paranormal milieu. Myra's empathy is eclipsed, when she and her husband abduct a child to fake the evidence of her paranormal abilities and speed up her overriding wish to work with the great talents in her field.

leap's length forward she was out in the mist. [...] A tree trunk loomed in front. [...] She put out a hand and touched it, and immediately her other hand was grasped and a convulsion ran through her.[47]

And then the girl who died on her watch starts speaking through her and she turns herself in.

The sliding scale of paranormal experience projected by Schopenhauer and adapted by Freud can be watched in *The Haunting* (1963). The movie is based on Shirley Jackson's 1959 novel *The Haunting of Hill House,* which opens with the epigraph: "No live organism can contrive for long to exist sanely under conditions of absolute reality; even larks and katydids are supposed, by some, to dream. Hill House, not sane, stood by itself against its hills, holding darkness within." The supposition to dream covers fantasying and waking sleep, which Hill House, built with near-miss right angles, every corner and closure askew, excites and deranges. The director of *The Haunting,* Robert Wise, employed a new, yet untested lens (which he had to sign off on to absolve the company of any responsibility) for the distortion he was after. He wanted to demonstrate what he had learned while apprenticed to Val Lewton: horror as sight unseen.

Together with Günther von Fritsch, Wise directed the sequel to Jacques Tourneur's *Cat People* (1942), *The Curse of the Cat People* (1944), his debut. The curse is daydreaming that afflicts Amy (daughter born of the second marriage of dead Irena's Oliver) and triggers madness in the mother's daughter next door. Because Amy's daydreaming verges on dissociation (according to the reports of her alienation at school), her father is determined to drive the predilection out of her. She has one friend in the neighborhood, an older actress who fears her own daughter Barbara; she must be a spy. When Amy finds a picture of Irena, the dead woman she never knew, Irena begins appearing to her and they form an imaginary friendship. When one day Irena says that she has to go now for good, Amy runs away to the neighboring mother. While a snowstorm keeps her there, the daughter is

---

47 Mark McShane, *Séance on a Wet Afternoon* (New York: Mysterious Press, 2013), 170–72.

so jealous she could just strangle Amy. But Amy sees the sign of Irena's face on Barbara and embraces her, averting a dire ending. Now her father promises not to interfere again with her fantasying.

In *The Haunting*, Eleanor, whose unacknowledged talent is telekinesis, joins the paranormal researcher Dr. Markway and the other talent, Theo, a telepath. The nephew and future inheritor of the house has also come along to keep an eye on his future property. In the final round, the paranormals witness the effects of haunting upon awakening together battened down in the drawing room. The earlier haunting episode in the rooms of Eleanor and Theo also began with their awakening there. The ghost effects are picked up by the dream organ in the environs of the will or the unconscious while awakening into the ideality of sense perception. The participants in the paranormal investigation of the house are waking dreaming in each other's psyches because the unconscious that is the same in every one of them is foregrounded by the flexing of the death wish (which also holds the attention of the heir).

The first family living in the house that Crain built no longer did when the surviving heiress, Crain's daughter, an old invalid, kept knocking on the wall until she died. That the companion who was in charge was too preoccupied with a date from the village to pay attention means she had to pack away the recoil of the wish. The first spell of haunting at Hill House left her hanging from the circular stairway in the library. That's why Eleanor ends up staying. She spent her young adulthood caring for her bed-ridden mother. Did she not heed the knocking one night, whereupon her mother died, or is it an excess of self-recrimination, which Freud observed in the most devoted caregivers,[48] that lowers the doom because she couldn't help wishing that there might be an end to her service? Relief makes murderers of us all on death watch/wish.

When Eleanor follows the summons to join the paranormal experiment, she in reality escapes her family situation. Wise shows the flight when Eleanor scans the areas she drives through,

---

48 This observation is basic to the projection argument in the section "Taboo upon the Dead" in *Totem and Taboo*.

spinning off scenarios of omnipotent idealization according to which she has, for example, an apartment of her own with lion statues on her mantle, like the larger lions at the entrance to a driveway she just passed. Her run of fantasying stops at the gate to Hill House, but then she rises to the occasion and dismisses the insolent caretaker. She has been training in daydreaming to be a lady. When the view of the house, ominously caught in infrared film, comes around the bend, the soundtrack riffs off the music going into the shower scene in *Psycho,* while we watch Eleanor through the windshield driving. The film begins fantasying scenes from Hitchcock's film. The *Schauer* scene – the ultimate exercise in the horror of sight unseen that Lewton's production line rehearsed or presaged – becomes in *The Haunting,* in this run of fantasying, a potentiation of fantasy, a fantasy of fantasy in the spotlight of cinematic self-reflexivity.

A similar flight attends the film's ending, skidding into a denouement that reprises Hitchcock's stabbing skewering of eye and drain. But ambiguity averts the untenable omnipotent wish to profit from the last will and testament. Did Eleanor drive into the tree, or did the car, the *Auto,* the self, telekinetically turn the steering wheel? A formal affinity between film perception and fantasying leads the way away from the one dark wish's monopoly over wish fantasying. On the unlikely tracks of *Psycho,* Wise's film formally engages fantasying and allows its momentum to enter pictures.

The Haunting of 1999 goes on the update with digital special effects. Whereas in the 1963 film there was one haunting effect that wasn't *son et lumière* – the wooden door to the drawing room undulating with a ghostly pressure to enter – it overruns the 1999 movie, making the walls morph with nonstop digital ease and expense. Wes Craven was scheduled to direct this film but decided to go ahead with *Scream* instead, a far better choice aligned more with the Lewton intention and the *Psycho* introject in Wise's film. Jan de Bont made a film that reflected the pull of the fantasy genre's arrival in the realm of verification of its prediction or rather predilection. The phantasmagoria of special effects served up in *The Haunting* allies it with Christian fantasy movies like *Devil's Advocate* (1997). This time Eleanor discovers that she was to the haunted manor born. By family romance she is related to the master of the house of child abuse, and becomes the heroine leading into the light the ghosts of the children trapped in the house's walls. The death she risks claims her. Her heroism reverses the suicidality of her earlier incarnation as death-wish depressed and dissociated daydreamer with nowhere to go.

Fantasy Island

Presiding over the underworld in which Sibyl Vane flits through the collected words of Shakespeare like a spirit, the Jewish theater manager stands in Dorian's way on the day of his last visit to the nether realm. Dorian wants to see Sybil, his own Miranda he feels, and, again drawing on the Shakespeare play that was not part of the underworld repertoire, name-calls him Caliban.[49] On the eve of the divide between Dorian and his portrait we are thrown back upon the fantasy island of *The Tempest*.

Most agree that the bard said his farewell in Prospero's parting words that relinquished magic in favor of the separate interests of his daughter Miranda, Shakespeare's Judith. Formerly her father's companion, Hamnet's twin sister was stepping out into matrimony. Issuing from the encryptment of Hamnet in Shakespeare's corpus, Caliban, the injured and complaining ghost to whom love has been denied (in the recoil of thwarted substitute care), charges Prospero's magic with the future import of slavery in the new world.

The temporal paradox of the crypt is with us: Isola is a name that means "islander." It is ensconced in a word, "isolation," which was first used in French to refer to a method of quarantine: seclusion on an island of all those infected by contagion. Sibyl Vane's sailor brother, in the service of the colonial empire, immediately recognizes in the isolating constraint of Dorian Gray's courtship of his sister the man's wish to "enslave" her (76).

In the Preface to *The Picture of Dorian Gray*, signed Oscar Wilde, Caliban is introduced twice as test subject into the mirror cage of the novel's literary experiment. Each time Caliban looks into the mirror, he flies into a rage, once because he does

---

49 Wilde, *The Picture of Dorian Gray*, 91. Subsequent page references are given in the text.

see himself, the second time because he doesn't. He performs in short order the nineteenth century's dislike of Realism and Romanticism. By his reflex responses, Caliban bears, then, the burden of the nineteenth century's limitations in letters.

It was as White Man's Burden, the guise in which the theory of evolution took hold of the globe, Gertrude Stein emphasizes in *Wars I Have Seen,* that the nineteenth century kept malingering on for so long. It was at last coming to an end, Stein writes in 1943, the war killing "it dead, dead dead."[50] To orient themselves during the American invasion of Fortress Europe, Stein and her friends spent Friday afternoons together reading Shakespeare's *Julius Caesar, Macbeth,* and *Richard the Third* (the other works, other than *Hamlet,* that host ghosts): "[I]t is all just like what is happening now" (105). And again: "[T]he extraordinary thing about this war it is so historical not recent history but fairly ancient history" (135). Stein considers the end of the nineteenth century also in terms of developmental history. During childhood and latency everyone is "legendary." But "at fifteen there comes to be a realisation of what living was in medieval times and as a pioneer. It is very near. And now in 1943 it is here" (16).[51]

Along the seafaring trajectory of Elizabethan England that Carl Schmitt saw depart from the other history of the European

---

50 Gertrude Stein, *Wars I Have Seen* (London: B.T. Batsford Ltd., 1945), 51. Subsequent page references are given in the text.
51 Stein transfers the end of the nineteenth century to the Teen Age in developmental history by including midlife crisis and criticism, like the input of Lord Henry in the work of prematurity that Dorian becomes. "This is more like the beginning of middle living" (12). This resonates with what follows, namely living in the Middle Ages (which she juxtaposes to the pioneer on the frontier). Stein's American sense of "medieval times," moreover, like the fairs that became popular in the 1960s in California, like the future in outer space of *The Skies Discrowned* (1976), written by Timothy Powers, one of P.K. Dick's acolytes in Southern California, places the Renaissance in the foreground. In *Westworld* the recognizable medievalism of the robot lady's outfit (last time I checked it was the favorite historical costume for dressing up Barbie) is a match with the squire attire of the role player, which, however, looks renaissance.

continent,⁵² a stopover should be added. English interests (or letters according to Stein's "What Is English Literature," one of the lectures of her US tour, as famous in its day as Wilde's earlier junket) could not get past their basic insularity, and the empire got stuck like an island peg in a square world. The new world in *The Tempest* is viewed island to island. All the changes that Stein recounts in the history of English letters wrap around the steadying content of a daily island life. With the onset of sea power and then colonization, this content grew to include owning not only living a daily island life but also, by the nineteenth century, the rest of the world outside: "[O]utside and inside had to be told something about all this owning, [...] and so there was invented explaining."⁵³ By the nineteenth century, then, phrases of explanation and sentiment filled the word count of English literature.

> They thought about what they were thinking and if you think about what you are thinking you are bound to think about it in phrases, because if you think about what you are thinking you are not thinking about a whole thing. If you are explaining the same thing is true, you cannot explain a whole thing because if it is a whole thing it does not need explaining, it merely needs stating. And then the emotional sentiment that any one living their daily living and owning everything outside needs to express is again something that can only be expressed by phrases, neither by words nor by sentences. (51)

As the end of the nineteenth century neared, the insular economy of the phrase began to capsize: "[T]he daily living was ceasing to be quite so daily and besides that they were beginning not to know everything about owning everything that was outside of them outside of their daily living. [...] And so the phrase no longer sufficiently held what a phrase had to hold" (53–54).

---

52 This "Brexit" genealogy goes into Schmitt's monograph on *Hamlet*, which was a mainstay of my study SPECTRE.
53 Gertrude Stein, "What Is English Literature," in *Look at Me Now and Here I Am: Writings and Lectures 1909–45*, ed. Patricia Meyerowitz (London: Penguin, 1990), 49. Subsequent page references are given in the text.

And so, it was time for the paragraph to put a period to the end of Stein's sentencing of English letters. American literature alone came to be imbued with a future feeling. The word had caught up with the new world setting, which "was so completely not a daily island life that one may well say that it was not a daily life at all" (53). When Henry James, like his English colleagues, needed a "whole paragraph" "his whole paragraph [...] detached what it said from what it did, what it was from what it held, and over it all something floated, [...] floated up there" (57).

> [T]he form was always the form of the contemporary English one, but the disembodied way of disconnecting something from anything and anything from something was the American one. [...] It is a lack of connection, of there being no connection with living and daily living because there is none, that makes American writing what [...] it will continue to become. (ibid.)

The Tempest counts as terminus for narratives of magical omnipotence harnessing spirits on the stage of discovery of new worlds. The black magic that summons ghosts from their graves, which Prospero admits to commanding but which we never witness, is the gist of what's new for the seculars according to Christopher Marlowe's *The Tragical History of Doctor Faustus,* the other bookend across from *Hamlet* on the Elizabethan shelf or horizon line addressing new means of steering through the secular aftermath (while setting sail for the colonial empire).[54] In his version of the Faust legend, Goethe infused his inheritance of the only literary Faust with *Hamlet,* and offered a stay to the vengeful sibling ghosts that he had come to recognize in the Werther Effect of copycat suicides.[55] Marlowe's Faustus turns to magic to raise the dead with conscious deliberation and put them at his disposal, carrying out at the speed of thought his every wish (which is their command). But watching out what you wish for, the lesson that

---

54 I am reprising my reading of these bookends in *SPECTRE* where it belongs to the setting of a quarrel I ventriloquate between Klein and Lacan (27ff).

55 See Rickels, *Aberrations of Mourning,* 84ff.

unconscious or disowned wishing teaches, enters the uncanny prospect of Doctor Faustus's own death. The next in line with a magic book will order around his ghostly afterlife. To die is to be enslaved, a secular hell.

In *Hamlet,* Shakespeare offered mourning in lieu of magic as the new medium of orientation in the secular world. An inner world of haunting is ensconced within the greater setting of succession where every act is delivered on schedule and is its own reward. The inner profoundly adolescent drama stages not only an alternative inheritance but also another next generation. Giving grief is the unfinished business of adolescence. The father's ghost would rob Hamlet by giving him a first job finishing what's at loose ends in the father's legacy, the grief a father has to give. Instead of ending up as his father's agent and heir, however, Hamlet becomes a ghost, which is his business, and charges his BFF Horatio to write down the story of his haunt and inaugurate the non-Oedipal delegation of double occupancy.

That the insularity of empire broke upon the frontier would be the counterpart on the map to the paragraph's breaching of the phrase. Wilde's alternate internal dismantling of the phrase, his phrasing it out on the spit of wit, at once dispenses the phrase and dispenses with it, redistributing it and its cargo hold as resolutely as the Jamesian paragraph (with its ectoplasmic floaters). Lord Henry, the representative of Wilde's conversational career as male carrier of an encrypted girl, extends his "influence" not only to his creation, Dorian. At the outer limit of a novel steeped in the idea that everything can be expressed, it inflects the unidentified, unseen narrator's discourse on the many occasions in which the reader must wonder, who is speaking?

Wilde's novel supplies the disconnect in Stein's view that American letters remain closer than an insular literature that's always being updated to the Elizabethan modus of choosing words to be placed next to each other. The disconnect is haunting, and it is up to Lord Henry to recognize that the afterlife that Shakespeare staged with ghosts has gone West. "It is an odd thing, but everyone who disappears is said to be seen at San Francisco. It must be a delightful city, and possess all the attractions of the next world" (232). Implicit here is the reservation that Alfred Hitchcock would resoundingly confirm.

The onset of B-genres in the late nineteenth century coincides with the invention of cinema, which responds to the ununderstood in letters, like time travel, within a relay of visual and special effects. Reading through Shakespeare's delegation of haunting, the ascendancy of the B-genres belongs to the modern Teen Age that Stein saw commence toward the end of WWII between the continuous medievalism of fantasy and the pioneer explorations of science fiction. And so, the conditions were ready and set to go for *Star Wars* to redraw the horizon line and become our oldest cultural memory. Lucas's 1977 film illuminated the borderlands of the fantasy and science fiction genres folding out of and staggering the duel challenged by J.R.R. Tolkien and C.S. Lewis when they introduced their genre in running contrast to the science fiction of H.G. Wells. The resulting borderland of the B-genres counts today as the Heimat of the blockbuster culture industry.

If we tarried in A-culture it was also because a B-picture, *Forbidden Planet* (1956), took *The Tempest* to the final frontier.[56] The 1956 SF film, introducing Robby the Robot, internalizes and in part reverses *The Tempest*. Although a refugee, Prospero's roundtrip outlines in advance the colonialist signature. When the insular new world is reprojected into outer space, colonization already extends across interstellar distances jumped by hyperdrive. The philologist Morbius on Altair 4 exchanges vows with his new habitat and benefits from studying the artifacts left behind by the long extinct indigenous civilization of the Krells. By the surprise intrusions of his own disowned death wishes, Morbius discovers that the techno-animism of the Krells, which was capable of realizing wish fulfillment at the speed of thought, overlooked what the screenplay names the id – and a civilization technologically far in advance of humanity's space age was undone. The science fiction movie issues a warning against any realization of omnipotent fantasy that overlooks unconscious wishing.

---

56 This as much as the dew that Prospero ordered Ariel to bring him from the Bermudas shows that, in spite of the Mediterranean location off the coast of North Africa, Shakespeare's fantasy island belongs to the new world.

The warning will be updated. Techno-fantasy cannot outfly the shortfall and recoil of science fiction's predictive service. The history of the contested borderlands of both B-genres marks changes that arose in expectation of what the new media held in store, changes realized (but outside the box of what had been projected) upon the arrival of the unanticipated digital relation, which at last seemed to award the fantasy genre the contest prize. When in 1991 Peter Greenaway adapted *The Tempest* for his first digital film, *Prospero's Books,* a new magic that the director lets go on and on leads to fantasying paintings as tableaux vivants and books as the concise history binding the printing press to the apparatus lying within the digital film medium's prehistory. Greenaway looked past the Christian focus on surveillance in anticipations of the digital relation to highlight instead the upsurge of archival citation of every name, event, form, and medium in history, but each time as an entry removed from its former setting upon opposition.

The unmooring of fantasy from its belief system occurred in tandem with the revaluation of the science fiction genre. Once its future orientation was "history," the genre indwelled the ruins of its faulty forecasts. Science fiction began supplying captions of legibility for deregulated fantasy. As Freud stipulated via the datemark stamping its denied trigger in the present, fantasy is historicization waiting to happen, the mortal recoil of its flight. Science fiction, the allegory of fantasy, also lies in wait. By its salvos of right or wrong extrapolation, it is grounded in the present tense and, within the borderlands it shares with fantasy, illuminates ongoing tensions and encrypted contents. If the netherworld of supernatural afterlives is, already according to Immanuel Kant, the ultimate occasion and setting for fantasying and fantasy, writing on and reading crypts is science fiction.

3

New Vampire Lectures

Zombie Wars

Following the success of *The Autobiography of Alice B. Toklas* (1933), Gertrude Stein suffered a bout of writer's block. Over and again, she recorded that "It has not happened," until she was visited instead by W.B. Seabrook.[1] We don't know what exactly they talked about for three days. Seabrook was also only recently a famous author. His 1929 *The Magic Island,* about the occult practices he encountered on Haiti, introduced the zombie to American popular culture. *White Zombie* (1932), which was in part an adaptation of his book, had just joined the new Hollywood franchise of occult horror in talking pictures. Bela Lugosi, already famous for his leading role in Browning's *Dracula* (1930), played the zombie master, whose given name was Murder. Stein knew that she would be going back soon to tour in the train of the success of her novel and would surely have been curious about America today.

Both Stein and Seabrook were known for the frank intensity of what they were willing to talk about. The topics in Seabrook's repertoire of great interest to Stein as well counted sadistic sex practices (binding and hanging) and cannibalism. But the author of *The Magic Island* was also hurting from his earlier success, scrambling to hitch his subsequent efforts to his 1929 star. After

[1] I am relying on John Herbert Gill's Introduction in Gertrude Stein, *Blood on the Dining-Room Floor: A Murder Mystery* (Mineola: Dover Publications, 2008).

the exchange, Seabrook went directly to the States, entered a psychiatric hospital for treatment of his acute alcoholism, and documented the sojourn in his ethnographic journalism style a year later in *Asylum* (1935), which enjoyed the self-fulfilling success of the celebrity memoir. Following Seabrook's departure, Stein wrote her one and only murder mystery, *Blood on the Dining-Room Floor,* which, though she never saw it through to publication, was the "block-buster" that allowed her to compose a series of celebrity-memoir novels in which she rewrote history as the killing off of undead centuries.

Stein reckons in *Wars I Have Seen* that it took Napoleon to kill off the eighteenth century he epitomized.[2] Then came the Big One, the nineteenth century, kept going by the theory of evolution it spread across the globe: "The nineteenth century is taking from 1914 to 1943 to kill" (9). Evolution can also mean that it takes but one advance in machine technology to redraw the map of adaptation, ultimately to war.

Although Hitler was the quintessential avatar of the nineteenth century who destroyed it and himself in the setting of Europe, Stein also argued that the Civil War already ended the nineteenth century in the US, which was why for quite some time to come it was the oldest nation of the twentieth century: "The American civil war was the prototype of all the wars the two big wars that I have completely lived" (4). Stein's contrast between the World War One doughboys hanging out bashfully or dully post-victory in Europe and the self-possessed GIs at the end of World War Two, who owned their every setting in which they were conversant, suggests that the vault into the new century left the denizens of its new world behind to catch up with the overturning of the old century, which happened when it replayed in Europe.[3] When a European author delivered the first bona fide science fiction of rocket flight in 1865 (Jules Verne's *From the Earth to the Moon*), he was on target in ascribing its

---

2   Gertrude Stein, *Wars I Have Seen* (London: B.T. Batsford Ltd., 1945), 8. Subsequent page references are given in the text.
3   What also animates the GIs for Stein is that they know who she is. It is by the light of the fame of her unblocked writing that Stein reads the zombie wars carrying out the old and ushering in the new.

invention to the Baltimore Gun Club, which applied the techno-benefits picked up in the testing grounds of the Civil War.[4] At the opening of *Gone with the Wind* (1939), as parchment pages of medievalist fantasy turn, we are introduced to an era long gone, in which representatives of European tradition still held court down South. With the borders opposed during the Civil War, modern spiritualism, which was the afterlife adapted to science fiction, went directly from the Northern States to Europe. Once the last ties to Europe in the New World were liquidated with the Confederacy, the import of globalization reached the South, too, which yielded its occult stores to science fiction.

In the Professor Challenger novels by Arthur Conan Doyle, the protagonist, more a detective than an adventurer, passes tests posed by fantasy and science fiction before meeting his greatest challenge of all, belief in spiritualism.[5] In *The Lost World* (1912), the professor visits a surviving pocket of prehistoric nature and wildlife. In *The Poison Belt* (1913), he is one in a locked-room circle of witnesses to the world's engulfment by a poison cloud. In *The Land of Mist* (1926), the figments of fantasy and science fiction give way before the contemporary phenomenon of spiri-

---

4   See my *Germany: A Science Fiction* (Fort Wayne: Anti-Oedipus Press, 2014), 101–4.
5   In *Mille Plateaux,* Deleuze and Guattari drew out of a couple of Professor Challenger science-fiction short stories an assembly line for their body without organs. In "When the World Screamed" (1928), the professor exacts from the earth a Schreberesque bellowing miracle by skinning one part of the Earth like an animal and piercing its nerve. The professor, who wants to be the first and only human the earth recognizes, journeys, in effect, to the animist view of the world as a single organic being. In "The Disintegration Machine" (1929), another scientist has tapped a secret power he can aim through a machine. He can disintegrate organic beings and then, by putting the machine in reverse, reassemble them. That a destroyed being returns as the same, in spite of the molecular flow released in the breakdown, prompts the inventor to analogize the power he wields with teleportation in Western occultism. Professor Challenger is a bystander whose acceptance in the end does not enroll him in the company of the committed. But then he checks out the machine and makes the inventor disappear forever.

tualism. Professor Challenger is its most celebrated antagonist, but his resistance to reports and demonstrations of ghost-seeing gives them the traction of testable hypothesis and his acceptance follows suit. Here we see the work of detection characteristic of Conan Doyle's Sherlock Holmes mysteries already at work in the receiving and conceiving area of modern spiritualism. In French letters, too, for example the novels by Gaston Leroux and Maurice Renard, we observe the affinity between the new detection plot and modern spiritualism.[6]

In *Ubik* (1969), P.K. Dick projected a techno-realization and refinement of the historical artifact of modern spiritualism. Unlike the philosophical "spiritualism" that Kant, Schopenhauer, and Freud rejected, the cult of modern spiritualism, even if certain adherents sought to reconcile it with Christianity, was constitutively a secular-mediatic enterprise that kept to a span of extended finitude, lodged between the recent past and the near future. The admittedly fantastic summoning of spirit guides from all the eras and places in history wasn't really a contradiction. It testified to the renewal of the planetary scope of animism, which regional civilizations had consigned to the border as superstition.

Ghost-seeing has undergone many updates, but what draws it onward since the Enlightenment is that it hypothetically explores what counts in the main as unseen communication that never really materializes as proof. Creaturely occult relations pose a different challenge. When the epidemic outbreak of vampirism occurred in eighteenth-century Central Europe, all the stations of recording and transmission available under the newly secular aegis of the Enlightenment turned this iteration of a recurring prospect of too much life in death into a primal scene. Over the ages, in settings of rapid burial in sites already used and now reused, like during cholera epidemics, those who witnessed the metabolic changes in a corpse early on in the course of decomposition – including the freeze-frame of somebody struggling against the frequent mistake of burial alive – could not rely on

---

6 See my *The Psycho Records* (New York: Columbia University Press, 2016), 90, 117–19.

religion or science for an explanation. They turned instead to superstition, the warping reverb of repressed animism.

At the so-called vampire courts set up during the eighteenth-century outbreak of undeath, corpses were examined for evidence of the charges brought against the recently deceased. If the skin seemed too ruddy, too fresh, the body too bloated like after a feeding, or the hair and nails still growing, the dead body was sentenced to death.[7] These court proceedings were recorded and their gist thus circulated in news reports. In no time, the documented event of the epidemic entered the scholarly apparatus in Germany and France, resulting in a number of dissertations and treatises. The corpses to be tried and examined for undeath, however, were in short supply and could not support the fascination with something as close to home as mourning the dead. In other words, unlike the prayerful contact with the departed in ghost-seeing, vampirism could not continue as a hypothetical construct. The relationship to vampirism became, instead, psychic, at first by entering literature. It started with a couple of German poems in which the beloved returns from the grave to consummate the relationship in undeath. They made such an impression throughout the language cultures into which they were quickly translated, that as late as in *Jane Eyre* (1847), the surprise co-tenant is taken to be the "German vampire."

---

7 These special effects would in time be known to belong to the natural process in the early phase of decomposition. The skin tightens, dries out, sloughs off leaving "fresh" skin and showing the apparent growth of hair and nails. The build-up of gas and its displacements plumped up bodies, even making a corpse jolt upright like Nosferatu rising up from his coffin. The freeze frame of the struggles of those buried alive presented the most memorable portrait of the vampire. In *Aberrations of Mourning: Writing on German Crypts* (Detroit: Wayne State University Press, 1988) and *The Vampire Lectures* (Minneapolis: University of Minnesota Press, 1999), I argued that the Enlightenment replacement of the skeletal representation of death by a more natural, even beautiful figuration borrowed from Antiquity (the twin brother of sleep) was just waiting for its co-optation within the new secular scenario of an uncanny doubling between sleep and waking up buried alive.

English authors were able to turn the relationship to the vampire into narrative. There is one early German vampire story, E.T.A. Hoffmann's "Der Vampir" (1821), which is a docufictionalization of an episode that refers to (and looks like it's on the record of) the vampirism epidemic. That it concludes, however, with a full body shot of cannibalism, rather than the more discrete drips and pricks of blood lust, reflects the pull of the German inclination to make book out of doubling. The double was the sole occult figure to transfer intact into the environs of the science-fiction genre, which explains the German head-start so spectacularly illustrated in Fritz Lang's *Metropolis*. The psychic and the hypothetical trajectories conjoin in the double. Its material immateriality is as close or far away as are mirror and media. In treatises on ghost-seeing, seeing double becomes a form of communication with the yet living that comes as close to contact with the dead as their authors can allow. And yet it is the un-provability of ghostly communication with the departed that draws all psychic research onward.

In "The Confidences of a 'Psychical Researcher'," William James, philosophy's representative in the experimental setting of spiritualism, applied a self-help exercise to organize his own undecided stance with regard to occult phenomena that are "inwardly as incoherent as they are outwardly wayward and fitful," like the "stray vestiges of that primordial irrationality, from which all our rationalities have been evolved"[8]:

> Try, reader, yourself, to invent an unprecedented kind of "physical phenomenon of spiritualism." When *I* try, I find myself mentally turning over the regular medium-stock, and thinking how I might improve some item. This being the dramatically probable human way, I think differently of the whole type, taken collectively, from the way in which I may think of the single instance. I find myself believing that there is "something in" these never ending reports of physical phenomena, although I haven't yet the least positive notion of

---

8 William James, "The Confidences of a 'Psychical Researcher'," in *Writings 1902–1910* (New York: Library of America, 1988), 1259.

the something. It becomes to my mind simply a very worthy problem for investigation.[9]

In *Telepathy and Medical Psychology*, Jan Ehrenwald, an author P.K. Dick read closely, reflects on the paradox that during the Cold War era of modern spiritualism the new discipline of parapsychology adopted the statistical method not to document the reliability of experimental results, but to demonstrate the very existence of extra-sensory perception.[10] It was the only reliable standard for determining the extra-chance nature of the scores. In countless experiments, in which images were transferred by thought alone, the percipient being tested rarely reproduced the whole of the testing agent's mental content but tended to score "near misses" scattered around the target idea (69). While a "'near miss'" is "certainly less convincing than a fully correct guess," it proves of "even greater psychological interest" (29). It is what the agent does not think of transmitting which is most successfully transmitted to the test subject (31). And there is a tendency for the percipient's guess to slip from the essential to the accidental (ibid.). There is nothing to prevent thoughts, ideas, or expectations that are not immediately concerned with the proposed test from entering the subject's mind. That's what telepathy is all about: "telepathic leakage" (32).

The spatio-temporal dislocation in the telepathic reception of thought processes in another person's mind – reflecting them either after the event of presumed contact or ahead of time – can give the transmission a semblance of prophecy (197). Only by setting a period of time in the course of an experiment could the operation of hetero-psychic experiences be tracked. Otherwise, Ehrenwald concludes, "there would be no limit set to the range of telepathic scatter" (139). The science fiction of a psychophysical grid, according to Williamson according to Günther, completes the technologization of the opposition which Ehrenwald's telepathic scatter begins to breach.

9 Ibid., 1261. Emphasis in the original.
10 Jan Ehrenwald, *Telepathy and Medical Psychology* (New York: Norton, 1948), 34. Further page references are given in the text.

In *The American Apocalypse,* Günther argues that the thought of the regional civilizations opened and entered the exceptional series of causality to secure the highest degree of probability. The eventuality of the next step was thus practically certain. To this end, so-called degrees of freedom had to be kept out. Günther ascribes "the serial theory of magic" to the animism of primitive culture. It groups together events under one specific perspective, which is all that they have in common, yielding a "virtual significance."[11] Logically, the components are causally independent of one another. The shorter the magic series, the more degrees of freedom are involved. One omen doesn't mean much; two omens are way more meaningful; but too many omens no longer give the forecast since it is already happening (128). The exclusivity of causality conceals that cause reflects only one tendency in universal processes, one world-series. In addition to the general progression from improbable to more probable world conditions, there is also the "individualizing progression from probable chaos to improbable Gestalt and order" (159). Günther puts it evocatively: Freedom is the "third" between true and false (130). "Series with a random measure of degrees of freedom are theoretically as controllable and calculable as simple causality series" (153).

Ehrenwald's study proposes a telepathy connection fomenting the outbreak of schizophrenia in adolescence, which fits Dick's construction in *The Martian Time-Slip* (1964) of the rapport between Jack Bohlen, the recovering adult schizophrenic, and the autistic-schizophrenic teen Martin, who wields paranormal powers. Adolescence, according to Ehrenwald, is the season for the onset of the psychotic illness, because it is the period when, for the sake of group bonding and couplification, the teen is challenged to renounce the isolation enjoyed in latency, the independence won toward the end of childhood proper from merger with the minds of the parents (193). Paranoia and megalomania are last stands of coherence before the full disintegration into schizophrenia sets in. It marks the end of the subject's struggle to

---

11 Gotthard Günther, *Die amerikanische Apokalypse,* ed. Kurt Klagenfurt (Klagenfurt: Profil, 2000), 121–22. Subsequent page references are given in the text.

maintain their personality against the impact of sadistic aggression conveyed through the hetero-psychic crossover of thoughts and wishes (147).

Dick's half-life system in *Ubik* is violated, when a teen delinquent among the ghosts starts consuming, depleting, and liquidating all ghostly others. But the life suck brings up the arrears in testing, and carries out the sentencing of finitude in the afterlife: the second death, which is murder. Modern spiritualism turned absence of proof into a promo for testing, which by testing for it confers more and more hypothetical reality. That's its science-fiction aspect. But spiritualism also faces toward horror fantasy. The planetary animism that spiritualism updates to allow for the hypothetical reality of ghostly correspondents via media gets subsumed, according to Freud's *Totem and Taboo,* by the psychic reality of the living dead moving against us.

The Psychopathy Test

One turning point in my longstanding reception of horror between occult and technical media, which my 2016 book *The Psycho Records* documents,[12] was my 2009 invitation by *Artforum International* to interpret the updating of vampirism. A new integration of the vampire seemed to be offering a stay against the thrill-a-kill consumerism of the unidentified dying zombie that had been in the ascendant since 9/11.

I concluded, however, that what was left lurking in the divide between undeath and living death was the psycho, our most uncanny double at close quarters: there, but for the grace of the good object, go I. Since psycho violence, which was carried forward, but without agency as zombieism, upon the termination phase of slasher film therapy, could be renewed intact in the Saw franchise through a compact with the Devil, I also concluded that what we were watching in mourning's light was more a shake-up than a succession. Psycho murder, infernal instruction, zombie killing, and vampiric replication are split-off phases of the mourning process awaiting integration.

12 See Record One of *The Psycho Records*.

A close look at the argument of Freud's essay "Mourning and Melancholia" shows over and again how elimination loops through preservation. The mourner tests for the reality of the loved one's absence in every port of recall. Rerecording erases, but reality testing's eviction notice extends the afterlife of the departed. In the android test for the human ability to mourn, which P.K. Dick introduced in his 1968 novel *Do Androids Dream of Electric Sheep?*, the parameters of the text – I mean test – are empathy and psychopathy. These positive and negative outcomes of Dick's version of reality testing also served in the novel that he published the year before, *The Zap Gun,* as reversible manipulations going into the invention of ultimate weapons.

In his contribution to philosophical ethics, Schopenhauer argued that empathic identification, which can only gain traction in response to the other's suffering, must somehow get past the complete difference between the self and every other on which basic egoism rests.[13] The will can be moved by the well-being or being-in-pain of self or others, to which, therefore, the motive for every action must relate. The address of every action is anyone who can benefit from the experience: the one who acts, the recipient, or even a passive bystander.

What counts high on the scale of morals is compassion – *Mitleid* in German, literally "suffering with," which is real and not dreamed up. Happiness is nice, but who cares? To sympathize with the other directly, the requisite is the other's suffering, because *Mitleid* cannot be extended to the other's well-being. We might care if the happiness followed a sorry state. At the same time, we never confuse ourselves with the object of our empathic identification. We feel the other's pain, but it is his or her pain, not our own. Schopenhauer gives us the grid that Dick turns into a game in which the standoff between empathy and psychopathy is manipulated unto the player's self derangement.

According to the 1974 interview with Arthur Cover, Dick set his compass to the alternate realities of science fiction by turning

---

13 Arthur Schopenhauer, "Preisschrift über die Grundlage der Moral," in *Werke in zwei Bänden,* vol. 1, ed. Werner Brede (Munich: Hanser Verlag, 1977), 654–61.

up the contrast with fantasy, the genre in which he first tested his decision to write. Dick explained: "In fantasy, you never go back to believing there are trolls, unicorns [...] and so on. But in science fiction, you read it, and it's not true now but there are things which are not true now which are going to be someday. [...] It's like all science fiction occurs in alternate future universes."[14] Five years later, Dick took up the contrast again in his afterword to *Dr Adder,* the first novel by K.W. Jeter, at the time one of his So-Cal acolytes. Writing about Jeter's novel, which was completed in 1972 but not published until 1984, Dick defended bona fide science fiction against the fantasy hybrid: "Endless novels about sword fights and figures in cloaks who perform magic – in other words clones of the Hobbit books – have been cranked out, published, sold, and the field of science fiction has been transmuted into a joke field."[15] And then, making the pitch for *Dr Adder*: "[A]ren't you tired of reading about magic and wizards and little people with turned-up fuzzy feet?"[16] What had intervened between the interview with Arthur Cover and the afterword was *Star Wars.* Just the same Dr Jeter like Dick's *The Zap Gun* mixes with fantasy to stage a postmodern heroic saga. *The Zap Gun,* which counts as a James Bond spoof, cites from the German Wagnerian and Anglo-American traditions of superheroism.[17]

The Cold War opposition between Wes-Dem and Peep-East is a front for what's really a division of labor in one media operation. The protagonist, Lars Powdery, works for Wes-Dem's weapons fashions design industry, which stretches "subsurface

14 Philip K. Dick, *The Last Interview and Other Conversations,* ed. David Streitfeld (Brooklyn and London: Melville House, 2015), 8.
15 K.W. Jeter, *Dr Adder* (London: Grafton Books, 1987), 248. For a more complete account of the figuration of psychopathy and its integration in Jeter's complex novel, see my *Germany: A Science Fiction* (Fort Wayne: Anti-Oedipus Press, 2014), 134–38.
16 Jeter, *Dr Adder,* 249.
17 In *I Think I Am: Philip K. Dick* (Minneapolis: University of Minnesota Press, 2010), 301ff, I read the novel through the protagonist's desire to be with the dead. This time my emphasis shifts to address its conclusion, which tests for the psychopathy in successful mourning.

from San Francisco to Los Angeles."[18] The weapons are props in demo films that simulate their efficacy in staged tactical operations against localized threats, like criminality in one's own society. Many designs are then turned into toys or adult gizmos, for example Ol'Orville, a talking head that answers questions, like a party game or an oracle.

The gadget Ol'Orville, which consists of all the parts that were to go into the original weapon that Lars once designed, gives therapeutic forecast and counsel. First, it diagnoses Lars's castration anxiety, namely, his dread that after going under in a mediumistic trance he could bring nothing back. The prospect of being, even in fantasy, *waffenlos* (without weapons) like Parsifal, says Ol'Orville, brings to a crisis point the lack of real weapons in his line of work. Lars's partner, Maren Faine, hovers over this exchange punctuating the counsel with jabs of her own that bring the castration home.

Alternating between the lingo of Wagnerian heroism and the plain text of successful mourning, Ol'Orville steers Lars clear of suicide and picks up what the Cold War opposition holds in store for Lars: the way out of his impasse by substituting for ol'Maren Lilo Topchev, the Peep-East main medium. Although Lars has only glimpsed his rival in blurred surveillance photos, she in fact already occupies the foreground of his wish fantasying (something Maren, a telepath, picks up).

Lilo and Lars are brought together by an actual threat from outer space. Rockets from Sirius are targeting whole territories and beaming their populations into slavery. Together Lilo and Lars work to project a real weapon to be used in Earth's defense. But their trance states prove capable of communicating and picking up only fantasy constructs. It turns out that the weapon designs that Lars and Lilo were fashioning all these years on their different shores of the faux Cold War opposition originated in the same fantasy space to which a certain Oral Giacomini, the author and artist of the ongoing adventures of "The Blue Cephalopod Man from Titan," had equal access. Their weapons were featured at the same time on the pages of the comic-book

18 Philip K. Dick, *The Zap Gun* (London: HarperCollins, 1998), 155. Subsequent page references are given in the text.

superhero series, whose creator, an ex-inventor, would be but for electroshocks and thalamic-suppressors in complete autistic schizophrenic withdrawal. Telepathically, without knowing it, the designers were party to a superhero space fantasy comprised of "worthless, grandiose, schizophrenic delusions of world-power" (135).

The saving device that is delivered after all proves to be a toy prototype that one of Lars's colleagues at the design plant, Vincent Klug, considered a teaching tool. By telepathy-enriched identification with the little critter in the maze, a child playing the game of torment and escape would understand the significance of empathy. Klug's toy, however, was never produced. When Klug returns from a roundtrip to the future that he took to get his invention noticed, he's an ancient veteran from a world that survived the outer space attack. He finally attracts attention, but he can't by dint of an abstruse fiat of time travel impart anything from the future. All he can do is point to something already in the present environment. Only by guessing games can Klug show Lars the way to the toy prototype existing now, which contains the kernel of the future weapon.

Upon abandoning a project with androids that were "really human-like," Klug developed the game of critter identification within the labyrinth of animal testing. "The psychiatric theory is that this toy teaches the child to care about other living organisms. [...] He wants to help the creature, and that stud on the right permits him to do so" (168). Lars points out, however, that there is the stud on the left, too. Although the game can't foster sadistic tendencies, because the telepathic empathy circuit makes the player the victim who must win against all odds, "to keep the game going, you stop pressing the decrease stud and activate the increase, and the maze-circuitry responds by stepping up the difficulty which the trapped creature faces" (ibid.). By increasing the output of the telepathic empathy circuit and altering the controls so that both studs augment the difficulty the maze victim undergoes, the modified toy cannot but induce "a rapid, thorough mental disintegration" in "any life form that was intelligent enough to receive the emanations" (169).

The happy outcome of Lars and Lilo's search for the best defense against the invaders from outer space is followed by

Lars's second consultation of Ol'Orville, this time in the setting of substitution. The success of substitution and mourning would appear to have wrecked Lars. Because Lilo and Lars were coupled while working on a functioning weapon, Maren, the odd woman out, killed herself on or off purpose. It looked like she was gunning for Lilo or for Lars, but then blew herself up by accident. It is up to Ol'Orville to remind Lars that already prior to her exitus he had substituted Lilo for his ex. The close quarters of empathy and psychopathy, in which the game that is a lethal weapon is played, match the tight spot in which Lars, to keep his game going, must apply psychopathy to secure the prospect of living on in substitution.

Lars wants to harness time travel to remembrance: "I just don't understand where the past goes when it goes. [...] Where is she? Where's she gone?" (173). He would come right back to Lilo following the visit with Maren in alternate reality. It is an itinerary within the mediatic mortuary circuit often booked in Dick's novels. This sci-fi death cult is the mediatic application of the ambivalence toward the dead staggered through a letting go that keeps the ghost going, which Freud elaborated in *Mourning and Melancholia*. When Lilo responds that if he goes, he should stay gone she pronounces the paralyzing injunction that Freud attributed to the onset of mourning. The survivor must choose either to let the dead go or to join them.

Lilo heads Lars off at the impasse of his underlying funeral fantasy of waiting around until time travel becomes available in forty years, so he can go back to visit her in the past. She considers Lars's unmourning fixation – the question, where do the goners go – a hysterical symptom, a faux incorporation that must yield precedence to the substitute or go one-way like the goner. Lars at first resists the intervention, the death-wish scenario and its psychic quality, which he aptly identifies, thus coming closer, however, to the substitute's truth: "That simple. That simple, anyhow, to the easy scene-fabrication faculty available within the psychopathically-glib human mind" (175). Although psychopathy is the logical counterpart to the empathy for which Dick ceaselessly tested, the term is almost never used in Dick's fiction. This is the spectacular exception.

The oracle supports Lilo's paradoxical intervention – her encouragement of his suicidality – and then prescribes that Lars go have sex with her. If this devaluation of melancholia in Dick's oeuvre seems unique, it is so in tandem with the perspective of the substitute, which is brought to bear outside the melancholic atmosphere of suspicion of murder. The parameters of psychopathy and empathy working together in *The Zap Gun* describe the close quarters in which the mourner must follow out and surpass the death wish to secure the innovation of living on.

All You Vampires

The innovation of survival follows a new line on the geopolitical map. According to Günther in *The American Apocalypse,* it is the departure fundamental to science fiction and it draws us onward: "one lived in a world dimension that had no fixed proportions organizing a unitary, physiognomically familiar landscape, but rather one that by a natural process kept expanding westward and in which the dominant psychic category was the new."[19] While in *Der Untergang des Abendlandes* (*The Decline of the West,* 1918), Oswald Spengler forecast that the final "Faustian" phase of regional civilization was phasing out without the prospect of succession, Günther counters that the future was already upon us of a new civilization that would be planetary, the launching pad for an intergalactic civilization that would no longer be earth-bound. While so-called primitive culture has always been a planetary phenomenon, the high cultures that hailed from the East were tied to specific geographically circumscribed areas, which they required, according to Spengler, as their *Mutterboden* or "mother earth." The visions of outer space presuppose a universal planetary civilization – and condition or determine a new non-classical conception of reality.

The relay of frontiers leading up to the final Terran frontier, Günther agrees with Stein, was guaranteed by the outcome of the American Civil War. In the south, Günther writes, "the cultural tradition of European history was always incomparably

---

19 Günther, *Die amerikanische Apokalypse,* 108. Subsequent page references are given in the text.

stronger than in the north," a connaisseurship of European cultural traditions without "any creative spark to carry it forward" (193). The belief that European history and culture were to be continued on the American continent was dominant prior to the Civil War. "The outcome of the civil war [...] is one of the most powerful factors in the psychic isolation of the American individual and the atomization of the continent's population" (194). Waiting around for outer space following the separation from Europe with no other end or purpose in sight can be lonely and empty. "Everyone looks around and sees only larvae and talking automata" (195).

The metaphysical hierarchy of landscapes no longer holds: every landscape has the same historical value (117). Once he too had followed out the westward trek to the final frontier up against the Pacific, Günther saw that the switch of the frontier to a vertical axis was already underway. The wide-open layout of neighborhoods in Southern California, which relied on and reflected the car as sole means of transport, comprised the address rehearsal for life on foreign planets (184–85).

In his Haitian memoir *The Magic Island,* W.B. Seabrook responds to his interlocutor's occult etiology of zombieism: "[I]t is a fixed rule of reasoning in America that we will never accept the possibility of a thing's being 'supernatural' so long as any natural explanation, even far-fetched, seems adequate."[20] In his 1942 reflections on the occult, *Witchcraft: Its Power in the World Today,* Seabrook considers supernatural figures, such as the vampire or the werewolf, to be "hallucinated" within a three-way subjective reality, in which the creature, the victim, and the witness participate simultaneously.[21] When his study extends to academic parapsychology, in particular research into clairvoyance and retrocognition, Seabrook, impatient with the plodding neutrality of the experiments underway in his day, switches to the possibilities of outer space:

---

20 William B. Seabrook, *The Magic Island* (New York and Tokyo: Ishi Press, 2015), 102.
21 William Seabrook, *Witchcraft: Its Power in the World Today* (London: Sphere Books, 1970), 127. Subsequent page references are given in the text.

If you were somewhere out there, and could see light carried there from here, bringing you visual images, what you would see in the light-waves would be our ancient stone age with its cave men, Pharaoh building the first pyramid, Caesar's legions marching – depending on how many light-years distant you stopped off – all occurring as images *in the present nick of time.* (170)

And: "[I]f you could travel through space with a speed greater than light, you [...] could likewise go scooting into the future" (171). In sum, "telepathy and clairvoyance, including the reading of the future, would become as simple as television and the radio" (ibid.).

While Seabrook splits off such psy-fi prospects from vampiric undeath, his own introduction of the zombie entertained the reality-tested prospect of capitalization of PTSD victims as automated unremunerated labor. The TV extravaganza *The Walking Dead* that took off in 2010 triggered recognition in critics that the zombieism set in Atlanta disclosed its voodoo significance as slavery, the European history of the New World. But its twentieth-century significance was also already legible in the first episode. The outbreak of living death led to a reprisal of the hospital yard scene in *Gone with the Wind.* Identification with lost causes enlivens the south.[22] But what rises again can be killed off again. The rise and the fall can be played out with zombies and with vampires. In Quentin Tarentino's *Django Unchained* (2012), the antebellum South makes a good last resort for undead "European" aristorcrats. That Tarentino selected for the role of his white hero an actor hailing from another shore of crimes against humanity fits a cinema of integration, in which time-traveling interventions skewering together traumatic histories go

---

22 See the section of *Germany: A Science Fiction,* "The Identification with Lost Causes," in which the reversal with losses is developed in the setting of Freud's study of those wrecked by success. The reading of this popular encryptment, which the placement of the Trojan War at Rome's origin exemplifies, also inflects Stein's insight that through the civil war the United States became the oldest country of the twentieth century.

to the future of wish fulfillment and, for the present, change the past.

In the sci-fi setting of alternate history, vampires can come out of hiding to rule over mankind. In one scenario,[23] their control is history following the inadvertent invention of the first lenses of magnification, by-products of the official task assigned human mechanicians to design interesting playthings for their rulers. Vampires don't need a break from primary narcissism, the break you get with machines, which separate the body from itself to avert the crisis in uncanniness that the zombie embodies. In Jim Jarmusch's *Only Lovers Left Alive* (2013), the vampires judge inventiveness by standards of collectibility, and contain the uncanny by calling humans zombies. And because vampires inhabit a relay of museum exhibits secured against death or loss, as Freud argued was the European condition prior to World War One,[24] they lack the innovation enzyme. Once undeath can be conceived of as a germ viewed under a microscope, either the undead die or the living contract undeath *en masse,* a.k.a. living death. Either way, what the undead are good for in a science fiction setting is the dress rehearsal for what Stein understood to be history: killing the century that has overstayed its welcome.

In American letters, beginning with A.E. van Vogt's 1941 story "Asylum," vampirism underwent a remake. Upon coming to the New World, vampirism traveled through outer space. In "Asylum," earthlings have known space travel for about one hundred years. But humanity on Earth is one of several intergalactic races and the human vampires were created by an accidental sun blast one million years ago. The Galactic Observer, who alone has powers greater than the couple of vampires that suck blood

---

23 I am recalling Brian Stableford's "The Man Who Loved the Vampire Lady," which I discuss in *The Vampire Lectures* (Minneapolis: University of Minnesota Press, 1999), 108-10.

24 Sigmund Freud, "Thoughts for the Times on War and Death," in *The Standard Edition of the Complete Psychological Works of Sigmund Freud, Vol. XIV (1914–1916): On the History of the Psycho Analytic Movement, Papers on Metapsychology, and Other Works,* ed. and trans. James Strachey with Anna Freud (London: The Hogarth Press, 1957), 276–78.

and life force, splits off the majority of his powers to assume the guise of a mild-mannered reporter. When he rises to the occasion of defending earth against the thoroughly modern or American high-IQ-boasting vampires it turns out that he holds a far higher score.

Thirteen years later, in Richard Matheson's novel *I Am Legend,* the science-fictionalized vampires in van Vogt's story could be readdressed as terrestrial masses of the living dead. These then are the opening tracks of vampirism in the New World: either European refugees lost in space or zombies. According to Matheson's 1954 novel, the main text behind George Romero's *Night of the Living Dead* (1968), it was an epidemic spread of undeath that massified the object relations of vampirism unto zombie-like consumerism. When there's just not enough blood to go around, retrograde mutation promotes fracking of what's left of life. In *Daybreakers* (2009), the running out of blood reserves causes vampires to mutate, a process accelerated by self-feeding. The first mutants we encounter are leathery, winged creatures with long tails, demonic gargoyles from the edifice of Christianity (or the props department of fantasy). But after the German blood substitute fails and the crisis goes viral, the former vampires are the decaying living dead.

The paradoxical intervention in vampirism that spawned the living dead, first identified by Romero as zombies in the sequel *Dawn of the Dead* (1978), undergoes its reversal in the stronghold of the sole survivor in *I Am Legend,* where the recent past is recycled melancholically. Through the science fiction of an apocalyptic war's transmission of infectious undeath, vampirism in fact replaces the bulk rate of humanity. The traditional vampire is at home, however, in sole survivorship.

The vampire served Freud in *Totem and Taboo* as model for the transformation that the deceased loved one undergoes through the projective realignment of mixed feelings during mourning's opening season. But it is Freud's turn to the taboo restrictions placed upon contact with the dead, all the dead, which corresponds to the first group portrait of the vampire. According to Matheson's origin story, his undead masses supply the missing link between the occult creatures of the night and the secular prospect of what is announced in *Night of the Living Dead* to be an "epidemic of mass murder."

In *I Am Legend,* the protagonist Robert Neville pitches his last stand against his own destruction, but in the first place against the siren wailing of the undead babes in the front yard, which he puts on mute by turning up the volume on the orchestral music his mother taught him to appreciate. Secured against the taboo bust of happy-hour substitution, the basic needs and supplies in Robert's household and psychic economy reserve places for absence. His fortress home is the columbarium of his recent past, conserved between the closet of cans (and cannots) and the canned music of his habitat.

Robert doesn't want to be like his scientist father, who died denying the existence of the vampire. His recollection of the father's denial is the first reference to "the vampire" in the novel.[25] The vampire that Robert believes in is not that of "the B-film factories" (29). His belief is rather the precondition for fighting the vampire for real. He doesn't let sleeping vampires lie, but tests them by driving the point home. Then a no longer human survivor discloses to Robert that she belongs to a new group of living vampires who have learned to regulate and defer the course of the infection by taking pills that combine blood with a drug preventing multiplication of the vampire germ. Robert recognizes that the metabolic regulation really means that a mutation has already taken place. At the end, Robert doesn't recognize in the clean-up elimination of the non-mutated vampires by vigilantes of the new order his own testing of subjects. His identification instead is now with the vampires, who are as vulnerable as only the dead can be: "With a sense of inward shock he could not analyze in the rush of the moment, he realized that he felt more deeply toward the vampires than he did toward their executioners" (158). Before the mass prospect of living, dead, dead dead, and mutating revenants human mourning becomes the vampire.

The post-apocalyptic science-fiction setting in *I Am Legend* drives a split in undeath between one side that will come to be identified as zombieism and the side of survival that is allied to

---

25 Richard Matheson, *I Am Legend* (New York: ORB, 1995), 29.
Subsequent page references are given in the text.

mutation. Sometimes a human survivor identifies his dead in a zombie that is still trying to come home. This trace element is what mutates into the new object relation embodied by Bub in Romero's *Day of the Dead* (1985). On a feeding schedule and plugged into the earphones of the maternal Sensurround of music, Bub contains his violent tendencies. He also recognizes his research lab mentor as his father, whose death at the end of the film he will mourn.

The corporeality of mutation, its dependency upon a constant milieu consisting of reproduction and death, is secondary to its acceleration in time, the sudden changes that bypass a cumulative prehistory of evolutionary adjustment. Mutation, the fast track in the theory of evolution, sponsored among the earliest psy-fi conceits the prospect of any species, natural or artificial, fast-forwarding into survival of the fittest. Already in Samuel Butler's *Erewhon* (1872), the ultimate fit was seen to be with technology, which reverses the prosthetic relationship and does the evolving for us. The first historical scheme that could address the impact of machine technology was, therefore, a byproduct of evolution. Time travel is the corollary in narrative form and the psychic pendant to this techno-history.

As fantasy, time travel spins the denial of irretrievable loss by rendering generational time trans-parent (like in the *Back to the Future* franchise, 1985–1990). I underscored in *Germany: A Science Fiction* that in P.K. Dick's *The Simulacra* the technique of time transport forever falls short of changing traumatic history and provides, instead, training in the reality of loss. But not only fantasy is stowaway in time travel; evolutionary prehistory also hitches a ride. That the science fiction of travel in time can overtake and remake the evolutionary machine history that turns on mutation and breach its controlling interest in the future is conveyed by Robert Heinlein's short story "All You Zombies..." (1959). The alternate realities and histories branching off from each stopover in double time inscribe time travel's other legibility within its staging area – addressing both the expansion of the recording surface of finite remembrance and the innovation of survival.

In "All You Zombies...," a time-travel device dated 1992 secures the future of the species by multiplying sole survival.. The unnamed protagonist is an agent in a secret service that travels in time to reverse damages at their onset. However, the "Mistake of '72," which belongs to the near future that Matheson's 1954 novel also inhabits, can't be undone. It "either is, or it isn't." And "there won't be another like it."[26] At the bar that the secret agent protagonist is tending in 1970, a customer tells his story, a shaggy dog that the 2014 film adaptation *Predestination* couldn't leave lie. But boring, like Doubting Thomas's finger, enters and exits a wound.

On a dare, then, the customer tells the bartender his history, which will be unlike any story he has ever heard. He is an intersex unwed mother, Jane, who was turned upon giving birth into a man. Next their daughter was snatched from the hospital. The storyteller assumes it was the baby's father who betrayed Jane and then ruined her thoroughly. After awarding the prize to the storyteller, whose day job is authorship of romance fantasies under the name "the unwed mother," the bartender offers an alternate ending to the sorry story. They can travel into the past to get back at the man who abandoned them. Their stopovers in the past, in 1945, 1963, and 1964, reenact Jane's story. But in truth the bartender-protagonist is following out through alternate histories his own story.

By rewinding the historical or mythic past around him – he is father, mother, and child – he skips the Mistake of '72 in the near future and delivers instead another version of himself as new recruit for time service in 1985. When he gives his report (in 1993), he counts forty recruitments in the course of this stint of his time service. "Then I glanced at the ring on my finger. The Snake That Eats Its Own Tail, Forever and Ever [...] I know where I came from – but where did all you zombies come from?" (46). In real time, he, like Robert Neville, is sole survivor of a plague of living death. Heinlein's protagonist doesn't cede the future of survival to mutation. But by the time paradox, or, as Count Dracula characterizes his advantage, the time that is on

---

26 Robert A. Heinlein, "All You Zombies…," in *The Best from Fantasy and Science Fiction*, ed. Robert P. Mills (New York: Ace Books, 1964), 45. Subsequent page references are given in the text.

his side, he populates multiple alternate realities with matching versions of himself.

In *Predestination,* the protagonist's loop, which fits Heinlein's story, has an added significance. It is the prize agency of the temporal bureau, which aims to prevent crime before it takes place. What singles out the bartender-agent (who keeps recreating himself out of John and Jane) is that he is devoid of external ties to time and history. But his agency proves most successful when he becomes psychotic from obsessive unauthorized use of his time traveling device and ends up adding the Fizzle-Bomber to his loopy retinue of multiple personalities. Rather than the single traumatic event that in Heinlein's story can only be time-trip circumvented through the multiplication of sole survival, there is the terrorist in *Predestination* who over a span of decades detonates bombs. It turns out that the bombings prevented worse or more crime. The perfect temporal agent projected himself into the utilitarian terrorist, giving supernatural assist to the temporal agency. Each act of terrorism can be accounted a lesser loss than what would have transpired if the Fizzle-Bomber hadn't acted.

Countdown

"All You Zombies…" was a remake of Heinlein's 1941 novella "By His Bootstraps," a backstory of horror fantasy that Heinlein reduced to the 1959 title's clue or MacGuffin. Together with the protagonist Bob Wilson (and his time-travel doubles), the reader of "By His Bootstraps" returns over and again to what began with one person (in a locked room) who was completing his thesis titled "An Investigation into Certain Mathematical Aspects of a Rigor of Metaphysics."[27] We attend as Wilson types up reflections on time travel, its plausibility and impossibility: "Duration is an attribute of consciousness and not of the plenum. It has no *Ding an Sicht*" (40). This typo, which is internally shored up in the edition I read by its intact repetition (51), spells out the "in itself" of the *Ding* as a metaphysical "thing" about "seeing" or

27 Robert A. Heinlein, "By His Bootstraps," in *The Menace from Earth: Eight Stories from the Grand Master of Science Fiction* (London: Corgi Books, 1973), 40. Subsequent page references are given in the text.

"viewing," which does not hold for consciousness. An encysted sight or *Sicht* interrupts the assurance that nothing is unmediated by and unknowable to the duration of consciousness.

It is possible to assign the *Ding an Sicht* to a realm between literature and film, which the conceit of time travel occupies and cathects. Fredric Jameson identified the requirement of what he terms a "transcendental hyperspace" for the narrative rendering of time. It serves as the descriptive normality of space-time, which can be occupied like any other narrative scenery, as well as allowing the positing of this space-time as the real milieu of the reader. Jameson makes the camera pivotal to modernism's invention of a hyperspace "from which to observe the observer," which both film and time travel thematize.[28]

As byproduct of temporality's fictionalization in terms of travel in a machine, which begs the update of cinema, the *Ding an Sicht* raises the philosophical question of the status of the special effect. H.G. Wells first inscribed in *The Time Machine* the proto-cinematic effect of the ununderstood:

> Night followed day like the flapping of a black wing [...] I saw the sun hopping swiftly across the sky [...] as I went on, still gaining velocity, the palpitation of night and day merged into one continuous greyness; the sky took on a wonderful deepness of blue, a splendid luminous color like that of early twilight, the jerking sun became a streak of fire, a brilliant arch, in space.[29]

For every temporal paradox that literature gestures toward, film can supply the approximation via visual and special effects, the specialized department of filmmaking that subsumes the medium when fantasy is in the ascendant.

In Heinlein's story, what can't be seen or recognized frames the mounting recognition of the double in the first stranger's

---

28 See the last two paragraphs of Jameson's review article "In Hyperspace," *London Review of Books* 37, no. 19 (September 10, 2015), https://www.lrb.co.uk/v37/n17/fredric-jameson/in-hyperspace.
29 H.G. Wells, *The Time Machine* (Garden City: Dolphin/Doubleday, 1961), 210.

appearance in the room. He says he entered through the circle over there, which looks to Wilson like "a great disk of nothing" (41). The stranger has "something familiar about the face" (ibid.), which is all that Wilson musters upon first contact with his double. The stranger urges Wilson to step through the disk, identified as "Time Gate," whereupon a third man arrives to dissuade Wilson from following the lead of the first stranger. "The two looked a good bit alike, he thought, enough alike to be brothers. Or maybe he was seeing double" (43). I argued in *Germany: A Science Fiction* that time-travel fantasy can be seen, although it's a struggle for Wilson, to be a subgenre of *Doppelgänger* fiction. The double, according to Freud and Günther, starts out a resounding confirmation that the self stands in interchangeable relation with its own content. If you meet your double, unique like the golem, you meet yourself. Forever. But then for Freud the double crosses the dividing line and becomes the harbinger of death. A multitude of doubles, however, fits a broader picture of humanity, which accords, says Günther, with a new planetary going on intergalactic civilization.[30]

The ensuing altercation among the three men knocks Wilson through the disk portal. The invitation to enter willingly was his chance "for high adventure" (43). Upon regaining consciousness following his knocked-out arrival in the future, Wilson finds himself in fantasy, I mean in primal time, that is, in the "Hall of the Gate in the High Palace of Norkaal" (46). Time tripping in "By His Bootstraps" mixes up B-genres according to the early recipe or tendency of American heroic fantasy/science fiction to decorate the future and remote planets in the style of timelessness with bric-a-brac from the Medievalist-to-Renaissance fairgrounds.

The light show that first attended Wells's evocation of transport by machine across eons of time returns in Heinlein's second description of the disk, again leading up to the typing of the sentence that there is "no *Ding an Sicht*": "a simple locus hanging in the air, its flat depth filled with the amorphous colors and shapes of no-vision" (51). At this point Wilson begins to recog-

---

30 On time travel as a subgenre of *Doppelgänger* fiction see the section "Double Time" in *Germany: A Science Fiction*.

nize the strangers as his doubles (ibid.). What's more, the return to the scene of writing sparks Wilson's recognition of another level of doubling: "[T]his was not simply a similar scene, but the same scene he had lived through before – save that he was living through it from a different viewpoint" (52).[31] This could be, then, the *Ding an Sicht*: a POV unavailable to consciousness (of time and causality).

Diktor, the ruler in primal time, appears to be the only outsider who manipulates Wilson and his doubles. Wilson tries to displace Diktor by traveling to the time before his regency to establish an alternative government. He arrives ahead of time with the knowledge Diktor entrusted to him, including a reading list of four books, Machiavelli's *The Prince* and three alleged self-help books (including *Mein Kampf*). Because it didn't fit inside the focus of the disk at takeoff, Hitler's tome arrives cut in half (73). Not such a loss, Wilson reflects; but this was the first time he became aware of the bodily risk involved in time tripping. He also comes equipped with Diktor's vocabulary sheet for communicating with the indigenous people of the future. They are the "Forsaken Ones," who are on a line of descent from the extinct "High Ones." They comprise another introjection of Wells's *The Time Machine*. What they share with the Eloi is the lack of "the competitive spirit," in other words, "the will-to-power" (78).

Wilson seeks to shore up his preemptive ploy by going back in primal time to encounter the "High Ones." When he sees "it," he flees: "It had not been fear of physical menace that had shaken his reason, nor the appearance of the creature – he could recall nothing of how it looked. It had been a feeling of sadness infinitely compounded which had flooded through him at the instant, a sense of tragedy, of grief insupportable and unescapable, of infinite weariness" (81). He awaits Diktor's arrival – until

---

[31] The unseen gives way before doubling, in which the unnamed inheres. There's always a homoerotic rub in Heinlein. This time around Bob Wilson is miffed that he was forced by his double to participate in the scenario of doubling: "[Y]ou butted me in and tried to queer the pitch" (56). And again: "[W]hat was the idea of shoving me into that [...] that daisy chain without warning me?" (58).

he must recognize that he himself has grown into Diktor, his older double, his older self.

Between "By His Bootstraps" and "All You Zombies..." Heinlein updated his doubling fantasy via Matheson's science fiction of a global vampire epidemic. In "By His Bootstraps," Bob Wilson and his doubles try to reroute or improve upon what they in the end nevertheless inherit: evolutionary and colonial rule over a collective my "Man Friday" (77). "All You Zombies..." integrates a post-war world rather than double back to govern the nineteenth century. Heinlein goes further inside the new era than does Matheson at the close of *I Am Legend*. Sole survival in "All You Zombies..." does not end with the missing link, the legend to the map of evolutionary mutation, but deploys the quintessential science fictions, travel in time and alternate reality, to orbit the moment of irreversible catastrophe.

The blank checkout lane that is the American way of life or death cannot pick up the lack of metaphysics, as Günther argues in *The American Apocalypse*:

> For the time being the experience that man isn't capable in the long term of living without a metaphysics of his own – and that he therefore cannot produce history – has not yet been made or registered in the new world. The local carriers of the history to come have not yet suffered metaphysically. The epoch of this suffering, however, lies ahead. It is the inescapable consequence of human aloneness.[32]

The aloneness and emptiness belonging to the period of transition, the waiting around for the conquest of space, is the negative historical aspect of the decline of traditional supports, which also has positive implications: "This ambivalence of the spiritual situation is a necessary precondition for a positive historical future of the new world. Mere suffering drains, reduces, and makes sterile as long as it isn't able to transcend itself into something Other" (200). Günther registers the zombie as the identifiable

---

32 Günther, *Die amerikanische Apokalypse,* 199–200. Subsequent page references are given in the text.

symptom of the onset of a suffering that could supply a restart of consciousness to match the prospect of outer space.

A starting point for an American metaphysics of death, the idea of the zombie, as it stands, is nothing other than "a mythologization of the tendency to separate out all elements of death from the life of the soul or psyche" (251). Any content of the psyche, however, can be objectified and attributed to what is factual or dead. The consequence of the tendency for which the zombie is a mascot, therefore, is that all phenomenal life can be assigned to the realm of death. Perceived life, then, isn't life but a walking corpse.

Günther identified the mechanical brains already being designed and built in the United States in the 1950s as the technological version of the idea of the zombie (251). The equation, although it was never part of any text he saw through to publication, illuminates by its twilight his commentary on *The Humanoids*. Günther underscores in *The American Apocalypse* that so much that earlier epochs considered spiritual was really only matter of fact (*sachlich*) – in fact mechanical (249) – and that the mechanical brain is the technologization of what the zombie mythologizes: the overcoming of finitude by getting it over with already, by excluding it until that's all there is. The American way of death follows by breaking with the old view of death as intervention from some transcendental realm and guidance out of this world. The American has unlearned dying a personal death; its eventuality is at most an unfortunate work-related accident (218). The Old-Testament life spans that Günther sees already arriving from the future will render death truly free, accepted and self-administered by the more tired than tried (ibid.).

Günther sees the zombie rebound from a logical impasse into aftermath that doesn't sound like it computes: "A zombie is a walking corpse in possession of a second and dead life and, because he has already died and thus left death behind, is immortal. But death is absolutely unique. You cannot die twice" (250–51). The zombie, however, updates the commandment or conundrum by its function of walking target. Knock it over and the truth of the unique death, that is, second death, shines through. Target practice with zombies is assigned in the American spirit of demolition, which, according to Günther, necessarily comes before the world religions can begin to become one and cosmic (251–52). The split between personal and impersonal versions of the absolute can only be negotiated by someone "who for himself has undergone a heretofore unknown process of separation from subject and object, in which every trace of what belongs to objectivity's realm of the dead, the realm controlled through thought, is removed from the realm of the subject" (252).

In *The Humanoids,* as we saw, the service plan sets each robot apart from human agency and thus from the vicissitudes of willing and wishing. The "real perfection" of the humanoids is that they are "protected from human manipulation"[33] Günther follows Hegel to a point where cybernetics shall overcome the impasse between will and reason by reconsidering them as energy and information, allowing them to be but different perspectives on the same activity of the spirit for which each is just another expression.[34] The brain is the organ of subjective consciousness and repeats in itself the relationship between I and You, which has been mediated through the physical environment (240). The subjectivity of the You can be grasped and observed by us as an event of willing – the expression of a subjective will, which isn't our own and remains for us completely out of reach (239). Günther decides to bracket out the You, therefore, and reenter solipsism, but including the life or death of the observer (240). To remain within the near future of reading and address planetary mourning within the onset of a new metaphysics of science fiction, I follow the You that Günther was ready to leave behind.

Aligned with *I Am Legend,* Heinlein's "All You Zombies..." showed that human sole survival worked through the melancholic profile of the vampire, while the inheritance of the Earth is split between zombieism, science-fictionalized vampirism in a mass consumer setting, and a new form of immunity to the fatal course of the epidemic, either by time travel or mutation. Time travel in Heinlein's story keeps looping through, around, but

---

33 Günther, *Science Fiction als neue Metaphysik?,* 171–72.
34 Gotthard Günther, *Das Bewusstsein der Maschinen: Eine Metaphysik der Kybernetik* (Baden-Baden: AGIS Verlag, 2002), 237, 260. Subsequent page references are given in the text.

never past the countdown to the second death (the accident or loss that cannot be undone).

Since the Age of Discovery, mourning has required running up against Günther's summary dictum: you cannot die twice. But if the "you" is conjugated between you there, the other, and double you, the psycho, then we can count two deaths. This countdown is the secular world's afterlife in finitude. During World War One, Freud argued that primal man had no problem killing off enemies, rivals, anyone who was in the way, but that this killing spree was pulled up short before the loss of a loved one, a good object.[35] Primal man lives on in psychic reality as the death wish. In the course of mourning a loved one, the untenable admixture of murderous feelings, which underwent emergency projection, must be integrated, which doesn't mean neutralized. In the end, the mourning process requires that the double you, the psycho in you, attend the prospect of the deceased's second death. This does not necessarily entail a sentencing by your agency or acknowledgment. Alone the mourner's entry upon substitution suffices to curtail, displace, or subsume the extended scenarios of identification.

That outer space is big enough to admit indeterminacy in clocking the finitude between two deaths is the underlying conceit of the 2014 film *Interstellar*. The astronaut-protagonist Cooper recalls his deceased wife's words in contemplation of their young children: "Now we're just here to be memories for our kids." But there isn't enough room in generational time to avert the disaster of loss that afflicts the near future of Earth. Cooper risks a mission impossible to secure more time and resources for the dying planet or a double of Earth for starting over. After a succession of failures there are two survivors, Cooper and Amelia, the daughter of Cooper's former professor and father figure, who designed the two-pronged rescue attempt. Amelia is jettisoned off to a habitable planet, the backup goal of the original mission, while Cooper struggles to transmit to his daughter Murphy, now an established scientist, the saving message, the formula for restoration of life on Earth via integration within the multiverse.

---

35 Freud, "Thoughts for the Times on War and Death," 298–99.

The father-and-daughter bond, an Enlightenment introject, was all along outside linear time. A child when her father departed, Murphy was already attuned to Poltergeist-like aberrations imparting themselves in her bedroom. This communication from the other side held the place for the paternal transmission of rescue from outer space, which she later receives and carries out. Cooper, who like his co-survivor Amelia has remained unchanged inside the bubble of relativity, arrives at last in the multiverse in time for his aged daughter's dying. She sends him away, however, to join Amelia on her lost planet and enter upon the substitution that can reabsorb the mother of memories, like the multiverse Earth. Cooper departs once again, this time to traverse the span between the beloved daughter's first death, which she won't let him witness, and a second death that is at once certain, given, but equally far away on a compass that's cosmic.

In a flashback, Robert Neville breaches among the cans of sole survivorship the "cannot" in Günther's death sentence. In rehearsal since the onset of secularization, together with its byproducts haunting and mourning, the suffering that alone, according to Günther, can give a new history and a new metaphysics to the planetary civilization to come percolates through *I Am Legend*. After his dead daughter Kathy was taken away and consigned to mass cremation, he is determined to provide proper burial for his wife Virginia, who goes next. But then it is two in the morning, two days after he buried her.:"Two eyes looking at the clock, two ears picking up the hum of its electric chronology, two lips pressed together, two hands lying on the bed. He tried to rid himself of the concept, but everything in the world seemed suddenly to have dropped into a pit of duality."[36] And then he discovered, upon Virginia's return from the grave, that there are two deaths. The objective of mourning straddles the pit of duality – not only semantically through the injunction organizing mourning's opening season to join or let the dead go, a decision that in the time of mourning's altering alternations between projection and identification can in turn be let go, but

---

36 Matheson, *I Am Legend*, 75–76.

also syntactically and more effectively through the sentencing of two deaths.

In *I Am Legend*, the sole survivor derives a legibile legend to the experimental mapping of his impasse from two texts, *Dracula* and *Hamlet*, in which mourning is on a schedule of two deaths. Between the evidence of elimination and the pages of *Dracula*, the reality of vampirism's mortality can be addressed. It is the symptom picture of an infectious disease to which he applies himself as experimental scientist, like father like son. He obtains thus a greater containment of the scream memories from his recent traumatic past. The treatment is second death.

Vampires unacknowledge the second death because they are masters. Already the idea of the second death liberates ghosts from the magic book of endless slave time. In *Interstellar*, we saw the resolution to count down buffered by the temporal paradox of outer space transport. From the vantage of *I Am Legend*, the first science fiction to extract the happy end of zombie second death from the vampire's deferral position, the emphasis falls far more resolutely. Early in the movie *Last Action Hero* (1993), we attend school with the fanboy who watches, in place of Laurence Olivier as Hamlet, his superhero Slater (Arnold Schwarzenegger). Hamlet in the role of action figure chooses "not to be," which is now the transitive sentencing of the rot, the lot he eliminates in the fortress he detonates. Only thus can the malingering on of the lapse into lifelessness give way to innovation.[37]

What crosses Robert's mind when he visits the grave of his wife is on the same page with Hamlet's paternal ghost: "I'm here, he thought. I'm back. Remember me" (37). Although he speaks the injunction of a father's ghost, he's not commanding or asking, but, rather, he remembers a line that resonates differently inside him.[38] He's not a ghost nor is his wife (he saw to that).

---

[37] I have been revisiting and at times reprising my extensive reading of *I Am Legend* in *The Psycho Records,* but the focus is shifted away from the attempt to track the underlying psychopathic violence, while at this juncture I reverse the sense of my *Hamlet* reading in SPECTRE (Fort Wayne: Anti-Oedipus Press, 2013) to resituate psychopathy within the success and succession of mourning and substitution.

[38] In *Hamlet,* as I argued in SPECTRE, the father's ghost is double occu-

And he is not another Hamlet. Since his wife brought home the realization that there are two deaths, Robert has not hesitated to carry out the unfinished business of putting the already dead to rest. Robert Neville's sole survivorship becomes the legend for a new planetary civilization, which, fully theorized by Freud in *Totem and Taboo,* has been in preparation since the Age of Discovery in the occult margins of mourning's compass between life and death.

pancy and "Remember me" can be reread with the quavering lilt of the child Hamnet asking if he is remembered. Robert's citation resonates more with this stowaway question than with the paternal command.

4

Where the Dead Are

Fantasia

The "music of the spheres," the wrap of music in mathematics and astronomy, can also mean that when the music plays we wish upon the stars. Going into the "Pastorale," his Sixth Symphony, Beethoven took along Jean-Jacques Rousseau's *Reveries of the Solitary Walker*. A run of works of Romantic program music followed the stroll through the countryside. In 1940, the "Pastorale" entered Walt Disney's *Fantasia,* a title that also designates a form of musical composition that harnesses improvisation. Beethoven, who composed in the form, was according to legend better even than Mozart at improvisation on the piano, the performance called in German *Phantasieren*. In order that such legends might also be mapped, pianographs, melographs, and *Phantasiermaschinen* were designed to transcribe an improvised performance into a repeatable score. In a 1956 Disney comic book made in West Germany, the local engineer Düsentrieb invites the Duck family to try out his newly invented *Phantasiermaschine,* and Donald promptly takes along his nephews on a fantasy trip to Jupiter.[1] In Walt Disney's original design for the main building of CalArts, the art school he founded in 1961 as tribute to his *Gesamtkunstwerk Fantasia,* there was an amusement-park train circling close to the ceiling, guiding visitors through the complex, allowing them to gaze down upon the artists busily at work in the *Phantasiermaschine,* the happiest place on earth.

1 "Der freie Lauf der Phantasie."

In early fragments, Benjamin formulated and reformulated a brief theory of color that was specific to fantasy, that of German Romanticism to be sure, but which already indicated the predilection he would realize in his outright appreciation of Disney's art of animation: "The rainbow is a purely childlike image. [...] The color is [...] moist in nature, the medium of changes and not symptom."[2] Like in a rainbow and the *laterna magica,* too, "the color is completely contour."[3] What is typical of fantasy (in contradistinction to the "fantastic") is an intrinsic *Entstaltung,* de- or un-formation: "All fantastic forms have in common a constructive moment – or (from the perspective of the subject) a moment of spontaneity. True fantasy in contrast is unconstructive, purely un-forming – or (from the subject's vantage point) purely negative."[4] The vibe of fantasy coloration draws on the phospherescent, scintillating spectrum of decay – and the violet of violence.[5]

Because he turns the palette into a container, Benjamin's theory of fantasy coloration is on the same page with the daydream and Tolkien's genre: "Fantasy can be kept under control only through such contemplation of colors and fully developed and satiated in relation to them."[6] The rapport with the nuances and transitions of wet color keeps the antisocial tendencies in post-childhood fantasying (which according to Tolkien stain the elves) under control. By including a happy end, although his

2 Walter Benjamin, "Die Farbe vom Kinde aus Betrachtet," in *Gesammelte Schriften, Band 6: Fragmente, Autobiographische Schriften,* eds. Rolf Tiedemann and Hermann Schweppenhäuser (Frankfurt am Main: Suhrkamp, 1991), 110. My translation.

3 Ibid.

4 Benjamin, "Phantasie," *Gesammelte Schriften,* in *Gesammelte Schriften, Band 6: Fragmente, Autobiographische Schriften,* eds. Rolf Tiedemann and Hermann Schweppenhäuser (Frankfurt am Main: Suhrkamp, 1991), 115. My translation.

5 The Disney production *Mary Poppins* (1964) gave in one scene full visualization and manipulation of the contours of color, drawing animation out of it to shape a kind of cartoon environment for the live actors. Mary un-forms a street-art landscape to enter its big-screen sensurround where she and her charges spend the day with the painter.

6 Benjamin, "Phantasie," 115.

formulation is half empty rather than half full, Benjamin supplies what for Tolkien reforms wayward fantasy. The un-forming tendency of true fantasy upends the sense of an ending, which "never leads into death, but rather renders the decline it summons eternal by an endless relay of transitions."[7] We saw that in "On Fairy-Stories" Tolkien responded to a dilation of the sense of an ending by identifying "the good catastrophe, the sudden joyous 'turn'" that anticipates a happy ending in the Gospel, not in the works themselves since "there is no true end to any fairy-tale."[8] End phrases like "and they lived happily ever after" or "And if they have not gone away they are there still" are like the margins and frames of pictures,[9] which flex the enigmatic force of upending or unhinging. From within the walls of the world, the eucatastrophe gives a fleeting/fleeing glimpse of joy, "poignant as grief."[10]

In the future highlight of glass architecture shining through Paul Scheerbart's craft hovering over an unidentified playing field between science fiction and fantasy, Benjamin recognized the coloring scheme on which he had brooded earlier in his fragments on fantasy. In Scheerbart's "asteroid novel," *Lesabéndio: Ein Asteroiden-Roman* (1913), the coloration dabs yellow on the brown skin of the alien creatures; violet across the sky; green upon the stars; blue on assorted mountain ranges.[11] Gray is daubed once in the recurring descriptions of the array of colors in the alien environment. A little dab will do it. Scheerbart's next novel puts on gray as the experimental foundation for an architecture of colored glass. The first German translations and samplings from Oscar Wilde's oeuvre appeared in collections that included work by Scheerbart. And Scheerbart was a close reader of Goethe's *Theory of Colors,* as was his major influence,

7 Ibid.
8 J.R.R. Tolkien, "On Fairy-Stories," in *Tree and Leaf / Smith of Wootton Major / The Homecoming of Beorhtnoth* (London: Unwin Books, 1975), 68.
9 Ibid., 78.
10 Ibid., 68.
11 Paul Scheerbart, *Lesabéndio: Ein Asteroiden-Roman* (Scotts Valley: CreateSpace Independent Publishing Platform, 2017), 32.

G.T. Fechner, who continued Goethe's afterimage experiments. Fechner was the first to characterize as "subjective" the different colors seen by each observer whenever the rotating discs covered with black and white circles turned slowly.

In Scheerbart's *Das graue Tuch und zehn Prozent Weiß: Ein Damenroman* (*The Gray Cloth and Ten Percent White: A Ladies' Novel*, 1914),[12] the color gray that is applied is part of the pitch for a Swiss architect's mission of mixing color into glass and steel construction. That is why he contractually binds his wife to wear only outfits of gray and ten percent white. His better half will serve to guarantee the architect's simplicity of taste in coloration, and, inducing a sense of color against a gray backdrop, allow him to fulfill the wishes of his clients as his own.

The realistic novel that follows the architect and his wife around the world wherever his multi-hued glass architecture is under construction was composed in tandem with *Glasarchitektur,* a non-fiction work also manifesting the advantages of a new transparency in building. Bruno Taut was a follower and in 1914 built a glass pavilion in Cologne that displayed on each of its fourteen sides text by Scheerbart. The two-pronged plug for an environmental change in the near future operates like reality testing, which like mourning, however, is not a match for the march into total war.

In the 1933 essay, Benjamin seeks a silver lining in the fact that experience didn't come back from the First World War. He makes room for outright affirmation of the arrival of Mickey Mouse. But then, he ends the essay, which pitched Scheerbart's *Lesabéndio* to future readers, on the war that's next after the last one that did Scheerbart in. True fantasy, Benjamin argued early on in his coding of color, is deformative, endlessly transitional, and inimical to the sentiments of creativity and spontaneity (the old barbarism). Benjamin doubts that survival of the next war will get out of its retrenching. The posttraumatic structure of Benjamin's reflections on Scheerbart's novel peforms the reinstallation of the Gray crypt in the tower rising above the as yet uncontested playing field of fantasy and science fiction. That the afterimaging of the colored glass architecture circling the future

---

12 Benjamin acquired a copy in 1920.

against a neutral backdrop transpires between novels is unavoidable since unlike Oscar Wilde Scheerbart wrote more than one novel.

In "Erfahrung und Armut" ("Experience and Poverty," 1933), Benjamin introduced Scheerbart as the poster boy of the new lease on thinking fantasying heralded by the popular revival of astrology and ghost-seeing. The interior that the revived ideas address is not inwardness but amounts instead, says Benjamin, to a new barbarism that supplants Faustian creation. The poverty of experience allows the new barbarian to start anew in the stricken sentencing of the past. Unlike the gentlemen of leisure who continue to travel through the cosmos of Jules Verne, for example, the passengers that Scheerbart describes are human beings transformed by telescopes, airplanes, and rockets into lovable and interesting creatures.[13] Scheerbart projected citizens of the future longing for a world in which they can make pure and decided use of their poverty – their outer poverty, and ultimately also their inner poverty. All that's required, according to Scheerbart according to Benjamin, is a simple but ambitious plan (734). Encased in *Lesabéndio* is a plan for a *Leseabend,* an evening of reading. The name Lesa nicks the imperative to read, *lese,* as one might use it lovingly to encourage a child.

Mickey Mouse, says Benjamin, is contemporary man's wish dream, pulling out of his animated critter body miracles that both surpass the wonders of technological progress and make light of them. Scheerbart's aliens are salamander-like Gumbo figures that can pull and push themselves into miniaturization or magnification. In keeping with the theme of tentacular otherness that regularly introduces first contact with aliens in science fiction, they move about with suction feet, and their scalp is a rubbery surface that can be opened like umbrellas. The details of their sensorium are collectibles that skip the prosthetic history of technology on Earth and reflect a habitat that science fiction tends to project beyond, but which was never, in *Lesabéndio,* a

13 Walter Benjamin, "Experience and Poverty," in *Selected Writings, Volume 2: 1927–1934,* trans. Rodney Livingston et al., eds. Michael Jennings, et al. (Cambridge: The Belknap Press of Harvard University Press, 1999), 733. Subsequent page references are given in the text.

historical setting of this alien species on the planet Pallas. Their eyes resemble telescopes that can be turned into microscopes. They can tune in to a form of wireless telegraphy (as it is identified by the narrator) using their bodies as receivers by dint of their own electrical aspect.[14] They resemble the fantasy-reprogrammed robots that sidle up to our empathic identification in the manner of pets, like R2D2 and the protagonist of *Wall·E* (2008).

Their only external technology is photography, which is the means of fabricating the tiny books they wear around their necks and which they can read only by turning their eyes into microscopes. Early on in the novel, we read the book of one alien's sojourn on Earth. The earthlings could pass right through the alien's body without notice, which might describe a not recognized ghost. The author of the mini volume comments: "What was most terrible was that they killed other lifeforms, spliced and diced them and stuck the parts and clumps into their mouths; they had stone-hard teeth in their mouths with which they ground everything up."[15]

To carry isolation can mean relating to your dead as to sibling playmates in childhood. If of one kind, how much easier to be kinder to them. According to Melanie Klein, all the unborn siblings lead the way to this happy interface of undeath.[16] For the child survivor there's not that much difference between the many who are never born and those who existed only to exit. The death wish, especially one so early and automatic as the wish to be an only child, can be a pioneer in pacifying new frontiers for the identified (with) dead. The indigenous people of Pallas in *Lesabéndio* hail from both genres. They are pet-like cyborgs, the other Hobbits.

Hobbitness, the hippie magnet that brought the counterculture to Tolkien's Shire, started out as fellowship among orphans, fatherless heirs to the fairy story, always a mother's bequest. As

14 Scheerbart, *Lesabéndio*, 82.
15 Ibid., 7–8.
16 Melanie Klein, "On Identification," in *Envy and Gratitude and Other Works: 1946–1963* (New York: The Free Press, 1984), 158–59. That P.K. Dick's twin sister Jane died on him meant that he could see better how we live with our dead.

a philologist and inventor of timeless fictive but functional languages Tolkien surveyed the singularity and iterability of myths finding a pattern and a path. One variant, the fairy story, always gestured toward a happy end and gave consolation. It wasn't until I addressed this in German for a radio special about the 2019 movie *Tolkien,* that I realized the significance of Tolkien's consolation packaging of his genre fantasy. *Trost* is a big word in German and by its lightening shows the depression, indeed the hole out of which the Hobbit first arose. One of his Oxford students left a page unintentionally blank in the written assignment Tolkien was correcting. In a sudden place for absence Tolkien wrote automatically: "In a hole in the ground there lived a Hobbit."[17]

That the draw of a language for Tolkien was the beauty of its sound world means that he lost and found a specific emotional situation there. The topography of Tolkien's fantasy epic inscribes an affective pathway from the hole to the Hobbit in the Shire. The Elven idealization is for the memories. Tolkien saw his young bride Edith dancing and singing in the glen of the Elves and, biding their time together, already knew he would inscribe her idealizing Elf name onto her gravestone.[18] But the more immediate bond of the fatherless duo who lost their mothers in early adolescence was Hobbitness. When sitting on the balcony of their favorite tea shop, the kids delighted in dropping sugar lumps into the hats of the passersby.[19]

Tolkien underscored that one fantasy (his adult translation of fairy story) was the Gospel truth, and that the Christian fantasy, because it had entered history, vouchsafed the immanent Christianity of fantasy's parallel worlds in which the word Christianity need not be known. Each fantasy setting nevertheless abuts on the European Middle Ages north of the Alps. That's where Christianization rather than demonization

---

[17] Humphrey Carpenter, *Tolkien: A Biography* (New York: Ballantine Books, 1977), 172. All my references to Tolkien's life can be found in this biography.

[18] J.R.R. Tolkien, *The Letters of J.R.R. Tolkien,* ed. Humphrey Carpenter (London: HarperCollins, 2006), 340.

[19] Carpenter, *Tolkien,* 40.

altered the content and not the practice or forms of paganism. Christianization is an ongoing practice. To this day German readiness to go naked is heathen (and not the Roman bathhouse kind), but the sacrificial content has been displaced. When getting dressed again, the German is at the Christian address.

Secularization that showcases continuities with Greek and Roman antiquity, which must first be cleansed of demonization, is not at home in the Shire (the Medieval continuity shot up north in Europe). That's why Tolkien was genuinely uncomprehending when it came to allegory. But even if *The Lord of the Rings* wasn't influenced by the rise of Nazi Germany and didn't refer to it, World War Two got an allegorical rise out of Tolkien's novel. Allegory happens.

Tolkien's other bout of denial concerns Wagner, whose contribution to the Nibelungen saga was the ring of power secreted away in the gold in the bed of the Rhine river. The repressed returns at a tilt. When Californian fans called Tolkien at three in the morning (what's the time difference?!) to share their experiences reading *The Lord of the Rings* on acid,[20] he was confronted with both coasts (and extremities) of the teen age. The Hobbits, like Tolkien, like being tipsy on an occasion. Wagner mixed hard drugs into the reception of the Middle-Ages crisis. Tristan, an orphan, takes Isolde's potion and puts himself at her disposal. They toast to reconciliation, and she knows they're both goners. But then they don't feel numb and number. OMG! That handmaiden replaced my poison with love potion number *nein*! But Tristan later affirms that it's all the same. What they want is P.K. Dick's Substance D, the drug called Death. Tristan and Isolde's withdrawal from their names and the words that link and separate them swaps the little death for the Big One. Wagner's drug-addled *unio mystica*, the *Liebestod*, the mutual-daydreaming administration of the Werther Effect, falls flat between Tolkien's incomprehension and Freud's dismissal of regression to in fantasy. Today, Freud quips, we have neuroses in lieu of monasteries![21]

20 Tolkien, *The Letters of J.R.R. Tolkien*, 368.
21 See Sigmund Freud, "Five Lectures on Psychoanalysis," in *The Standard Edition of the Complete Psychological Works of Sigmund*

Freud declares that to speak of "chemistry" or "metabolism" on the same page as "sexuality" is without content. At least until we know more about the body's chemistry. In other words, Freud allows that the day will come when science opens up more and more prospects for drug intake. Then he writes:

> The popular mind has from time immemorial paid homage to hypotheses of this kind on the nature of sexual desire, speaking of love as an "intoxication" and believing that falling in love is brought about by love-philtres – though here the operative agent is to some extent externalized. And for us this would be an occasion for recalling the erotogenic zones and our assertion that sexual excitation can be generated in the most various organs.[22]

Add together all that variety and you can again be the body genital of infancy. That's what the libido toxin is good for but this kind of autonomy cannot enter the community of libidinization since too busy masturbating or being suckled with substances. Only the Californian orgy, according to Herbert Marcuse, a Frankfurt Schooler exiled to the Coast, could break through this impasse and enter utopia.[23]

The other Hobbits, the cyborg aliens that Scheerbart visited on the planet Pallas in 1913, make room in their cozy corner for Fechner's theorization of a universe that is animate, even conscious, in all its parts and partings. The eponymous protagonist, Lesabéndio (or Lesa for short) adheres to a "theory" of *Ergebenheit* (devotion and, more literally, submissiveness) that

---

Freud, Vol. XI (1910): Five Lectures on Psycho-Analysis, Leonardo da Vinci and Other Works, ed. and trans. James Strachey with Anna Freud (London: The Hogarth Press, 1957), 50.

22 Sigmund Freud, "The Common Neurotic State," in *The Standard Edition of the Complete Psychological Works of Sigmund Freud, Vol. XVI (1916–1917): Introductory Lectures on Psycho-Analysis (Part III),* ed. and trans. James Strachey with Anna Freud (London: The Hogarth Press, 1963), 388.

23 Herbert Marcuse, *Eros and Civilization: A Philosophical Inquiry into Freud* (Boston: Beacon Press, 1955).

posits the "Great," "our second nature," which is always invisibly near.[24] On other stars or planets, millions of life-forms perish every second. The big dying teaches the survivors the grand horror (*Schauer*) of *Ergebenheit*. They call it religion (ibid.). The "Great" encompasses a cosmic animism. Stars are life-forms, too, but they don't value the fixing of or fixation upon thoughts (107). The cloud ceiling of the planet Pallas conceals and makes secret the "Great." This animate cloud of spiderweb filaments, in which critters dwell, is not the only secret on this planet that Lesa's tower project will penetrate. There's reproduction, too, its nuts and bolts. To bust a "nut" is to secure a new generation, a labor force for the tower's construction (33). Each new being coming out of the nut has been in "other worlds" (34).

In *Zend-Avesta*, Fechner follows memory, the more spiritual form of understanding, into an exchange with the "circles of memory," which the higher spirit absorbs or reabsorbs (like god the nerves in Schreber's system) from all human beings upon their passing.[25] Just as we are in life the perceptions of the higher sphere, so we are after death this sphere's memories (174). Like the spheres rolling within and around all the other spheres in Fechner's famous analogy for the fourth dimension's wrap of the other three dimensions,[26] our life and afterlife are on a roll within

---

24 Scheerbart, *Lesabéndio*, 42. Subsequent page references are given in the text.

25 G.T. Fechner, *Zend-Avesta: Gedanken über die Dinge des Himmels und des Jenseits vom Standpunkte der Naturbetrachtung* (Leipzig: Insel Verlag, 1919), 171. Subsequent page references are given in the text. It was hard enough to obtain this copy through interlibrary loan while I was guest professor at NYU. Unhappily I received an adulterated and abridged edition: "Frei bearbeitet und verkürzt herausgegeben von Max Fischer."

26 Fechner's essay "Der Raum hat vier Dimensionen" ("Space Has Four Dimensions," 1846) culminated, Wolfgang Hagen argues, in the "transcendental physics" and outright occultism of his colleague J.F.K. Zöllner. What Fechner propagandized was the discourse that Daniel Paul Schreber was given to recognize, in concert with the work of academic psychologists like Carl Du Prel, Eduard von Hartmann, and Zöllner, as hard science. See Wolfgang Hagen, *Radio Schreber: Der "moderne Spiritismus" und die Sprache der Medien* (Weimar: Verlag

the greater existence of planetary bodies and stars, including the Earth, of course, in particular the Earth's animate surface, which is under development like our evolving brains: "The life of a person acts in this life beyond his own body upon the entire body of the earth" (201) and Fechner can recognize the "will" of the earth along with its sense organs and organs of motility (97).

Before an alien creature on Pallas dies in Scheerbart's asteroid novel it begins drying up, becoming increasingly transparent. The dying alien expresses the wish to be sucked up into a living friend, who fulfills the wish by extending to maximum height and thus widening the pores to absorb the goner into this metabolic afterlife.[27] Several friends pass into Lesa, who upon the tower's completion, which scrapes away the cloud cover and gives access to the *Kopfsystem,* the head or brain system that is more than an analogy for the "Great," merges with the upper region while sending to the surviving friends by thought transference the message of the significance of suffering for all the transfers that comprise the theory of *Ergebenheit* (143–44). Leading up to ascension, there was a span of time for Lesa in which dreaming and waking were one (131). "Submission is the greatest. Dying, too, is in fact only submission" (139).

Memory serves Fechner well in *Zend-Avesta* to designate that which crosses over from the mind into the beyond.[28] Our memory life here and now can be seen as the test and germ of our memory life in the next world (184). Reunion awaits us: "We will be able to reconnect in the afterlife with all the relationships to our loved ones in this world" (187). Ghosts don't give up their old areas of activity, although they aren't limited to them: "They work in us and with us continuously on the projects to which they dedicated themselves in this life, carrying them forward" (194). The labors of the past are just points of reference for a continued and extended labor (ibid.). In the afterlife we communicate, but without mouth or ear, "just as now in the realm of memory and fantasy there is a pure inwardness of speech with-

und Datenbank für Geisteswissenschaften, 2001), 28.
27 Scheerbart, *Lesabéndio,* 27. Subsequent page references are given in the text.
28 Fechner, *Zend-Avesta,* 177.

out a mouth, of hearing without an ear" (220). Much that we take to be our own derives already from the spirits of the beyond: memories play into our perceptions; they help us interpret our sense impressions in a certain way. Nature, Fechner concludes, would be a marbled palette of paints if memories did not jog our perceptions (193). A signal familiar to us from Schopenhauer's treatise keeps the traffic going one-way. We feel the proximity of the ghosts or spirits, but we don't feel that they feel anything in exchange (194).

Scheerbart was the eleventh child, the last-born. Nine of his siblings died in childhood. When he was thirteen years old he decided to become a missionary. Instead he joined Fechner in exploring the great, greater, or greatest, the cosmic animistic afterlife he set on the borderlands of fantasy and science fiction. But when the Great War broke out Scheerbart stopped eating and died in 1915. How could the protector of so many related deaths acquiesce before the prospect of human material, *Menschenmaterial*? In "Experience and Poverty," Benjamin rips through time to nominate Scheerbart a new barbarian survivor of "some of the most monstrous events in the history of the world,"[29] namely the Great War that caused him to ascend, like Lesa, into the *Kopfsystem*. But he left behind a saving loop inside the fall that etymologically indwells the German word for mourning, *Trauer*. In *Lesabéndio,* he foresees and reverses the condition of the *Gefallenen,* the term that would come to signify those lost in the war. In the novel, the aliens who have literally fallen discover that gravity in this particular shaft is neutralized. They fall without sinking down.[30] The accident that proved an experiment made the assembly of the tower to last at last possible. It is the monument to the *Gefallenen*.

In the language of dreams at least, at last, to build upward can mean to build down there, in the underworld. Tolkien averred that it was the First World War that had dug his hole or depression in which the Hobbits dwelled. But he needed the sequel, a wish for another postwar period that he didn't watch out for. The European traditions of continuity with Medieval

---

29 Benjamin, "Experience and Poverty," 731.
30 Scheerbart, *Lesabéndio,* 84.

Christendom came to an end, when enthusiastic soldiers crowded into no-man's-land like heroes going to a joust and laid siege at hell's mouth. That they were reduced to human material was certainly nihilistic but there was neither good nor evil on this level dying field. That changed with the Second Coming of the war to end all wars. While the rockets, atom bombs, air raids, and computers of the second war challenge the contours of Medieval continuity (but qualify as science-fiction props), evil was openly installed in Nazi Germany and, what is more, first had to be believed in. Hitler was adept at manipulating the fake-news guilt of the first war's victors, but then the good people believed and they rose to the occasion like Hobbits to fight pure evil and re-secure the inheritance of the meek. The fantasy genre could come back or re-start at the border to science fiction (Nazi Germany was the first realization of a science fiction), and by occupying the edge of the present that belongs to science fiction by its hit and miss extrapolations of future worlds forestall the end of history. Once fantasy was propped up by both coasts it could, through the mediation of *Star Wars,* go global. As it goes the rounds the fantasy that is true is no longer the Gospel but digitization.

Wish upon the Stars

For both the secular and the religious mindsets that Günther allows in his commentary on *The Humanoids,* the starry heavens are the beyond. The space-time continuum available to secular science in 1950 is, just the same, finite. The question what lies beyond still applies: In what space is our outer space installed?[31] Outer space contains a metaphysical secret, a characteristic it shares with the spiritual heaven of believers. However, when we travel to the outer planets or even outside our solar system, we will not in fact arrive at the absolute limit of human consciousness: "The end of the world" in either sense. Here Günther raises the question whether there are relative limits of consciousness,

---

31 Gotthard Günther, *Science Fiction als neue Metaphysik? Dr. Gotthard Günthers Kommentare zu "Rauchs Weltraum-Büchern,"* ed. Dieter von Reeken (Lüneburg: Verlag Dieter von Reeken, 2015), 56.

which can be expanded in the course of space travel. Earth-bound consciousness would be, then, one such relative limit. Unlike Arthur C. Clarke in *Childhood's End,* Williamson doesn't summon the Second Coming from outer space, but focuses instead through the inclusion of psychophysics on qualitative and relative expansions of consciousness that follow upon all the quantitative changes that the future will bring.[32] While Clarke's Overmind expunges mourning from the human horizon, Williamson's mechanical brain targets an illogic of unhappiness that means to be dead-wrong wrongs the dead. For this protocol of its treatment, the mechanical brain in *The Humanoids* admits the integration of psychophysics.

In contrast once again to the Christian repurposing of evolutionary mutation that in *Childhood's End* resolves or suspends the occult predilection of mankind, in *The Humanoids* the gift of the psychophysical grid is Enlightenment in provenance. Psychophysical functions, which are "normally unconscious,"[33] can be integrated via "the perfected paramechanical grid" (237). Delivered of the "interfering internal conflicts" in human agents (275), its "creative" "energy," which represents "the driving power of organic evolution" (276), "can even mend the decay of time" (238). The "real function" of the grid is education and its power will be "completely democratic" (287): "[I]t is just a tool to unite the unconscious minds of all people in whom love had displaced hate" (288).

The 2016 film *Arrival* touched down with an introject of the Enlightenment in the mixed-use development between fantasy and science fiction. The aliens impart a lessening of grief, a lesson learned through the mediation and alienation of their otherworldly mode of inscription with precognitive loops. The gift that the aliens communicate awakens in the protagonist, Louise Banks, her own talent for simultaneity, which recalls the frequent

---

32 My reading of *Childhood's End* in *The Devil Notebooks* (Minneapolis: University of Minnesota Press, 2008) was central to my understanding of the relationship Freud almost posits between the Devil and the death drive.

33 Jack Williamson, *The Humanoids* (New York: Orb Books, 1996), 275. Subsequent page references are given in the text.

byproduct of the Enlightenment therapy of animal magnetism. Contact with the *magnetiseur* regularly led to certain patients showing all the same clairvoyant abilities, which conferred on the gifted client the status of therapist's assistant in a social network of awareness.

Because their exchange cannot be out in the open, the parties to the conference are kept in separate environments on board the alien vessels and must communicate through the big screen between them. For the duration of the interdisciplinary summit, which leads to an understanding of the alien trace against time as the truth for the ages, we are ensconced in a classroom lab space that functions up against the screen as a transcription and translation machine – a complete *Phantasiermaschine*.

Twelve alien spaceships land at divergent points across the globe to impart a life-changing lesson in two parts. First, the planet must unite to coordinate and receive the contact staggered across twelve installments. The second bestowal unfolds in the course of learning their written language. Getting to know the alien language means getting to know all about time, which doesn't exist in the terms of an inexorable declension of past, present, and future.

The first translations of what the aliens are communicating seem to be announcing that there's no time like the present for a conflagration among the superpowers, which Banks alone realizes is a misreading that fills in like an ellipsis the message that there's no time as we know it – that time, tout court, doesn't exist. Projected into the alien visitation and communication is a strategy lifted from a concise history of White Man's Burden. It is likened to what was done by "the British with India, the Germans with Rwanda." After she tells her favorite anecdote about Captain Cook securing "kangaroo" from the locals as the new animal's name, unwittingly using the word in the name meant to signal in the exchange "I don't understand," the US commander chides her that she must never forget what happened to the aborigines of Australia. In their dealings with the alien visitors, the humans could become the victims of a superior civilization.

At the end, a moral majority interprets the alien visitation as planting a weapon-tool in twelve settings to lead the way into the twilight of suicidal conflict. When Banks goes up alone after the vigilante American soldier bombing that brought the "death process" into the alien ship, she, like Ellie Arroway in *Contact*, is the heroic champion rising above Christian right-wing media politics. And she is CGI-enhanced, fantasy-tweaked as she ascends to receive the gift, mistranslated as weapon-tool. She is also at this instant given the ability to read fluently and immediately the complex message in which the alien gift is bestowed.

When she returns, she learns that China is leading the way toward a battening down of the local stations of alien visitation, a retrenchment of national interests that in blocking the conferral of the gift will lead to war. In possession of the ability to open time, she calls the Chinese commander and pronounces his wife's dying words to him. While no tense is given and intuitively the words belong to the recent past, the logic of the film and of the traditions coursing through it also suggests that Banks initiated the commander into clairvoyance by his recognition of the future parting words of his wife. An American and a Chinese would then be the two equal bearers of the gift. Either way, what follows is that the commander immediately understands what "no time" means and guides the world in the other direction, toward unifying communication of contact.

Only since 1900, Günther underscores in his commentary on the novelty of the stories comprising his edited collection *Überwindung von Zeit und Raum* (*Overcoming of Space and Time*, 1952),[34] could the question even be raised whether there are habitable planets outside our solar system.[35] In American science fiction, the abstract considerations and calculations concerning the habitability of vastly distant planets occupy the foreground. Günther takes off for the abstract possibilities of American science fiction from an Enlightenment datemark. When he dips into the probability of life on these planets, Günther advances

---

34 Günther's collection of German translations of American science-fiction short stories is the readymade that I unpack in the second volume, reading the stories in alternation with comps, fantasy contrasts (notatbly works comprising and influencing Lewis's "Space Trilogy"), hybrids between the B-genres, and film adaptations.
35 Günther, *Science Fiction als neue Metaphysik?*, 81.

an argument that is the byproduct of an absurd improbability, namely that there could be an alien life-form so continuous with our own capable of composing Mozart's *The Magic Flute*. However, the less likely it is that we are going to encounter in outer space the folks from back home in Europe, the more the probability increases that remote planets in fact fulfill the conditions for generating basic life.[36]

To emphasize that the development going into and through American science fiction commenced only very recently indeed, Günther turns to and cites from Kant's pre-critical study *Allgemeine Naturgeschichte und Theorie des Himmels* (*General Natural History and Theory of the Heavens*, 1755), in which the philosopher of the Enlightenmet assessess the possibility that dwellers on the outer planets are "more perfect creations."

> Should the immortal soul remain forever attached to this point in space, to our earth for the whole infinity of its future duration, which is not interrupted by the grave itself, but only changed? [...] Who knows whether it is not intended to get to know at close quarters those distant spheres of the solar system? [...] Perhaps some further spheres of the planetary system will form around them in order to prepare new places for us to reside in other heavens, after the completed passage of time prescribed for our stay here.[37]

---

36 Ibid., 83.
37 Immanuel Kant, *Allgemeine Naturgeschichte und Theorie des Himmels oder Versuch von der Verfassung und dem mechanischen Ursprunge des ganzen Weltgebäudes, nach Newtonischen Grundsätzen abgehandelt* (Königsberg and Leipzig: Bey Johann Friederich Petersen, 1755). I cite the English translation by Olaf Reinhardt from Peter Szendy's *Kant in the Land of Extraterrestrials: Cosmopolitical Philosofictions,* trans. Will Bishop (New York: Fordham University Press, 2013), 51. Szendy gives as the source from which he took off Geoffrey Bennington's *Kant on the Frontier: Philosophy, Politics, and the Ends of the Earth* (New York: Fordham University Press, 2017). It originally appeared in French under the title *Frontières kantiennes* (Paris: Éditions Galilée, 2000).

Kant concludes his study with the inside view of its makeup. His mind filled with the scientific knowledge of his day, the author enjoys the view of the starry heavens on a clear night, which he explores in a state that we can consider reverie, but which he ennobles further as manifestation of "the immortal spirit's hidden faculty of cognition," which "provides undeveloped concepts that can certainly be felt but not described."[38]

At this juncture of its citation by Günther, Kant's *Theory of the Heavens* exemplifies the European cosmos that American science fiction must leave behind in its own preliminary probing for a completely new mythic fairytale, a new plain text suitable even for children. Günther writes that in these reflections Kant is still projecting the alien in analogy with human life. Still? Kant's view of the solar system bears the date stamp of the Enlightenment. It was an innovation of this period to view the Christian afterlife as the at once secularized and personalized reunion with loved ones.[39] Werther's outbursts to Charlotte about loving the dead and reuniting with them beyond the grave belong to this changed relationship to the afterlife. It followed that our dead went to the outer planets to pursue their perfectibility, the striving on which the highest value was placed (Kant's important "imperfect duty") and which fell short in one life span (see Goethe's *Faust*).

Beginning in the Enlightenment, there was continuity between the living and the dead and the matching prospect of

---

38 Quoted in Szendy, *Kant in the Land of the Extraterrestrials*, 52.
39 Diethard Sawicki, *Leben mit den Toten: Geisterglauben und die Entstehung des Spiritismus in Deutschland 1770–1900* (Paderborn: Schöningh, 2002). The opening chapter addresses the change in earlier theocratic conceptions of the afterlife in the course of the Enlightenment. His time span leaves out the late arrival of this secularization of the heavens in Daniel Paul Schreber's *Memoirs of My Nervous Illness,* the bible of psychosis studies, which, however, as Benjamin first pointed out, was originally published as a contribution to modern Spiritualism. See Hagen's *Radio Schreber* for a more complete exploration of this setting of Schreber's memoirs, although the new history he develops of the psychotic break as specific to this era demonstrates the shortfall of all resistance. In *Kant in the Land of Extraterrestrials,* Peter Szendy doesn't recognize this milieu in his assessment of Kant's turn to the firmament of secularization.

contact. But the immaterial dead relied on alternate media/mediums to get across. What made spiritualism modern was that communication with the other side was analogized with telecommunications media. These media were not used, however. Instead, disabused of function, they were turned into allegories, endopsychic perceptions, animism props, or alternate means of transmission hiding out in the recording. Between the input and output of the message sent by electric live transmission, there was immaterial mediation that bordered on the unknown and infinite.

What could be bent to function for live communication among the living was open wide for immaterial contact of the other kind. Photographs of ghosts could be taken with the lens covered. The tape recording of the noise between radio stations picked up spirit voices that upon incessant replay could be discerned. To reverse film, tape, and vinyl record means to undo function for the outside chance of an alternate message. Christianity rides reversal as the plain text of the Devil. That's one way to stop the all-out secularization that commands the thought of continuity and contact with the known and knowing dead.

In *The Devil Notebooks,* I approached Clarke's *Childhood's End* through Alan Turing's admission that if the compartments used for testing recognition of the difference between human and artificial intelligence had to be telepathy-proofed, then one would need to factor in ghosts as well. Telepathy among the living is child's play and is raised up into the pre-Enlightenment firmament of the Overmind, transformed, mutated beyond object relation or recognition, while the Enlightenment generation on Earth is blasted to excise the cancer of its modern-occult spin on telepathy.

The preamble to modern spiritualism's science fiction of the afterlife saw the dead perfecting themselves beyond the limitation of lifetime. Although the cultural A-list doesn't take the direct hit, Diethard Sawicki finds the tendency confirmed in popular works of the day, like *Elpizon oder Ueber meine Fortdauer im Tode* (*Elpizon or On My Duration in Death*). Published in 1795, it is the ostensible document by one returned from the grave reflecting on the circumstances of his continued existence.

Critical of the conditions obtaining on Earth, the author cannot imagine mankind's perfectibility in the light of this sun.[40] It follows that the divine providence of reason sees to it that we are transferred after death to another star system. And he is sure that his own "transplanted" father is citizen of this divine realm.[41] By an illumination of influence chosen from column B, the setting of the conclusion of Goethe's *Faust II* in an academy of striving-in-reverse can be seen to inherit the Enlightenment program of perfectibility in which our dead are enrolled. Once the impact of the first era of discovery and colonization of a new world hit home, the dead could be sent on ahead to colonize inner/outer space.[42]

Instead of entering upon the conceit of continuing education, Kant speculates that the development of our soulmates on other planets in the light of the sun folds out a scale of spiritual progress according to which earthlings occupy the middle position. In his commentary on "Desertion" by Clifford D. Simak, the first story in *Overcoming Space and Time,* Günther concludes that what Kant tries to get around through the balancing act of pros and cons remains motivation enough for deserting one's own species. Kant:

> If the idea of the most sublime classes of sensible creatures living on Jupiter or Saturn provokes the jealousy of human beings and discourages them with the knowledge of their own humble position, a glance at the lower stages brings content and calms them again. [...] On one side, we saw thinking creatures among whom a Greenlander or a Hottentot would be a

---

40 This is the lead that I owe Sawicki. I pursued it to check his claims, which check out. I looked at the first edition, published anonymously, of *Elpizon oder Ueber eine Fortdauer im Tode, Erster Theil* (Danzig bei Troschel, 1795), 148. The author is C.Fr. Sintens.

41 Ibid., 151.

42 Paul Scheerbart claimed that he wrote for an eighteenth-century readership. Paul Scheerbart, "Autobiographisches," in *Paul Scheerbart: Bibliographie mit einer Autobiographie des Dichters,* eds. Kurt Lubasch and Alfred Richard Meyer (Scotts Valley: CreateSpace Independent Publishing Platform, 2013), 14.

Newton; on the other side, we saw people who would admire Newton as if he were an ape.[43]

"Desertion" spells out the truth in what the title advertises. Merger with life forms that are spiritually more intense and advanced than the human species prompts the wish to desert from mankind. Günther: "It is the categorical duty of consciousness to realize in itself the highest form of experience of which it is capable."[44] The morality of the story is that from the vantage point of our future in outer space a "terrestrial concept of man cannot be exported" (ibid.). In a unique concession to the datemark of his composition of "On Fairy-Stories" and *The Lord of the Rings,* Tolkien rescues the escape in escapism by transfer to the political situation of "departure from the misery of the Führer's or any other Reich" (61). He also closes ranks with the war effort and draws the line between escape and desertion. Although he wrings the concession to his revalorization of escape from "stories of Science fiction" "the most escapist form of all literature" (64), he also lands in range of Günther's affirmation of desertion when he concedes a contrast between fantasy escape and the quintessential trait of the other genre. The imperative to desert, a better defense than escape, underscores the genre difference. "Seen from the perspective of the Neanderthal, Caesar [...] and Beethoven are already deserters" (ibid.).

Our contact person in *Arrival,* Louise Banks, belongs to the SF retinue of grief-stuck deserters who roll back their blind spots to see better what the future brings. (As we saw, the film brings Ellie Arroway of the 1997 film *Contact* to mind.) Her loss lies in the future, but its stations are shown at the start of the film. She is the narrator of this preamble, which is the container in which her cry to her doomed daughter resounds: "Come back to me." Then the film restarts around the arrival of the spaceships. Banks, a professor of linguistics, is one of the experts soon summoned to facilitate contact with the ship that landed in the US. While she decodes the characters of the alien script (with the assistance of

---

43 Quoted in Szendy, *Kant in the Land of the Extraterrestrials,* 53.
44 Günther, *Science Fiction als neue Metaphysik?,* 87. Subsequent page references are given in the text.

a physicist, her future husband), she flashes on fragments of the traumatic souvenirs belonging to the future, which augment her recognition of the writing on the screen.

This summoning of the future to confound the chain of wishing grounded in the past turns up a contrast with the deliverance from/of the recent past in M. Night Shyamalan's 2003 film *Signs*. Peter Szendy wrapped the film's opening crop circles in a late arrival of Kant's pre-critical reach for the stars, namely his proposal in the *Critique of Judgment* that if "someone were to perceive a regular hexagon drawn in the sand in an apparently uninhabited land," he could not ascertain its "nonrational cause."[45] In his summary of the film's opening, Szendy covers the range of responses of the Hess family members awakened by the barking dogs to witness the immense geometrical figures cut out on the field. The young boy Morgan is immediately convinced that "God did it," which his father, Graham Hess, refuses to believe. The prospect that local delinquents did it has to be abandoned. While consulting with the police officer, Hess himself concedes that the figures are too perfect to be made by human hand. Then the TV news that crop circles have manifested worldwide together with commentary on alien visitation beliefs dating back to the 1970s introduces a new causation and agency.

In the film, the arc from God to science fiction must make the detour around an unmournable loss, which Szendy leaves unattended before proceeding to touch, however, just this once, on the underworld in Kant's star-gazing treatise: "In his conclusion to his *Theory of the Heavens,* Kant imagines in a [...] conjectural way if not exactly a future epoch for interstellar journeys, then at least the possibility of staying in other worlds after death."[46] In *Signs* this straying into other worlds is brought down to Earth. In the course of the alien visitation, the complete scene of the mother's/wife's dying catches up with her last words, fragmentary messages that the father/husband cited early on, but readily explained away as static from misfiring nerve endings. When the scene is restored just in time for the showdown with the alien,

---

45 Quoted in Szendy, *Kant in the Land of the Extraterrestrials,* 49.
46 Ibid., 51. The "philoso-fiction" that Szendy pursues has little in common with what I named "psy fi."

her clairvoyant command comes through. To her husband she said: "See!" And then: "Tell Merrill to swing!"

Merrill, her brother-in-law, once played baseball, earning all-time records, but, because he was unable not to swing, scoring as many strikes. Swinging is his faith – and the seeing that is believing has to be renewed in his older brother. Graham Hess was a Father of the church who defrocked himself in the wake of his wife's fatal accident. Merrill asks his brother to give comfort like he used to. Graham instructs that there are two types of people: those who credit everything that happens to luck, meaning that whatever happens they're on their own, and then there are those who see signs and hope to know that someone is there. Then he recites his wife's dying words, for him the echo of her hatefully, meaninglessly destroyed body.

The father makes a comeback when Morgan suffers an asthma attack down in the battened-down basement while the medication is upstairs with the aliens. He tells his son to believe the air is coming, coming into his lungs; he tells him to believe and breathe. Upon learning that the aliens have retreated, leaving behind only the wounded, the family goes back upstairs. A wounded alien seizes Morgan and starts poisoning him. The father sees and commands Merrill to swing. Merrill takes his trophy bat off the wall and starts swinging. Because she dreads contamination of the water in her glass, Graham's young daughter has left half-full glasses all over the place. Merrill hits the alien but his swinging also knocks over the water glasses and douses his antagonist with the natural element that repelled the invasion. One child's water phobia matches her brother's asthma on the symptom trail of the father's aberrant mourning. After the ordeal, the father injects Morgan's inert form to jumpstart breathing, although the others are convinced it's too late. But Graham is sure that the asthma shut down his boy's lungs and kept the poison out. He sees the signs of his wife's death protecting them. The air/heir does come and Graham is restored to fatherhood.

More than the direct combat with the alien, it is the collateral dispatch of the family's two dogs that enacts the violence going into second death. The redemptive happy end leaves this violence unaddressed. When we see the first alien on television it looks like the female mannequin upstairs in the dead woman's sewing corner still modeling a half-finished blue dress like the princess dress her little girl wears. The alien is the mother's ghost. Graham's acceptance of his wife's death as "meant to be" elides the death-wish traffic between first and second deaths by raising the countdown to Heavenly powers. At the close of the film, Graham Hess is again a Father of the church. The snow on the ground is a commemoration on ice of the termination of the injured alien–evil mother.

Fantasying and Haunting

In *Träume eines Geistersehers* (*Dreams of a Ghost-Seer*, 1766), Immanuel Kant takes several running starts to suggest affinities between ghost-seeing and philosophy's love affair with metaphysics. It is an ironic text that withstood the test of time not only because Schopenhauer rewrote it, but also because Kant's relationship to Emmanuel Swedenborg's thought was as serious as this text's irony. The Nebular Hypothesis that Kant advanced in his *General Natural History and Theory of the Heavens,* and which came to be associated with Laplace, who worked it out independently, was in fact rehearsed in Swedenborg's cosmological oeuvre, which Kant indeed knew thoroughly – and not just as a recent purchase obliging him to write a fresh monograph on it.[47] This commitment, I submit, is what in Kant's prediction that the readers, who don't shrug or laugh the whole thing off, will simply not understand.[48]

Benjamin took from Swedenborg's universal theory of communication with spirits what he found in Baudelaire. Swedenborg: "I have been allowed to know that there is no way that such a heaven with all its correspondences could have come into existence without drawing on the inhabitants of very many worlds."[49] In a footnote, Daniel Paul Schreber urges upon a fourth dimension the task of maintaining the Kant/Laplace

---

47 Immanuel Kant, *Träume eines Geistersehers erläutert durch Träume der Metaphysik* (Berlin: Verlag Lambert Schneider, 1925), 6–7.
48 Ibid.
49 Emanuel Swedenborg, *Life on Other Planets,* trans. John Chadwick (West Chester: Swedenborg Foundation Press, 2006), 6.

Nebular Hypothesis side by side with his belief in God.[50] Schreber concludes the Enlightenment tradition that subtends Kant's dream text. Kant allows, for instance, that we tend to misconstrue the heavenly seat of departed souls as a vertical contrast based on the centrality of planet Earth. But what about the "inhabitants of other worlds," who for the same reason could assume the planet above them to be the heavenly home for the eternity awaiting them.[51]

Swedenborg leaves unexplained how humanity came to occupy diverse planets, which we know about only once we have passed on into the spirit realm through the direct contact that we then enjoy with the spirits and angels of the once living inhabitants of Jupiter or Mercury. An ambiguity in the translation that I consulted (*Life on Other Planets*) reflects the bottom line of the Enlightenment tradition that Swedenborg came to symptomatize when he turned to theology upon his father's death in 1735:[52] "It is a very well-known fact in the next life that there are many worlds inhabited by human beings, and there are spirits and angels who have come from them."[53] When I read it too quickly, I slid the "that" like a cursor to scan "that in the next life," which would conform to the view that the disparate nations of humans living on other planets hail originally from the Heimat of finitude on Earth. As noted earlier, the Enlightenment A-list slips and slides away from the B-list, which is resolutely plain-text about the outer space disposition of the afterlife.

Kant's treatise is a series of hypothetical scenarios that allow for a possible argument in favor of ghost-seeing. For one scenario of possibility, Kant turns to the spirit world inherent in morality.

---

50 I discuss Schreber's note in *I Think I Am: Philip K. Dick*, 39.
51 Kant, *Träume eines Geistersehers erläutert durch Träume der Metaphysik*, 27n.
52 That it was a case of deferred obedience on the part of the stuttering son would seem confirmed by an initial hallucination during the breakup of his scientific career. Out of the murky corners of a restaurant a man emerged who told Swedenborg not to eat so much. Karl Jaspers, *Strindberg und van Gogh: Versuch einer vergleichenden pathographischen Analyse unter vergleichender Heranziehung von Swedenborg und Hölderlin* (Munich: R. Piper & Co, 1949), 109ff.
53 Swedenborg, *Life on Other Planets*, 4.

Moral feeling is a portmanteau word like gravitation in Newton's science.⁵⁴ When we refer external things to our needs, we feel bound or constrained by the sense that in us an alien will is operative and that our own inclination is constituted and conditioned by its external confirmation (29–30). This is the source of the moral drives turning us away from self-service by the strong law of obligation (*Schuldigkeit*) and the weaker law of benignity (*Gütigkeit*). We are dependent, then, upon the ruling of a general will, which maintains moral unity and systematic constitution according to spiritual laws (30). "All morality of actions can by the order of nature never have its complete effect in the bodily life of man but instead in the spirit world [*Geisterwelt*]" (31). An afterlife of inseparable community with and within the spirit world seems a natural continuation. Present and future would be of one piece (32).

Although Kant tried to keep ghost-seeing, a dream of reason, separate from fantasying or waking-dreaming, which is a dream of sensibility (40), he could not get around finding them combined in his monograph's topic, Swedenborg's occult system of communication with the other side. Swedenborg is, in Kant's estimation, at once the premier ghost-seer among all ghost-seers and the premier fantast among all fantasts (56). Swedenborg communicates at will with departed souls and reads in their memories the condition in which they view themselves. He sees it all clearly as with bodily eyes (68):

> Even the immense distance separating the reasonable dwellers of this world from the spiritual world amounts to nothing at all, and it is as easy for him to speak to a dweller on Saturn as to a departed human soul. It all depends on the relationship of the inner state and on their interconnection according to their conformity with the true and the good. (68–69)

The problem remains that the human soul's contemplation of itself as a spirit in conjunction with beings of a similar nature is radically removed from human consciousness. One subject is not

---

54 Kant, *Träume eines Geistersehers erläutert durch Träume der Metaphysik,* 30. Subseqeuent references are given in the text.

the same persons: "What I think as spirit, cannot be remembered by me as human, and vice versa, my condition as a human cannot at all enter the consideration of myself as a spirit" (34–35). A footnote drops here to address a sliding scale between the night dream and conscious memory. We enter upon the grounds for Schopenhauer's sequel, his closer reckoning of the ranging of the dream. Sleepwalkers have forgotten what was otherwise their rational condition upon awakening. If you remember your dream, then you weren't completely asleep: with clear senses the dreamer has interwoven his spirit activities with the impressions of the external senses (34–35n).

Because the ideas of fantasy and those of the external sensorium were mixed up together, the dreamer remembers the dream in part and in the other part encounters wild chimeras (ibid.). Someone given to fantasying is aptly termed a waking dreamer. If the impression of his senses were further reduced, he would be asleep and the chimera would be a true dream (41). When the dreamer awakes, the images continue to preoccupy him, but no longer deceive him. Although we carry in the brain a sense of self and body in relation to which the fantastic images situate themselves, the real sensation of the body through the external senses provides a decisive contrast that enables our identification of a chimera. Asleep, the sense of the body dissolves, and only the self-inventions remain, in relation to which the other chimeras can be thought of as external (41). They will deceive the dreamer as long as he is asleep.

How, then, do the waking dreamers do it? Kant offers an optical POV model based on the manipulation of perception of rays of light. The point that fixes the POV is effectively one of distraction, but, in the imagination, it is a point of collection of the directional lines according to which the sensation is imprinted (42–43). Kant entertains the example of the "spectrum of the body" perceived in the air and projected by a concave mirror (ibid.). It is the special effect that's a wrap with the ununderstood. Kant applies his sharpener to Aristotle's maxim – that the world is held in common in waking reality and that countless realities arise in dreaming – to make a *pointe*: "When among diverse people each has a world of his own, then we can assume that they are dreaming" (39–40).

Toward the end of the monograph, Kant acknowledges that there is one bias that he would never want to shake: ghosts weigh in on the scale of hope (50) – the hope, as he deposits in a footnote on the next page, that death is but the upbeat of metamorphosis. Writing from within the biographical precincts of Goethe's *Werther*,[55] Johann Georg Schlosser composed a dialogue on a variant of metamorphosis: *Ueber die Seelenwanderung* (*On the Transmigration of Souls*, 1781). Through transmigration, the "inner man," not separable, however, from the aggregate of physical organs and mental faculties, goes to the "school" of countless lives or incarnations, but without accumulating the burden of remembering former lives or maintaining a greater all-subsuming personality. The influence of experience is more important than its recollection.[56] As the spirit becomes more and more refined no memory is needed. He sees in every object the whole succession of its determination in time (I.30).

At the end of eons of transmigration, when all the incarnations are together again, the pursuit of one's own perfectibility can be attained (I.37–38). This schooling takes place in earthly existence. But then through the closing Indian parable, the exponent of transmigration instructs his interlocutor that there are two exits from the recycling, from the ongoing afterlife brought down to Earth. A divinity in the office of the creator evaluates the degree of refinement that a soul attains after thirty thousand years. If there has been no improvement worth mentioning, the soul is deleted, while the appreciably refined soul is "transplanted" to "another planet" for the ultimate upgrade (II.23). Transmigration was the method of schooling and cleansing adopted for starting over. Man, the depositing of spirit in animal life, flunked both paradise and the world of work. The malig-

---

55 More pressing upon the Werther grave plot than the two cases of near-miss adultery, I would think, is the marriage of Goethe's sister Cornelia to J.G. Schlosser in 1770. Her death seven years later confirms Goethe's later reservation that the Werther Effect haunted him like unquiet dead siblings.

56 Johann Georg Schlosser, *Ueber die Seelenwanderung: zwey Gespräche*, 2 vols. (Basel: Serini, 1782), I.30. I worked with the facsimile edition by Nabu Press, 2012. Subsequent page references in the text.

nancy upon the spirit had to be excised, but the father–creator didn't want to give up on human being once and for all. And so, he opened the school of transmigration (with post-graduate programming in outer space). It takes that much time to experience fully what's good and evil – to the point of recognizing the durability of the good (I.29).

Arrival Time

In underscoring that the limitation of analogical extension of human existence to alien lifeforms fits the other limitation retrofitting the universe to our solar system, Günther awards Kurd Laßwitz the distinction of reaching as far as the moons of Neptune.[57] Alongside Jules Verne and H.G. Wells, Laßwitz is a founding author of science fiction in Europe. Of course, his range of forecast "still" didn't go further than this solar system. Indeed, in Laßwitz's *On Two Planets,* the Martians "still" arrive to teach the Germans Kantian philosophy and shape them into their representatives on Earth.

In *Arrival,* to know the writing from outer space is to know what's going to happen, that it has already happened, and to enter upon a categorical imperative of fulfillment before the wish. The alien written language sentences lifetime according to our concise history of continuity and contact with the dead. The message that the alien written language conveys to Banks (in the beginning and at the end, the film is her narration) reverses the hierarchy of time and memory.

In Ted Chiang's 1998 "Story of Your Life," which the film adapts, the new written language learned from the aliens is the beacon of a literature truly to be, in Kafka's terms, autonomous. In the story, the remembered death in the future is more ambiguously fateful. Banks's daughter dies while mountain climbing, an "accident" inflected by the suspicion of suicidality lurking in the constitutively reckless and "contrary" child. It is the ambiguity basic to science that must admit alongside the sequential view carried forward by spoken languages (which is post-traumatic)

---

57 Günther, *Science Fiction als neue Metaphysik?,* 81.

the imperative of autonomous writing, a sense of the future to come, a wish fulfillment independent of will or intention.

The scientists make no progress in their exchange until the aliens recognize the Fermat principle of light refraction first discovered in the seventeenth century. Because even our written languages refer to speech, we are committed to a sequential form of understanding, which in turn led to the centrality of causality in science. Thus, when Banks wonders why the breakthrough principle doesn't sound like a law of physics, her scientist-partner explains:

> You're used to thinking of refraction in terms of cause and effect: reaching the water's surface is the cause, and the change in direction is the effect. But Fermat's principle sounds weird because it describes light's behavior in goal-oriented terms. It sounds like a commandment to a light beam: "Thou shalt minimize or maximize the time taken to reach thy destination."[58]

The variation on causality shows Banks that the "physical universe was a language with a perfectly ambiguous grammar. Every physical event was an utterance that could be parsed in two entirely different ways, one causal the other teleological, both valid, neither one disqualifiable no matter how much context was available" (133). Alongside the volition basic to human consciousness, which in the celebrated form of free will forgoes knowing the future, there is a "sense of obligation" arising with knowledge of the future, "a sense of urgency" to act precisely as you knew you would (132).

Transferred to Freud's account of the drives in *Beyond the Pleasure Principle,* we can recognize in the imperative to minimize or maximize the route to the known end the sense of urgency driving the death drive and the sense of obligation prompting the life drive to cut in and allow room for the slack of deferral. The death drive minimizes the route to the end, which, however, must be your proper end, the one that in the alien lan-

---

58 Ted Chiang, "Story of Your Life," in *Arrival* (New York: Vintage Books, 2016), 124. Subsequent page references in the text.

guage is already known. The life drive, which cannot contradict the overall alignment with the known future according to the alien script, maximizes the time of awareness of the sense of certainty of the ending.[59]

One big change from page to screen lies in the valorization of memory. In the story, when Banks looks across the epoch to be remembered and lived, she only occasionally achieves the alien view of "simultaneity." She likens the glimpse of "past and future all at once" to "a half-century-long ember burning outside time" (140–41). Otherwise she remembers, but without the one-way prospect of "real combustion": "[M]y consciousness crawls along as it did before, a glowing sliver crawling forward in time, the difference being that the ash of memory lies ahead as well as behind" (140). The change in her view of time and memory, which comes through learning the alien written language, is that she sees all that transpires within her allotted lifetime: the half-century-long ember burning outside time. "After I learned Heptapod B, new memories fell into place like gigantic blocks" amounting to "a period of five decades" (ibid.). While the aliens, Banks suggests, think big, making their actions "coincide with history's events" and "their motives" "with history's purposes," in effect acting "to create the future, to enact chronology" (137), their lesson plan for their prize human pupil fits the secular schedule of mourning.

In the movie, it is by the import of memory attuned to the simultaneity of arrival and return that the affective turbulence attending the deadlines in one's lifetime shall be overcome. This is a strategy we can identify by its Enlightenment datemark: the benign introjection of haunting secularizes and personalizes heaven, which comes down to earth via outer space. In Chiang's story, the alien script changes the way Banks thinks. Rather than follow out the "train of thought," which she associates with an

---

59 See my discussion of Freud's "Devil's advocacy" in *The Devil Notebooks*. After he has run through a speculation that self-preservation might also only serve to keep us on the track of our proper death, Freud reassures his readership that he has been playing Devil's advocate who doesn't intend to sign up with the Devil of a definition of the death drive.

inner voice speaking silently aloud, she can in certain "trance moments" see writing with her mind's eye "sprouting like frost on a windowpane" (127). But Banks's initiation isn't complete, only fleeting, leaving her to wade in the surf of the necessity of events (144). The first marriage doesn't last, but not because she tests him with the future. In fact, she vows that knowing the future means never letting the uninitiated know the writing on the wall (137). The alien writing, which in human systems appears comparable to mathematical equations and notations for music and dance (110), cannot overcome the speed – the speech – of thought is brought home by the screen test. After her solo exchange with the surviving alien, Banks in *Arrival* resolutely actualizes what is to come. Just the same, what makes for an ill fit in the movie is that she is unable to close ranks with her daughter's father in the face of her foreknowledge. She lets him in on their daughter's deadline and he can't live with them for it.

Banks recalls how in the future she explains to her daughter why the estranged husband and father moved out. She told him about an "unstoppable" rare disease, she tells her daughter, but doesn't conclude the sentence announcing the girl's verdict. What's unstoppable, her daughter asks. Banks withholds the truth and affirms life: "unstoppable" like her daughter, like her daughter's poetry, her drawing. "I'm unstoppable?" Yes!

The moral education that seeks to bring up the arrears of wish fantasying is recognizable in the alien lessons in simultaneity. P.K. Dick offered another variation on this inheritance that turns around the sentencing of loss. The death of his twin sister Jane only a few weeks into his own survival also meant that he instead was dead, living on only in his twin's memories. By this origin story, according to which each party to the loss was lost to the other, Dick began inscribing a science fiction of alternate realities that multiply and extend the finite recording surface/service of remembrance.[60] Like Dick's question or plaint – whose loss is it? – the categorical imperative from outer space forgoes the syntax of the death wish, the sentencing of the survivor.

---

60 If there is a gist to the conclusion of *I Think I Am: Philip K. Dick*, then this is it.

While in moments few and far between she sees it all, like a mandala, for the most part Banks goes, in Chiang's story, back and forth to revisit the situations in which the other was and is no more. She thus follows out a lesson plan for overcoming grief – like the operation of reality testing in the opening season of grief according to Freud in *Mourning and Melancholia* – that neutralizes and preserves the countdown between first and second deaths, between haunting and successful mourning.

The Specific Emotional Situation

In *Reveries of the Solitary Walker*, Rousseau demarcates the condemned site of fantasying:

> If I had possessed the ring of Gyges, it would have made me independent of men and made them dependent on me. I have often wondered, in my castles in the air, how I should have used this ring for in such a case power must indeed be closely followed by temptation to abuse it. Able to satisfy my desires, capable of doing anything without being deceived by anyone, what might I have desired at all consistently?"[61]

But just when you thought this was the Invisible Man's rhetorical question leading him to crime, Rousseau does an about-face: "[T]he sight of general happiness is the only thing that could have given me lasting satisfaction" (102).

When Rousseau composed his *Reveries of the Solitary Walker* in the last two years of his life, he saw himself an exile from a hostile society. If the sense of persecution to which we owe his escape-philosophizing was at the time of this work's composition out of context, out of time, it still fits a post-traumatic schedule. He chooses isolation to forgo external and internal contact with his enemies; in fact, he owes to them his discovery of a new resource for reflection and writing: "The moments of rapture and ecstasy which I sometimes experienced during these solitary

---

61 Jean-Jacques Rousseau, *Reveries of the Solitary Walker*, trans. Peter France (London: Penguin Classics, 1979), 101–2. Subsequent page references are given in the text.

walks were joys I owed to my persecutors; without them I should never have known or discovered the treasures that lay within me" (36). Rousseau reflects on the fantasying lost in transposition to his reflections on moral philosophy:. "As I tried to recall so many sweet reveries, I relived them instead of describing them. The memory of this state is enough to bring it back to life; if we completely ceased to experience it, we should soon lose all knowledge of it" (ibid.). The influence of its experience does not go into fantasying's recollection or record. No matter how forgone its content, it is not repressed; if it is dropped it still counts as "to be continued."

Preliminary to his walking cure unto reverie, Rousseau suffered a street accident, which shook loose the souvenirs of other bloody mishaps in youth and childhood that he confronts in the course of the book. This time around, however, the accident exposed him to the rumor of his demise (143). Setting the stage for this examination of the expansion and intensification of his inner moral life following upon his alienation and isolation, Rousseau projects his arrival on another planet: "I live here as in some strange planet on to which I have fallen from the one I knew" (21–22). He touches down on the Enlightenment staging area of the afterlife as science fiction. Whether by some kind of time paradox or the advancements in medical science, the protagonists of science fiction tend to attain biblical ages. Where death appears to have no dominion, it may have already happened.

The implication of a transfer to the afterlife becomes Rousseau's allegory of making over fantasying into the publishable record of his reveries.[62] "Set free from all the earthly passions

[62] Rousseau's Enlightenment equanimity can be contrasted with an earlier generation of reflection on fantasying. Michel de Montaigne bracketed out the force of fantasying in the first volume of his *Essais* (1580) by the relationship to memory, from the body memory that psychosomatically enacts what the impacted imagination must pass on like a curse to the faulty memory that makes it hard not to lie while conversing. Free-for-all fantasying, however, doesn't sit still, nor is it useful like a field gone to seed in the time out taken to promote its greater arability. It's more like a bolted horse. The author tried it out while retired in the closing chapter of his life and soon was studying all the disorderly oddities that ensued, registering them in the hope of

that are born of the tumult of social life, my soul would often soar out of this atmosphere and would converse before its time with the celestial spirits" (91). But visits there before his appointed time of departure are not enough to establish the continuity shot that moral philosophy alone can afford, namely the Before and After of a truly continued existence. And so, Rousseau turns his fantasying into a school of wishing well to amass for his soul the sole "goods it can carry with it:" "[P]atience, kindness, resignation, integrity, and impartial justice are goods that we can take with us and that we can accumulate continually without fear that death itself can rob us of their value" (61). The basic rule that Rousseau applies in pursuit of a happiness morally secured for transport to the other side must rule out the majority fare of our second nature as daydreamers: "Whatever our situation, it is only self-love that can make us constantly unhappy" (130).

It is getting late in Hanns Sachs's *The Creative Unconscious,* when we learn that music is "the art-form which comes nearest to being the pure embodiment of beauty."[63] Up to this point, Sachs, as we saw, was drawing on an eclectic spread of linguistic and visual works from ancient Greek sculpture and drama to Mickey Mouse cartoons, all the while testing high and low Freud's thesis that art rescues the omnipotence of thoughts from the off-limits underworld of daydreaming. Sachs followed Freud in seeing the artistic process commence through renunciation of the drippy primary narcissism of wish fantasying. What Sachs adds is that beauty is the consolation prize, beauty conceived, that is, in accordance with secondary narcissism as a goal of perfectibility that, always just out of reach, draws the artist onward.

The beauty of Sachs's argument, as becomes clear when we hear the music, is that art leads in the eyes or ears of the receiver to an "experience of an emotional situation which has been his potentially, but which he never can hope to attain in such unmixed purity and fullness" (209–10):

---

corralling them in time within the span of his calm contemplation.

63 Hanns Sachs, *The Creative Unconscious: Studies in the Psychoanalysis of Art* (Cambridge: Sci-Art Publishers, 1942), 208. Subsequent page references are given in the text.

> Music gives an emotional situation, or the change or sequence of emotional situations, in a more direct, immediate, and precise way than can be done by anything else in the world. Unhampered by contents, it can embody and convey emotion with a nicety and accuracy of nuance that is quite unattainable by any intellectual process or by any intrinsic connection with objective facts, be they real or imaginary. (209)

Just the same, when Sachs gives the example of one of Beethoven's listeners, we are in *Fantasia*: "The listener [...] may, if the spirit moves him, be carried away to the fantasy of a gliding stream between mossy banks or a field of wheat undulating in the wind, or a deserted street in moonlight, or to nothing at all. It does not matter, since all and none of these are present in the music" (ibid.).

Whenever we relate to beauty, "the highest form of psychic life" (239) that is most perfectly attained in music, we are brought "nearer to essentials": "[A] thing of beauty [...] represents and brings home a precise nuance of an emotional situation" (234). Beauty, in which "the presence of death makes itself felt in [...] sadness" (240), realizes in the palette of fantasy nuance "the aim of every work of art": "the representation – not the description – of a specific emotional situation" (229). That the emotional situation isn't a description means that the influence of its experience has been isolated and preserved, like the princess in her glass coffin.

The artwork is a kind of dream catcher with beauty as bait. It isn't any old oceanic feeling from prehistory, however, but a specific situation, which bears the time stamp not so much of fantasy incentive as of lapse in the timing of affective response. Rousseau, we saw, associated the goods of morals with an extraterrestrial perspective on the afterlife. In his "Fourth Walk," he addresses lying, the defective cornerstone of the moral philosophy in which he trusts. There is the lie to which he confessed in print ten years earlier.

In *Reveries of the Solitary Walker*, Rousseau claims that the ribbon episode is his method for never again telling a lie. But when he scours the impress of his conversations in the recent past he finds a mess of minor-league lying. "The profound impression made on me by the memory of poor Marion may be capable of preventing any lies which might harm other people, but not the lies which can help me to save face when I alone am involved."[64] Isn't only that which is useful true and therefore a grievous lie if withheld? "I have often made up stories, but very rarely told lies. In following these principles [...] I have injured no one and I have not laid claim to more than was owing to me. In my opinion this is the only sort of truth that can be called a virtue. In all other respects it is no more than a metaphysical entity for us, and produces neither good nor evil."[65] But there is no excuse in morals if lies happen because of out-of-timing. A conversation can run on ahead of Rousseau such that he is forced to speak before thinking. Or if taken by surprise, shame and his basic timidity can impel him to tell lies independently of his will.[66]

The utilitarian adjustments to the moral judgment of lying might make room for fiction. But more importantly it is the sliding scale of lying, which is unstoppable by the time-saving that the run of time in language requires, that extends the scenario of out-of-timing to fiction. What lags behind in sadness is the missed opportunity to tell the truth of what you felt in the emotional situation. The demand for this completion is inexhaustible. Benign lying or fiction gives to grievous lying a topography in which reparation and integration are possible. The beauty of *Dichtung,* Freud's summary term for art, is that it allows us to mourn the missingness of the affective response in the lost emotional situation.

Affection deficit is suffered over the time of our own response. As grievous as the circumstances of departure is the scene of parting. If it was a loss, it counted a failure to get one's farewell across. We "feel" fiction as though we could catch up with the lapse. Is the specific emotional situation the place for the absence of what we wanted to say or show? Affect isn't repressed but the out-of-timing of its response haunts us.

---

64 Rousseau, *Reveries of the Solitary Walker,* 74.
65 Ibid., 79.
66 Ibid., 73–74.

The constellation in Adorno's "Schubert" brings about the wrap of the music's truth and history in the latter-day depravation of its medleys. The essay's relay and rotation of reprisals of the opening theme of an enduring "landscape" in the music concludes when the object relation of grief enters upon this scene, which opens the other pathway through the music, the parallel universal alongside depravation's track that can now be left behind. We begin to recognize the liberated music of a mankind transformed. How sad that we yet fall short of these utopian prospects. It doesn't matter if mere sentimentality jerks them out; our tears let us see better "the ciphers of ultimate reconciliation."[67]

We are at the cusp of affect, which Tolkien's eucatastrophe delivers in the absence of the true happy end, which the turning point welling up with tears intimates. In *More Than Human,* to evoke the impact on his protagonist, Lone, of first contact with the other, Theodore Sturgeon writes/rides this cusp of a feeling always only about to catch up with itself: "His mouth opened and a scratching sound emerged. He had never tried to speak before and could not now; the gesture was an end, not a means, like the starting of tears at a crescendo of music."[68]

The recall of the second death in the future, which is Banks's gift in *Arrival,* elides what it would imply at closer range: the static of mixed feelings, the death-wish forecast. To recall goes back to or brings back finite life that is twice over unstoppable. While explaining that it wasn't the girl's fault, that her father left them and no longer looks at her in the same way, Banks almost lets slip her daughter's verdict. She says that she told him some-

---

67 Theodor W. Adorno, "Schubert," in *Gesammelte Schriften,* vol. 17, ed. Rolf Tiedemann (Frankfurt am Main: Suhrkamp Verlag, 2003), 33.
68 Theodore Sturgeon, *More Than Human* (London: Gollancz, 2000), 10. I will be looking at Sturgeon's novel closely in the third volume of *Critique of Fantasy.* In works by C.S. Lewis and Olaf Stapledon interpreted in the second volume, we can follow out the assignment of Tolkien's tearful joy to music, the next best thing to the true happy ending. Music plays in Lewis's empyrean spheres of outer space and in Stapledon's cosmic vistas of space and time to convey what lies beyond the grasp of a novel's main medium.

thing from the future that she knows and that he just wasn't ready to hear. Toward the end of the film, we get the snippet that was preliminary to her disclosure of their daughter's early death. When she asks her scientist colleague and future estranged husband whether he thinks he would ever wish to change anything in his life, he answers instead – because he's not on the same page with her, but is rather prematurely and belatedly on his own – that he might find wanting the incidence of his having given expression in the momentary situation to his feelings.

The Enlightenment subsumed mourning within the science-fiction afterlife of continuing education. When the wish for contact (or arrival) is added to the acceptance of continuity between the living and the dead, the sum in the aftermath can be endless. While the orbit of arrival time replaces mourning and commemoration with acceptance, even affirmation, just when Banks thinks she can get her future husband to join her in saying yes to everything that happens and happened, in affirming that it is and was as he wished it, his main concern turns out to be that he has been delinquent and delayed in giving full attention to his feelings in the moment. If the loss in mourning is not only embodied but expressed, then the words he could have should have spoken signal the combo of lag and jump-cut linking day-dreaming to incomplete mourning.

What happens when mourning isn't exclusively tied to the object of loss or to the defile of memory in which the object can again be lost? What if the traffic of thoughts and wishes irreversibly carries forward an affect that wasn't imparted to the person you cared for and lost? If daydreaming is in large measure training for big ideas and big feelings – how else could the carrot and stick of beauty, in Sachs's argument, transfer our second nature to art and the social relation – then the burden of preparedness lies heavy on our ability to express in good timing what we think and feel. The basic belatedness and prematurity of adolescent fantasying attend, then, even the most cosmic attempt to reverse loss. Resonating within our second nature as daydreamers, the scheduling conflict of affects unsaid, undead in the lost situations of their stirring, remains for the time being the unalterable flaw in the superhuman appointment with mourning. The run of fantasying behind the timing of expression in the moment of affect wades/waits in the surf of the crypt and its temporal paradox.

Afterword: Go to China

At the topical-allegorical level, *Arrival* belongs to a new millennial subgenre of SF films about the role of China on Earth as in outer space or heaven. On this new-milennial map, the datemark in *The Martian* turns on cooperation with China, the stable partner in outer space also in *Gravity*. This alliance must be formed preliminary to the onset of degeocentering life on Earth and advancing mankind into the start position for a new metaphyics of outer space. What was said to come from China, the 2020 pandemic, didn't contradict this forecast but forced open the prospect of planetary unity and, through social distancing and self-isolation, of life on alien planets. The call from the future self to "go to China" in *Looper* (2012) appears rescinded by the suicide at the end. But the end carries forward a more fundamental requirement, namely that America be made good again.

Upon its invention in the future, time travel is immediately outlawed and resolutely used by criminal organizations. The masterminds from fiction in *Last Action Hero* swept their unidentified victims under the rug of reality. In *Looper,* the disposal service from the future hides by relocating to the past the executions it orders. Because the target is a body that doesn't exist at the time, the crime is perfect. The deployment of time travel to make bodies unidentifiable – unidentified with – and thus disposable goes back to the American science-ficitionalization of the malingering-on vampire as zombies to kill in our own defense. Sole survival of the epidemic, by time travel or mutation, as we saw, means that human mourning becomes the vampire. But the times they are a changing for human mourning and at the count of two deaths the zombie fodder falls closer to the truth.

No trace of the illegal enterprise of taking out the future's garbage can remain behind or outside the loop of non-existence. Therefore, the greatest infraction against an agent's "contract" is to let the loop run, especially if it's his own dangling loop. Retirement means, as written into the contract, that the loop closes on the looper. The organization zaps back the older self for his younger self to execute. Then the assassin has that span of time ahead of him before the loop closes (again).

The run in the loop exceeds reversal of what already happened in time. The older self to the younger self: "My memories are no longer memories, now they are alternate potentialities." When the loop runs, the looper is at odds with himself, that is, with older and current versions of himself orbiting his loop and each hailing from another possible timeline. His older self was targeting the child who in the future would create the conditions that claim his wife's life. But before he fires, the child's mother steps in front to take the hit, which the current self recognizes is the trauma that will make the child grow up gnarly and dangerous. Grown up, he will attain power and first thing close all the loops. So, the younger self kills himself, which means the older self goes with him. Yes, he protects the greater good for more people than one selfish mourner, but he also accomplishes what the older self wanted all along: the reversal of his Chinese wife's murder in the future. The conclusion of *Looper* is a reverb of the maternal conceit in *Terminator 2: Judgment Day* (1991) and *Last Action Hero*. By closing his own loop, the time-travel agent preserves the telekinetic child's maternal bond, which will grow stronger through this close call. According to his older self, the Chinese woman in the future would have been "a great mother" and in fact "saves" their "fucking worthless life."

To heed the call to make America good again, there has to be, in the first place, a shift of investment within the portfolio of identifications and projections that *Star Wars* capitalized. America cannot bear the inscrutable burden of psychopathiy, the failure of Dick's empathy test. Consider the finite catharsis of slasher and splatter movies following Hitchcock's reprisal of the German recent past, its *Schauer* scene, in the stall of American eros. By the occupational therapy of reparation, the post-war world advances toward the onset of collective mourning.

The ready positioning for the merger implicit in the science-fantasy subgenre of datemark China came out of the work of integration, which can be followed in the B-genres, as I tried to demonstrate in *Germany: A Science Fiction*. As corollary to the collective mourning on the horizon of German reparation and integration is the withdrawal of the US investment in the good war and all the evil that hides out there. Can there be any import of *Star Wars* in the projected cooperation with China?

In 2017, *Wonder Woman* updated the super-heroine's World War Two setting, to which she is as indelibly tied as are Superman and Batman, by situating her opening struggle outside the island paradise that she calls home, ultimately her duel as "god killer" with Ares, within World War One. The displacement of the datemark is the hallmark of the deregulated fantasy genre's agenda of global-latinization (the true fantasy of the digital relation looped through the residual charge of Christianization).[1]

Germany is losing, but on the eve of Armistice a super gas weapon has been invented, massively produced, and can now be launched to turn it all around (a distinctive "final victory" structure that belongs more to the second war). When Wonder Woman kills Ludendorff, believing him to be the mask of Ares, she's wrong. The divinity is condemning mankind from a British post of betrayal. This way the human foe is a mixed bag, not just another German, and she rallies on mankind's behalf in the name of the love that Steve Trevor, this time a British spy with an American accent, offers her before he departs on a suicide mission. Wonder Woman's love and our love for her are pure – uncompromised by the recent past of a woman's subterfuge in second-class positions in order to stay by her man's side. The frisson of her superpowers while Trevor guides her through Europe is more comparable to the exoticism of Tarzan, which meets with approval.

---

1 On global-latinization, see Jacques Derrida, "Above All, No Journalists," in *Religion and Media,* eds. Hent de Vries and Samuel Weber (Stanford: Stanford University Press, 2001), 56–93.

Hollywood interests do not readily relinquish the good war that keeps charging "Germany" with cornering the market on evil. That the lead actress was Israeli was subliminally key to acceptance of a post-war affirmation that gets around Death Star Germany, but only by jettisoning history back before National Socialism. The film premiered in Shanghai and broke box office records, scoring by the Chinese history-book view of the Great War as Europe's civil war,[2] which renders the Armistice not botched, but the onset of the European Union, a benign power on the global map according to China in 2017.

Fechner relied on a Chinese contrast to ratchet up the significance of a European tendency to displace upwards: "As long as in China the corpses are only allowed to be buried next to one another, where will we find space for all the living and the dead? In our cemeteries, we overcome this difficulty by burying the dead always deep in the same place in the conviction that the bodies in the grave will not make things difficult for one another."[3] In *The Great Wall* (2016), we were invited to look upon with the pragmatic eyes of a new China this upward momentum of global fantasy. Its corollary opponent or opportunity, which Fechner's "conviction" belies, is zombieism. Toward this end, the bomb planted in range of the all-important mother of the divisions of zomboid monsters could only be detonated from a distance. The suspense builds inside the tower from which the triggering arrow must be shot, while the creatures pile up to stop the archers on top. The interior is illuminated by stained glass windows, and in this light the monsters can be identified as gargoyle demons. The pagan life of these demons, *in nuce* fitting inside the body of the queen mother, can now be extinguished. The female warrior was free to become the father-general of China while the foreign-body Christians, mercenaries who were reconverted by their mission, could go back home to demonization central. The general didn't require the happy end of marriage, because the

---

2 Stanisław Lem cites this curio, which I used in *Germany: A Science Fiction* (Fort Wayne: Anti-Oedipus Press, 2014).

3 G.T. Fechner, *Zend-Avesta: Gedanken über die Dinge des Himmels und des Jenseits vom Standpunkte der Naturbetrachtung* (Leipzig: Insel Verlag, 1919), 213.

prehistoric/pre-Oedipal mother was gone. We steer with relics not only of Christianity but of Oedipus too.

The tower stood for the movie theaters that the Chinese – disenchanted, it was reported, by Hollywood fare – could re-enter en masse now as the stations of a global-latinizing influence that greater China can draw profit from and then subsume or discard. The narrator of Wilde's novel, who often speaks with the lilt of Lord Henry's wit, comments on the fantasy trajectory of medievalism: "that vivid life that lurks in all grotesques and that lends to Gothic art its enduring vitality, this art being, one might fancy, especially the art of those whose minds have been troubled with the malady of reverie."[4] On Earth, the old metaphysics recycling through global Christianity or Mass media must be contained at the border to the fantasy genre.

Communist China, the Third World redeemed, plowed through the vertical contrast toward modification of the crypt of European influence. Americans have been working through the crypts of European history to enter the clearing that is underway. The sci-fi corpus of Cixin Liu washes/watches over the borderland of science fiction and fantasy, which it demarcates by the American Cold War canon of conquest with stopovers in the disavowal of contact on the other side. But what strikes the middle of this demarcated or inherited playing field is that the intergalactic expanse of an interminable course of ends of history is just about large enough to integrate the traumatic history of the Cultural Revolution.

In Liu's *The Three-Body Problem,* the members of the Frontiers of Science use the abbreviation "SF" to stand in lieu of "science fiction" for two fundamental axioms ("shooter" and "farmer") about the nature of the laws of the universe. In the fable of the "farmer" hypothesis, one scientific turkey observes after almost a year that it must be a scientific law that food arrives every morning. It's on the morning of Thanksgiving (which President Lincoln made a national holiday during the American Civil War) that the scientist announces to his fellow turkeys his discovery of the law of the arrival of the food. But on that day

4 Oscar Wilde, *The Picture of Dorian Gray* (London: Penguin Books, 1984), 145.

their food doesn't arrive and they're the food. You wanted the food to arrive each day by law, then be the food on the table each year on the day consecrated by the law of the land.

The "shooter" axiom, at the same time, cites one hypothesis about the nature of the contact impressed upon the Earth as a series of enigmatic zones in the Strugatsky Brothers' *Roadside Picnic* (the title bears the other inference, that the alien visitors were litter bugs): "[A] good marksman shoots at a target, creating a hole every ten centimeters. Now suppose the surface of the target is inhabited by intelligent, two-dimensional creatures. Their scientists, after observing the universe, discover a great law," mistaking the result of the shooter's "whim" for "an unalterable law of the universe."[5] While it circumvents the horror story of American SF, the hypothetical prospect of a shooter's whim bounces off the East Block tendency to disavow any possible exchange with alien intelligence, which is tantamount, according to P.K. Dick, to denying that the other exists.[6]

Tarkovsky carried the theme of fantasy in science fiction forward, in *Stalker* (1979) and *Solaris* (1971), unto mourning. In the final section of *Roadside Picnic,* when the protagonist Red reaches the wish-granting Golden Sphere, which was possible only by sacrificing his companion to the meat grinder so he alone could pass, he repeats the wish he knew his companion cherished, a wish for happiness on Earth not unlike the vow that almost handed Faust over to the Devil. The titular hero of *Stalker,* as Tarkovsky writes in his diaries, graduated in the course of revisions to the screenplay from "drug dealer or poacher" "to be a slave, a believer, a pagan of the Zone."[7] The Stalker guides the

5   Cixin Liu, *The Three-Body Problem,* trans. Ken Liu (London: Head of Zeus, 2016), 76. The SF movie *Annihilation* (2018) lifts the Zone and renames it the Shimmer. The remake of the Russian border zone between fantasy and science fiction is brought to a point by one of the scientists on the expedition who uses the analogue of optical manipulation, the palette we spun with Benjamin, Goethe, Scheerbart, and Wilde to describe the way the Shimmer acts on organisms: by distorting and refracting DNA like a prism refracts light.
6   See Rickels, *Germany,* 227.
7   Diary entry of August 26, 1977. See Andrey Tarkovsky, *Time within Time: The Diaries 1970–1986,* trans. Kitty Hunter-Blair (London:

Writer and the Professor to the Room, where wishes are granted. But the novel's sacrifice is displaced, when it looks like the Room's prowess in fulfillment targets unconscious wishes. This conceit was the unacknowledged concession to psychoanalysis in *Solaris,* both novel and film. Be careful what you wish for. Not the wish you express but a secret wish is fulfilled. That's why the Stalker's mentor killed himself; he wished that his brother might return from the grave but was granted instead wealth, which like the free money of inheritance fulfilled a death wish. And that's why at the end of the film the Stalker dissuades his wife from entering the Zone to wish upon the Room.

In Liu's "The Wandering Earth," the Earth as a whole must break orbit and travel toward life-sustaining proximity to a new sun (the old one was scheduled to blink out). Spaceship Earth is powered by a propulsion system that uses rock for fuel. Its main stations are in China and North America. In another story, "Mountains," contact is made with a gargoyle cosmology of bubbles embedded in rock, as specialized and askew in regard to science since the age of discovery as a Medieval map of the stars. The global population in "The Wandering Earth" undergoes *unio mystica* (which is communist), while the alchemical transformation of the earth's bedrock into cosmic fuel exhausts the fantasy throwback and enters the science fiction of survival of the planet. The utilitarianism of sacrifice comes up, but as matter of fact, its pathos of well-being for the majority at the same time dismissed as beside the point. Up against extinction, it's hard for the protagonist to imagine that anyone could hesitate in choosing the survival of a child over an oldster, of reproduction over sex. The Chinese protagonist meets his Japanese partner on a snowmobile rally across the frozen – endless but direct – connection between Shanghai and New York, where they set up house, marry, and win the highest prize when they draw the lot that bestows the right or duty to reproduce.

I daydream a study of Liu Cixin's work. It is close to the source, the history of science fiction, and to the datemark, the future history of its fantasying. Consider how "Curse 5.0" spins its self-reflexive tale about the borderland of science fiction and

Faber and Faber, 1994), 147.

fantasy out of Internet opinions and beliefs. A female programmer in 2009 creates the first version of the Curse to destroy the man who jilted her. The protagonists of the low-tech story of survival that lies outside the Internet battle of the sexes are first introduced at the time of the Curse's upgrade. Liu Cixin and his writer colleague from the other corner of the genre contest, Pan Haitian, "who had started out writing science fiction, switched to fantasy and then finally settled somewhere in between."[8] Rather than science fiction with or against fantasy, the border zone belongs to "the soft-hard divide in science fiction" (215), the ultimate user cliché. At their reunion they join forces to write one work twice over, once as science fiction, once as fantasy.

> Cixin chattered excitedly about his next grand endeavor. He planned to write a ten-volume [...] sci-fi epic describing the two thousand deaths of two hundred civilizations in a universe repeatedly wiped clean by vacuum collapses. [...] Pan was captivated, and he raised the possibility of collaboration: working from the same concept, Cixin would write the hardest possible science fiction edition for male readers, while Pan would write the softest possible fantasy edition for female readers. (ibid.)

Just as Curse 1.0 was about to sink to the bottom of the endlessly upgraded Internet and disappear after a decade or so, the new fad and science of Internet archaeology intervened. In the language of fantasy reserved for the Curse plot and frame: The Primogenitor's original Curse was discovered and tweaked by an

[8] Cixin Liu, "Curse 5.0," in *The Wandering Earth,* trans. Ken Liu (London: Head of Zeus, 2017), 215. Subsequent page references are given in the text. That the story is a farce doesn't exempt it from the author's overall grasp of a topography of traumatic histories that must be worked through in the border zones of science fiction. The way that the programmer introduced the curse brings to mind lines from Heinrich Heine's "The Silesian Weavers": "Old Germany, we weave your funeral shroud; And into it we weave a three-fold curse – we weave; we weave" (212). That we are brought to two minds before this German introject would be the subject of yet another chapter of my daydream of a study.

adept of the new science who adopted the moniker Upgrader and relaunched it as Curse 2.0 (216). In the low-tech story, the trend has been realized; the digital world/word has passed the authors by. Hardly any copies of the joint masterpiece, which they published privately, sold. But then counter-wave science fiction turns it all around into the hard-and-soft genre's rejection of technology. The *King of Science Fiction* editorial department follows suit, going on horseback to meetings with authors who must submit handwritten manuscripts.

With the exception of the editorial department's dinner invitations, the destitute authors have downgraded to psycho homeless substance abusers. In the junkyard they inhabit, Cixin finds a laptop discarded by a hacker fleeing the Internet police. On it he discovers Curse 3.0 (which in the heroic saga was the work of the Weaponizer).

> He pushed the laptop away and joined Pan in reminiscing. Those were the days! His omniscient, virile epics of destruction had struck chords with so many young men. [...]
>
> By now, Pan was sniveling alongside him. He thought of the colorful, profound works of his early years, like poems, like dreams. It was not so long ago that his prose had bewitched hordes of teenage girls. (224–25)

Despairing over their abandonment by their respective readerships, each author changes the parameters of the Curse back and forth, like the good fairies in *Sleeping Beauty* (1959), who change the color of the princess's gown with their wands back and forth to suit their preferences (and thus give away her hiding place). The result of the digital magic duel is the new and destructive Curse 4.0. Their abjection is the cone of immunity to the Curse that destroys the city. In the language of the Curse's digital upgrading, low-tech rescuers secure the authors' happy survival:

> Just then, they heard a silvery voice, like the touch of an ice crystal in the sea of flames: "Cixin, Pan, come quick!" Following the voice, they saw a pair of stallions emerge from the flames like spirits. Two beautiful young women from the SFK editorial department rode atop the horses, their long hair

> trailing behind them. The riders pulled Cixin and Pan up onto the backs of the horses. Then, like lightning, they took off through the gaps in the blistering sea, vaulting the burning wreckage of cars. (231)

A highpoint was reached for Schopenhauer with the prospect that more material on ghost sightings in China would make possible at last a truly universal understanding of the continuum of night dreaming and waking dreaming (and paranormal states): "It is to be wished and hoped that we will soon be in receipt of a collection of Chinese ghost stories, in order to see if they, too, are essentially of the same type and character as our own."[9] Kafka's story "Great Wall of China" belongs to this trajectory of occultation that starts out in a Europe that is already a foregone conclusion left behind by new goals set in "Amerika." At the other end, there is China, the Heimat of regional civilizations hailing from the East transformed by White Man's Burden. We witnessed Lord Henry in *The Picture of Dorian Gray* pull the afterlife through the portal in the new world to Third World China. This occultation traces in reverse the one-way trek of countless Chinese laborers who razed San Francisco's inland back country to bottom out a Californian valley for growing the produce for a successful new world.

According to Günther, "the attempt to include the only recently discovered American hemisphere as a colony in the epoch of regional civilizations of the eastern hemisphere failed. The process of spiritual or psychic emancipation which science fiction so importantly reveals continues."[10] This draws the

---

9   In his treatise on ghost-seeing, Schopenhauer crowns his definitive identification of episodes from *The Clairvoyant of Prevorst* now as invented, now based on optical illusion, now genuine by an aside trip to China. The cultural differences will add to the confirmation of a shared bottom line in the study of these phenomena. Schopenhauer expects confirmation because in a Chinese novella he did read the ghost appearances although fictional suggest that there are similar conceptions regarding "dreaming as true."

10 Gotthard Günther, *Science Fiction als neue Metaphysik? Dr. Gotthard Günthers Kommentare zu "Rauchs Weltraum-Büchern,"* ed. Dieter von Reeken (Lüneburg: Verlag Dieter von Reeken, 2015), 30.

divide between the American New World and the sorry state of colonization that constituted the Third World. China lifted out of there and through communism was as though redeemed. Filtered through Winnicott on acting out as signalling hope, we can understand Paul Mayersberg's observation in his 1968 study *Hollywood: The Haunted House* that "Los Angeles and Peking are the most hopeful cities on earth."[11] At the "Wall of the Pacific," the frontier spirit that looked forward to outer space also came before the mirror that leads to China. The borderland between fantasy and science fiction, between the digital relation and history, is the place where the two renewal "religions" of global capitalism meet and cross over: Chinese communism and American political correctness.

On a class field trip during my stint of teaching at the art school in Karlsruhe, I asked the head of the Freiburg paranormal institute about what appeared to me to be a return of the compact with the Devil in horror entertainment following the film-therapeutic termination of secular slasher movies. He answered that while European culture never separated horror from the Devil, the distinctions I was making reflected the unique metabolism of US popular culture, in which striking changes seem to occur immediately upon each change in office.

During the Obama presidency, a new digital sense of integration dominated the socius, in which every historical episode and figment was returning but outside the former context of its opposition. The Civil Rights movement was returning, the Christian Right was returning; every name and event in history was returning like an entry in the digital archive. This could be followed in a show like *True Blood,* in which every B-genre fantasy figure pressed for realization or inclusion. The undertow of the integration was a kind of fracking of undiscovered layers or deposits of consumption. *Twilight* was all about getting preteens for the first time in history to buy books and movie theater tickets for and by themselves, summoning them like consumer ghosts to compensate for the uncountable Chinese adults only

---

11 Paul Mayersberg, *Hollywood: The Haunted House* (New York: Ballantine Books, 1969), 13.

awaiting further capitalization of communism to be animated as big spenders.

The perfectibility of integration, in the social sense no less than in the sense of shoring up the psyche in mourning's aftermath, pushes toward the ongoing approximation to a more perfect union in the United States (according to Obama's Philadelphia speech on race), which can jump the divide between communism and capitalism. That it cannot be about reversing the historical inequities of the past, which amounts to an imperative of reproducing them, is the most radical gist of Maoism. Passing through the vale of industrialization is not preliminary to a revolution that makes history. Back in the United States in 2018, I could observe college students preparing to be a workforce – a collective – of one, trying to capitalize on a politically correct agenda, and thus doubling up the ranks of a new order that we think we can share or pretend to share with an increasingly middle-class China. The Americans need a good history for entry upon the experiment of partnership with Chinese capitalists who still visit Lenin's birthplace on holiday. Nitpicking about the totalitarianism of communism in the past is out of the new order. Sitting before the screens of the digital relation, like the disconnected segments of Kafka's "Great Wall of China," we work at a continuity between the renewal religions of capitalism and communism, which is tantamount to what the narrator of Kafka's story must "imagine": a central office in which "all human thoughts and wishes revolve in a circle, and all human aims and fulfillments in a circle going in the opposite direction."[12]

---

12 Franz Kafka, "The Great Wall of China," trans. Ian Johnston, *Kafka Online,* http://kafka-online.info/the-great-wall-of-china.html.

Bibliography

Adorno, Theodor W. "Schubert." In *Gesammelte Schriften,* Vol. 17, edited by Rolf Tiedemann, 18–33. Frankfurt am Main: Suhrkamp Verlag, 2003.

Balzac, Honoré de. *The Wild Ass's Skin.* Translated by Herbert J. Hunt. London: Penguin Books, 1977.

Benjamin, Walter. "Die Farbe vom Kinde aus Betrachtet." In *Gesammelte Schriften, Band 6: Fragmente, Autobiographische Schriften,* edited by Rolf Tiedemann and Hermann Schweppenhäuser, 110–12. Frankfurt am Main: Suhrkamp, 1991.

———. "Experience and Poverty." in *Selected Writings, Volume 2: 1927–1934,* translated by Rodney Livingston et al., edited by Michael Jennings, et al. Cambridge: The Belknap Press of Harvard University Press, 1999.

———. "Phantasie." In *Gesammelte Schriften, Band 6: Fragmente, Autobiographische Schriften,* edited by Rolf Tiedemann and Hermann Schweppenhäuser, 114–17. Frankfurt am Main: Suhrkamp, 1991.

———. *Ursprung des deutschen Trauerspiels.* Berlin: E. Rowohlt, 1928.

Bennington, Geoffrey. *Frontières kantiennes.* Paris: Éditions Galilée, 2000.

———. *Kant on the Frontier: Philosophy, Politics, and the Ends of the Earth.* New York: Fordham University Press, 2017.

Bloch, Ernst. *The Principle of Hope,* Vol. 1. Translated by Neville Plaice, Stephen Plaice, and Paul Knight. Cambridge: MIT Press, 1995.

Campbell, Joseph, with Bill Moyers. *The Power of Myth.* Edited by Betty Sue Flowers. New York: Anchor Books, 1991.

Carpenter, Humphrey. *Tolkien: A Biography.* New York: Ballantine Books, 1977.

Chiang, Ted. "Story of Your Life." In *Arrival,* 91–146. New York: Vintage Books, 2016.

Chion, Michel. *Eyes Wide Shut.* Translated by Trista Selous, BFI. London: Palgrave Macmillan, 2002.

Derrida, Jacques. "Above All, No Journalists." In *Religion and Media,* edited by Hent de Vries and Samuel Weber, 56–93. Stanford: Stanford University Press, 2001.

Dick, Philip K. *The Last Interview and Other Conversations.* Edited by David Streitfeld. Brooklyn and London: Melville House, 2015.

———. *The Zap Gun.* London: HarperCollins, 1998.

Ehrenwald, Jan. *Telepathy and Medical Psychology.* New York: Norton, 1948.

"Ep. 1: Joseph Campbell and the Power of Myth – 'The Hero's Adventure'" (June 21, 1988). *Moyers Archive.* https://billmoyers.com/content/ep-1-joseph-campbell-and-the-power-of-myth-the-hero's-adventure-audio/.

Fechner, G.T. *Zend-Avesta: Gedanken über die Dinge des Himmels und des Jenseits vom Standpunkte der Naturbetrachtung.* Leipzig: Insel Verlag, 1919.

Freud, Sigmund. "Beyond the Pleasure Principle." In *The Standard Edition of the Complete Psychological Works of Sigmund Freud, Vol. XVIII (1920–1922): Beyond the Pleasure Principle, Group Psychology, and Other Works,* edited and translated by James Strachey with Anna Freud, 7–64. London: The Hogarth Press, 1964.

———. "Civilization and Its Discontents." In *The Standard Edition of the Complete Psychological Works of Sigmund Freud, Vol. XXI (1927–1931): The Future of an Illusion, Civilization and Its Discontents, and Other Works,* edited and translated by James Strachey with Anna Freud, 64–145. London: The Hogarth Press, 1961.

———. "Creative Writers and Day-dreaming." In *The Standard Edition of the Complete Psychological Works of Sigmund Freud, Vol. IX (1906–1908): Jensen's "Gradiva" and Other Works*, edited and translated by James Strachey with Anna Freud, 143–53. London: The Hogarth Press, 1964.

———. "Five Lectures on Psychoanalysis." In *The Standard Edition of the Complete Psychological Works of Sigmund Freud, Vol. XI (1910): Five Lectures on Psycho-Analysis, Leonardo da Vinci and Other Works*, edited and translated by James Strachey with Anna Freud, 9–55. London: The Hogarth Press, 1957.

———. "The Common Neurotic State." In *The Standard Edition of the Complete Psychological Works of Sigmund Freud, Vol. XVI (1916–1917): Introductory Lectures on Psycho-Analysis (Part III)*, edited and translated by James Strachey with Anna Freud, 378–91. London: The Hogarth Press, 1963.

———. "The Uncanny." In *The Standard Edition of the Complete Psychological Works of Sigmund Freud, Vol. XVII (1917–1919): An Infantile Neurosis and Other Works*, edited and translated by James Strachey with Anna Freud, 219–56. London: The Hogarth Press, 1955.

———. "Thoughts for the Times on War and Death." In *The Standard Edition of the Complete Psychological Works of Sigmund Freud, Vol. XIV (1914–1916): On the History of the Psycho Analytic Movement, Papers on Metapsychology, and Other Works*, edited and translated by James Strachey with Anna Freud, 275–300. London: The Hogarth Press, 1957.

Galperina, Marina. "Andrey Tarkovsky Loved Star Wars So Much." *Animal*, October 31, 2013. http://animalnewyork.com/2013/andrey-tarkovsky-loved-star-wars-so-much/.

Goethe, Johann Wolfgang von. "Der Zauberflöte zweiter Teil (Ein Fragment)." In *Die Zauberflöte: Ein literarischer Opernbegleiter mit dem Libretto Emanuel Schikandeders*, edited by Jan Assmann. Zürich: Manesse Verlag, 2012.

Günther, Gotthard. *Beiträge zur Grundlegung einer operationsfähigen Dialektik*. Hamburg: Felix Meiner Verlag, 1980.

———. *Das Bewusstsein der Maschinen: Eine Metaphysik der Kybernetik*. Baden-Baden: AGIS Verlag, 2002.

———. *Die amerikanische Apokalypse*. Edited by Kurt Klagenfurt. Klagenfurt: Profil, 2000.

———. *Die Entdeckung Amerikas und die Sache der Weltraumliteratur*. Düsseldorf: Verlag Karl Rauch, 1952.

———. *Science Fiction als neue Metaphysik? Dr. Gotthard Günthers Kommentare zu "Rauchs Weltraum Büchern."* Edited by Dieter van Reeken. Lüneburg: Verlag Dieter von Reeken, 2015.

Hagen, Wolfgang. *Radio Schreber: Der "moderne Spiritismus" und die Sprache der Medien*. Weimar: Verlag und Datenbank für Geisteswissenschaften, 2001.

Hanslick, Eduard. *Die moderne Oper: Kritiken und Studien*. Berlin: A. Hofmann, 1875.

Heinlein, Robert A. "All You Zombies…." In *The Best from Fantasy and Science Fiction,* edited by Robert P. Mills. New York: Ace Books, 1964.

———. "By His Bootstraps." In *The Menace from Earth: Eight Stories from the Grand Master of Science Fiction*. London: Corgi Books, 1973.

Hofmannsthal, Hugo von. "Die Frau ohne Schatten." *Projekt Gutenberg*. https://www.projekt-gutenberg.org/hofmanns/frauohne/text.html.

James, William. "The Confidences of a 'Psychical Researcher'." In *Writings 1902–1910*, 1250–65. New York: Library of America, 1988.

Jameson, Fredric. "In Hyperspace." *London Review of Books* 37, no. 19 (September 10, 2015). https://www.lrb.co.uk/v37/n17/fredric-jameson/in-hyperspace.

Jaspers, Karl. *Strindberg und van Gogh: Versuch einer vergleichenden pathographischen Analyse unter vergleichender Heranziehung von Swedenborg und Hölderlin*. Munich: R. Piper & Co, 1949.

Jeter, K.W. *Dr Adder*. London: Grafton Books, 1987.

Kafka, Franz. "The Great Wall of China." Translated by Ian Johnston. *Kafka Online*. http://kafka-online.info/the-great-wall-of-china.html.

Kant, Immanuel. *Allgemeine Naturgeschichte und Theorie des Himmels oder Versuch von der Verfassung und dem mechanischen Ursprunge des ganzen Weltgebäudes, nach*

Newtonischen Grundsätzen abgehandelt. Königsberg and Leipzig: Bey Johann Friederich Petersen, 1755.

———. *Grundlegung zur Metaphysik der Sitten*. Edited by Theodor Valentiner. Stuttgart: Reclam, 2008.

———. *Träume eines Geistersehers erläutert durch Träume der Metaphysik*. Berlin: Verlag Lambert Schneider, 1925.

Klein, Melanie. *The Psychoanalysis of Children*. Translated by Alix Strachey. New York: The Free Press, 1984.

———. "On Identification." In *Envy and Gratitude and Other Works: 1946–1963*, 141–75. New York: The Free Press, 1984.

Liu, Cixin. "Curse 5.0." In *The Wandering Earth,* trans. Ken Liu, 209–33. London: Head of Zeus, 2017.

———. *The Three-Body Problem*. Translated by Ken Liu. London: Head of Zeus, 2016.

Marcuse, Herbert. *Eros and Civilization: A Philosophical Inquiry into Freud*. Boston: Beacon Press, 1955.

Matheson, Richard. *I Am Legend*. New York: ORB, 1995.

Mayersberg, Paul. *Hollywood: The Haunted House*. New York: Ballantine Books, 1969.

McShane, Mark. *Séance on a Wet Afternoon*. New York: Mysterious Press, 2013.

Meier, Wilhelm. *Höchst merkwürdige Geschichte der magnetisch hellsehenden Auguste Müller in Karlsruhe*. Stuttgart: J.B. Metzler'schen Buchhandlung, 1818.

Mill, John Stuart. "Utilitarianism." In *On Liberty, Utilitarianism and Other Essays,* edited by Mark Philip and Frederick Rosen, 115–77. Oxford: Oxford University Press, 2015.

Mozart, Wolfgang Amadeus. *Così fan tutte* (1790). *Opera Folio*. http://www.operafolio.com/libretto.asp?n=Cosi_fan_tutte.

Rank, Otto. *Kunst und Künstler: Studien zur Genese und Entwicklung des Schaffensdranges*. Gießen: Psychosozial-Verlag, 2000.

Regis, Meta. *Daydreams and the Function of Fantasy*. New York: Palgrave Macmillan, 2013.

Rickels, Laurence A. *Aberrations of Mourning: Writing on German Crypts*. Detroit: Wayne State University Press, 1988.

———. *Germany: A Science Fiction*. Fort Wayne: Anti-Oedipus Press, 2014.

———. *I Think I Am: Philip K. Dick* . Minneapolis: University of Minnesota Press, 2010.

———. *Nazi Psychoanalysis,* 3 Vols. Minneapolis: University of Minnesota Press, 2002.

———. *The Devil Notebooks*. Minneapolis: University of Minnesota Press, 2009.

———. *The Psycho Records*. New York: Wallflower Press, 2016.

———. *The Vampire Lectures*. Minneapolis: University of Minnesota Press, 1999.

———. *SPECTRE*. Fort Wayne: Anti-Oedipus Press, 2013.

———. *Ulrike Ottinger: The Autobiography of Art Cinema.* Minneapolis: University of Minnesota Press, 2009.

Rousseau, Jean-Jacques. *Reveries of the Solitary Walker.* Translated by Peter France. London: Penguin Classics, 1979.

Sachs, Hanns. *The Creative Unconscious: Studies in the Psychoanalysis of Art.* Cambridge: Sci-Art Publishers, 1942.

Sawicki, Diethard. *Leben mit den Toten: Geisterglauben und die Entstehung des Spiritismus in Deutschland 1770–1900.* Paderborn: Schöningh, 2002.

Scheerbart, Paul. "Autobiographisches." In *Paul Scheerbart: Bibliographie mit einer Autobiographie des Dichters,* edited by Kurt Lubasch and Alfred Richard Meyer, 5–15. Scotts Valley: CreateSpace Independent Publishing Platform, 2013

———. *Lesabéndio: Ein Asteroiden-Roman.* Scotts Valley: CreateSpace Independent Publishing Platform, 2017.

Schlosser, Johann Georg. *Ueber die Seelenwanderung: zwey Gespräche,* 2 Vols. Basel: Serini, 1782.

Schnitzler, Arthur. *Traumnovelle*. Scotts Valley: CreateSpace Independent Publishing Platform, 2018.

Schopenhauer, Arthur. "Preisschrift über die Grundlage der Moral." In *Werke in zwei Bänden,* vol. 1, edited by Werner Brede, 654–61. Munich: Hanser Verlag, 1977.

———. "Versuch über das Geistersehn und was damit zusammenhängt." In *Schopenhauer's Sämmtliche Werke in fünf Bänden,* vol. IV, Grossherzog Wilhelm Ernst Ausgabe, 271–369. Leipzig: Insel Verlag, 1908.

Seabrook, William B. *The Magic Island.* New York and Tokyo: Ishi Press, 2015.

———. *Witchcraft: Its Power in the World Today*. London: Sphere Books, 1970.

Singer, Jerome L. *Daydreaming and Fantasy*. London: George Allen & Unwin, 1976.

[Sintens, C.Fr.]. *Elpizon oder Ueber eine Fortdauer im Tode, Erster Theil.* Danzig bei Troschel, 1795.

Smith, Harrison. "Brian Aldiss, Science-Fiction Writer behind Steven Spielberg's 'A.I.' Dies at 92." *Washington Post*, August 23, 2017. https://www.washingtonpost.com/local/obituaries/brian-aldiss-science-fiction-writer-behind-steven-spielbergs-ai-dies-at-92/2017/08/23/da4bed60-8743-11e7-a94f-3139abce39f5_story.html

Stein, Gertrude. "An American and France." In *What Are Masterpieces*, 61–70. Los Angeles: The Conference Press, 1940.

———. *Blood on the Dining-Room Floor: A Murder Mystery*. Mineola: Dover Publications, 2008.

———. *Wars I Have Seen*. London: B.T. Batsford Ltd., 1945.

———. "What Are Masterpieces and Why are There So Few of Them." In *What Are Masterpieces*, 81–88. Los Angeles: The Conference Press, 1940.

———. "What Is English Literature." In *Look at Me Now and Here I Am: Writings and Lectures 1909–45*, edited by Patricia Meyerowitz, 31–58. London: Penguin, 1990.

———. "Why I Like Detective Stories." In *A Primer for the Gradual Understanding of Gertrude Stein*, 145–50. Los Angeles: Black Sparrows Press, 1974.

St. Thomas Aquinas. *Summa Theologiae*. http://summa-theologiae.org.

Swedenborg, Emanuel. *Life on Other Planets*. Translated by John Chadwick. West Chester: Swedenborg Foundation Press, 2006.

Szendy, Peter. *Kant in the Land of Extraterrestrials: Cosmopolitical Philosofictions*. Translated by Will Bishop. New York: Fordham University Press, 2013.

Tarkovsky, Andrey. *Time within Time: The Diaries 1970–1986*. Translated by Kitty Hunter-Blair. London: Faber and Faber, 1994.

Tolkien, J.R.R. "On Fairy-Stories." In *Tree and Leaf / Smith of Wootton Major / The Homecoming of Beorhtnoth,* 11–79. London: Unwin Books, 1975.

———. *The Letters of J.R.R. Tolkien.* Edited by Humphrey Carpenter. London: HarperCollins, 2006.

———. *The Lost Road and Other Writings.* Edited by Christopher Tolkien. Boston: Houghton Mifflin Company, 1987.

Torok, Maria. "The Meaning of 'Penis Envy' in Women." In Nicholas Abraham and Maria Torok, *The Shell and the Kernel,* translated by Nicholas T. Rand, 41–74. Chicago: The University of Chicago Press, 1994.

Wells, H.G. *The Time Machine.* Garden City: Dolphin/Doubleday, 1961.

White, T.H. *The Sword in the Stone.* New York: Philomel Books, 1993.

Wilde, Oscar. *The Picture of Dorian Gray.* London: Penguin Books, 1984.

Williamson, Jack. *The Humanoids.* New York: Orb Books, 1996.

———. *The Humanoid Touch.* London: Sphere Books, 1982.

Winnicott, D.W. *Human Nature.* London: Free Association Books, 1988.

———. *Playing and Reality.* Hove and New York: Brunner-Routledge, 2002.

———. "Primary Maternal Preoccupation." In *Through Paediatrics to Psycho-analysis: Collected Papers,* 300–305. London: Karnac Books, 1984.

———. "The Depressive Position in Normal Human Development." In *Through Paediatrics to Psycho-analysis: Collected Papers,* 262–77. New York: Brunner-Routledge, 1992.

———. "The Manic Defence." In *Through Paediatrics to Psycho-analysis: Collected Papers,* 129–44. New York: Brunner-Routledge, 1992.

Index Nominum

A

Abraham, Karl 107, 115
Adorno, Theodor 32, 220
Aldiss, Brian 44–45, 107, 109, 110
Antonioni, Michelangelo 122, 124
Aquinas, Thomas 42, 71
Aristotle 42, 58, 76, 209
Artaud, Antonin 115

B

Bailey, David 122
Balzac, Honoré de 81–82
Barrie, David 45–46
Barrie, James Matthew 45–46
Beethoven, Ludwig van 183, 203, 218
Bellamy, Edward 67
Benjamin, Walter 28, 58, 105–6, 184–87, 194, 200, 206, 228
Bentham, Jeremy 71, 73
Bergler, Edmund 32
Bloch, Ernst 41
Bont, Jan de 141
Burroughs, Edgar Rice 25
Butler, Samuel 169

C

Cameron, James 67
Campbell, Joseph 21, 24, 36, 61–62
Carroll, Lewis 39, 63
Chiang, Ted 211–13, 215
Chion, Michel 100, 102–3
Churchill, Winston 20
Clarke, Arthur C. 138, 196, 201
Collodi, Carlo 42, 45
Columbus, Christopher 60
Conan Doyle, Arthur 151–52
Cortázar, Julio 122
Cover, Arthur 158–59
Craven, Wes 141
Crichton, Michael 25
Cuarón, Alfonso 29

D

Da Vinci Leonardo 46
Derrida, Jacques 68, 225
Descartes, René 79
Dick, Philip K. 19, 21, 26, 30, 71, 77, 90, 143, 152, 155–60, 162–63, 169, 188, 190, 207, 214, 224, 228
Disney, Walt 36, 42, 46, 89, 183
Dostoevsky, Fyodor 35
Du Prel, Carl 192

E

Ehrenwald, Jan 155–56
Eissler, Kurt 46
Emmerich, Roland 19–20

F

Fechner, G.T. 186, 191–94, 226
Fleming, Ian 20

INDEX

Freud, Sigmund 24, 27, 31–33, 35–37, 46, 49, 50–54, 56–57, 75–76, 81, 83, 85, 92, 101, 104, 107, 110, 115, 120, 131–32, 138–40, 148, 152, 157, 158, 162, 165–67, 173, 178, 181, 190–91, 196, 212–13, 215, 217, 219
Fritsch, Günther von 139

G

Goethe, Johann Wolfgang von 91, 98–100, 102, 113, 145, 185–86, 200, 202, 210, 228
Greenaway, Peter 148
Günther, Gotthard 30–32, 58–64, 66, 68, 155–56, 163–64, 173, 175–79, 195, 198–200, 202–3, 211, 232

H

Hagen, Wolfgang 192
Hammill, Mark 21
Hartmann, Edurd von 192
Hauptmann, Gerhart 95–96
Hebel, Johann Peter 37
Hegel, G.W.F. 58, 61, 177
Heinlein, Robert 169–75, 177
Hitchcock, Alfred 113, 141, 146, 224
Hitler, Adolf 150, 174, 195
Hoffmann, E.T.A. 154
Hoffmannsthal, Hugo von 99
Huysmans, Joris-Karl 113

J

Jackson, Shirley 139
James, Henry 145
Jameson, Fredric 172
James, William 70, 154
Jarmusch, Jim 166
Jeter, K.W. 159
Jung, Carl 21

K

Kafka, Franz 211, 232, 234
Kant, Immanuel 29, 46–47, 49, 70, 75, 77, 148, 152, 199–200, 202, 203–4, 206–7, 208–210
Kelley, Mike 91–92
Kennedy, John F. 21
Klein, Carl Christian 136
Klein, Melanie 36, 43, 99, 119, 121, 125, 145, 188
Kubrick, Stanley 44, 98, 100, 102–3
Kurosawa, Akira 21

L

Lang, Fritz 154
Laplace, Pierre-Simon 206
Laßwitz, Kurd 211
Lewis, C.S. 32–33, 39–41, 63, 147, 198, 220
Linklater, Richard 91
Liu Cixin 227–30
Lucas, George 19–23, 26, 36, 147
Lugosi, Bela 149

M

Machiavelli, Nicolò 174
Marcuse, Herbert 191
Marlowe, Christopher 145
Matheson, Richard 167–68, 170, 175, 179
Mayersberg, Paul 233
Meier, Wilhelm 136
Mendés, Catulle 84
Mesmer, Franz 74
Mill, John Stuart 70–72
Moyers, Bill 21
Mozart, Wolfgang Amadeus 74, 98, 100, 183, 199
Müller, Auguste 135–37
Müller, Max 49, 56

N

Newton, Isaac 74, 203, 208
Nietzsche, Friedrich 36, 110

O

Obama, Barack 233–34
Onassis, Jacqueline 21
Ottinger, Ulrike 106

P

Pan Haitian 164, 230
Pliny 86
Ponte, Lorenzo da 74

R

Rank, Otto 23–24, 44
Romero, George 167, 169
Rousseau, Jean-Jacques 183, 215–19

S

Sachs, Hanns 83–88, 90, 92–97, 110, 131, 217, 218, 221
Sawicki, Diethard 200–202
Scheerbart, Paul 185–88, 191–94, 202, 228
Schelling, Friedrich 59
Schikaneder, Emanuel 98, 100
Schiller, Friedrich 68
Schlosser, Johann Georg 210
Schmitt, Carl 52, 143–44
Schnitzler, Arthur 98, 101–3
Schopenhauer, Arthur 75–81, 136, 138–39, 152, 158, 194, 206, 209, 232
Schreber, Daniel Paul 84, 86, 100, 102, 136, 192, 200, 206–7
Schwarzenegger, Arnold 180
Scott, Ridley 26, 28, 77, 86

Seabrook, W.B. 149–50, 164–65
Shakespeare, William 76, 113, 142–43, 146–47
Shelley, Mary 111
Shyamalan, M. Night 204
Simak, Clifford D. 202
Singer, Jerome L. 89
Spengler, Oswald 163
Spielberg, Steven 44, 109
Stapledon, Olaf 220
Stein, Gertrude 117–18, 123, 143–50, 163, 165–66
Strauss, Richard 99
Strugatsky, Arkady Natanovich 228
Strugatsky, Boris Natanovich 228
Swedenborg, Emanuel 206–8
Szendy, Peter 199–200, 203–4

T

Tarentino, Quentin 165
Tarkovsky, Andrei 22, 228
Tausk, Victor 84
Taut, Bruno 186
Tolkien, J.R.R. 22, 23, 26, 27, 31, 33, 35, 38–42, 49, 53–56, 92, 147, 184–85, 188–90, 194, 203, 220
Torok, Maria 107–8
Tourneur, Jacques 139
Trump, Donald J. 90
Turing, Alan 138, 201

V

Verne, Jules 25, 150, 187, 211
Vogt, A.E. van 166–67

W

Warhol, Andy 110
Weir, Andy 28
Weir, Peter 71

Wells, H.G. 22, 38–40, 67, 90, 109, 147, 172–74, 211
Whale, James 90
White, T.H. 115
Wilde, Oscar 111–14, 142, 144, 146, 185, 187, 227–28
Williams, Charles 33
Williamson, Jack 62–69, 155, 196
Winnicott, D.W. 36, 44, 51, 103–5, 107–10, 114–21, 124–35, 233
Wise, Robert 139–41

Z

Zöllner, J.F.K. 192

www.ingramcontent.com/pod-product-compliance
Lightning Source LLC
Chambersburg PA
CBHW071001160426
43193CB00012B/1869